Party People
Communist Lives

Explorations in Biography

£1-50

Lawrence and Wishart Limited
99a Wallis Road
London
E9 5LN

First published 2001

Copyright © This collection the editors 2001
Individual chapters © the individual authors 2001

The authors have asserted their rights under the Copyright,
Design and Patents Act, 1998 to be identified as the author
of this work.

All rights reserved. Apart from fair dealing for the purpose
of private study, research, criticism or review, no part of this
publication may be reproduced, stored in a retrieval system,
or transmitted, in any form or by any means, electronic,
electrical, chemical, mechanical, optical, photocopying,
recording or otherwise, without the prior permission of the
copyright owner.

Cover pictures show, in descending order from highest:
Bill Rust, Jack Gaster, Dora Montefiore, Margaret McCarthy,
Willie Allan and Arthur Reade. For assistance with the cover
illustrations, special thanks to Ian MacDougall, Viola Reade,
Karen Hunt and the National Museum of Labour History.
While we have made every effort to trace copyright holders,
any we have overlooked will be acknowledged in future
editions.

British Library Cataloguing in Publication Data.
A catalogue record for this book is available from the British
Library

ISBN 0 85315 936 X

Text setting Derek Doyle and Associates, Liverpool
Printed and bound by Bookcraft, Midsomer Norton

Party People
Communist Lives

Explorations in Biography

Edited by John McIlroy, Kevin Morgan
and Alan Campbell

Lawrence & Wishart
LONDON 2001

CONTENTS

Preface

We live in the golden age of biography. Despite the hostility of the rich and famous – and not a few university intellectuals – the appetite of the reading public for this ever-expanding genre appears insatiable. And it is a genre that is expanding not only in volume but in its concerns and sophistication. While much contemporary biography remains within orthodox parameters, there has also been a wealth of new approaches and subjects. The claims of marginal, intriguing, subterranean and exotic subjects have been increasingly asserted, and there has been widespread critical discussion on the nature of biographical writing. Critics have pointed to the complexities of human identity and the tendentiousness of its recreation; to the validity of competing versions of the past; and to the nuances of the interpenetration between biographers and their subject. There has also been discussion on the fragility of the frontiers between art and history.[1]

Communists have strong claims on the marginal and intriguing, and they have also boasted their fair share of subterranean and exotic lives. Yet Communist historiography has in the main been impoverished by its disregard of biography. Thus in Perry Anderson's magisterial memorandum on Communist history published in 1981, the nearest he got to biography when listing the five main types of work was 'Memoirs', and these were largely 'official-anecdotal'.[2] However, as Kevin Morgan demonstrates in the first chapter of this book, things are looking up. Historians of communism are beginning to avail themselves of the possibilities of 'life history', even if they have scarcely explored the potential of the headier approaches to it.

This collection reflects this new interest in Communist people. Drawing upon the CPGB archives in Manchester and Moscow, it brings together newly researched essays on a variety of figures from the early years of British communism. The contributors share a belief that writing biography can be an exciting and rigorous way of writing history, one which restores the flesh and blood, the inspiration and perspiration, to Communist lives; it is also a form which gives proper weight to human agency as well as its constraints. The book arises, more specifically, from our involvement in an Economic and Social Research Council project at the University of Manchester, which is concerned with elaborating a prosopography of British communism. We realised at an early stage that the quantitative depended on the qualitative: there was a need to explore the complexities of individual life histories and their construction, since aggregation and broader analysis depend on such work for their consistency and richness.

Existing biographies have most often concentrated on the leading figures of British communism. But even within these parameters, they have documented in detail the lives of only a limited number of the leadership cohort. There thus remains a need to deepen and extend our understanding of the human dimension of the party through a further scrutiny of the party elite. And if we are to properly people the party and recover the full range of its activities, there is also a need to go beyond this group, to depict the lives of the 'second level' – 'ordinary' members, birds of passage and heretics. The biographical form provides a structure and vantage point which facilitates a more intensive exploration of the world of communism, and enables a deeper consideration and reconsideration of important problems and neglected facets of Communist history, through the eyes of protagonists.

In this spirit, we have brought together nine brief studies of Communist lives, focused on the years 1920-40 and embracing the first two decades of party activity. As editors, we have in common a preference for biography which eschews reductionism and the dilution of complex experience to historical parables; which attempts to integrate the private and political; and which seeks to recuperate the background, values and motivation of party activists. We share the view that politics is central to the exploration and depiction of Communist lives, although our understandings of what constitutes the political naturally vary. There are also differences of interpretation as to the weight to be attached to the party's Russian connections and Comintern membership from 1920, though all are agreed that these are factors of immense significance.

In affirming the differentiation as well as the unity of British communism, the individualisation of biography raises issues of personal motivation and responsibility as well as the significance of political structures. If it reminds us of the selfless commitment to building a better world of many of the party's members, it also directs us towards an exploration of the relationship of many leading figures, and some 'ordinary' ones, to the policies of the Soviet Union and the crimes of Stalinism. Of course there was a complex interplay between commitment and complicity; and while the blanket use of the term Stalinist can obscure the passions, the longings, 'the teeming contradictory life', of Communist activists,[3] the Stalinism of the party's leading cadre must also be recognised. For they were, in the words of Edward Thompson, 'agile in casuistry and reinforcing their control by distinctively Stalinist procedures'.[4]

One of the major issues raised by this collection is the use to be made of this concept of Stalinism when analysing Communist lives. While the main concerns of the historian are with documenting, analysing and understanding, two of the editors of this book believe that British Stalinism requires judging. The third is also concerned with how judges acquire their authority, and with how Stalinism relates to notions of leadership and authority found in other socialist traditions. There has therefore been no unanimity, no party line, governing the contributions assembled here, and this applies equally to the contributions of the editors themselves. The essays collected here deal with a range of activists, take a variety of forms and contain diverse arguments. We hope that readers will feel that they also tell interesting stories and shed new light on the history of communism in Britain.

To assist readers less familiar with this period of communist history, we have compiled a list of mini-biographies of many of the people mentioned in the text (see 'Who's who', pp240-7). For frequently used abbreviations see p8.

Finally, we would like to express our gratitude to our contributors for their efforts, to Linda Lawton for her sustained assistance, and to Sally Davison of Lawrence and Wishart for her faith in this book. Thanks are also due to all those who took part in the workshop on Communist Biography which we organised at the University of Manchester in June 2000.

John McIlroy, Kevin Morgan and Alan Campbell, November 2000

NOTES

1. For stimulating explorations of new approaches to biography see, for example, the recent novels of Antonia Byatt: A.S. Byatt, *Possession: a romance* 1990; A.S. Byatt, *The Biographer's Tale* 2000.
2. P. Anderson, 'Communist Party history', in R. Samuel (ed), *People's History and Socialist History* 1981, p145.
3. E. Hobsbawm, 'Problems of Communist history', in E. Hobsbawm, *Revolutionaries* 1973, p11.
4. E. P. Thompson, 'The poverty of theory or an orrery of errors', in E.P. Thompson, *The Poverty of Theory and Other Essays* 1978, p329.

Abbreviations

AWA	Amalgamated Weavers' Association	*NL*	*New Leader*
BSP	British Socialist Party	NLS	National Library of Scotland, Edinburgh
BUF	British Union of Fascists		
CC	Central Committee	NSA	National Sound Archive
CI	Communist International	NUGMW	National Union of General and Municipal Workers
CPA	Communist Party of Australia		
CPGB	Communist Party of Great Britain	NUM	National Union of Mineworkers
CPI	Communist Party of Ireland	NUSMW	National Union of Scottish Mine Workers
CPSU	Communist Party of the Soviet Union		
		NWCM	National Workers' Committee Movement
Comintern	Communist International		
DPC	District Party Committee	OUA	Oxford University Archives
DW	*Daily Worker*	PB	Political Bureau
ECCI	Executive Committee of the Communist International	PL	Proudfoot Letter
		Politburo	See PB
FCO	Foreign and Commonwealth Office	PRO	Public Record Office, London
		RGASPI	Russian State Archive of Socio-Political History
FKCMA	Fife, Kinross and Clackmannan Miners' Association		
		RILU	Red International of Labour Unions
GARF	State Archive of the Russian Federation		
		RPC	Revolutionary Policy Committee
IE	Inner Executive	SDF	Social Democratic Federation
ILP	Independent Labour Party	SLC	Scottish Labour College
ILS	International Lenin School	SLP	Socialist Labour Party
Inprecorr	*International Press Correspondence*	*SW*	*Sunday Worker*
IWSA	International Woman Suffrage Alliance	SWCC	South Wales Coalfield Collection
		SWMF	South Wales Miners' Federation
IWW	Industrial Workers of the World	SWML	South Wales Miners' Library, Swansea
LBC	Left Book Club		
LM	*Labour Monthly*	TMM	Textile Minority Movement
LMU	Lanarkshire Miners' Union	TUC	Trades Union Congress
LRD	Labour Research Department	UK	United Kingdom
MAM	Memorial Archive, Moscow	ULF	University Labour Federation
MFGB	Miners' Federation of Great Britain	UMS	United Mineworkers of Scotland
MIC	Miners' International Committee	USF	University Socialist Federation
ML	Mitchell Library, Sydney	WBCG	Workers' Birth Control Group
MM	Minority Movement	WCG	Women's Co-operative Guild
MMM	Miners' Minority Movement	WCML	Working-Class Movement Library, Salford
MPL	Methil Public Library		
MRU	Mineworkers' Reform Union	WEA	Workers' Educational Association
NAC	National Administrative Committee	WI	Writers' International
		WIIU	Workers' International Industrial Union
NATO	North Atlantic Treaty Organisation		
		WIR	Workers' International Relief
NCLC	National Council of Labour Colleges	*WL*	*Workers' Life*
		WSPU	Women's Social and Political Union
NEC	National Executive Committee		
NMLH	National Museum of Labour History, Manchester	YCI	Youth Communist International
		YCL	Young Communist League

Parts of People and Communist Lives

KEVIN MORGAN

I

'But their habits of faith, of zeal, and of union seemed to multiply their numbers.' So wrote Gibbon of the early Christians, and if one adds to these qualities the flair for self-promotion which Eric Hobsbawm detected in the Fabians, and a habit of record-keeping unequalled by any other organisation of the left, one has the beginnings of an explanation for the recent revival of interest in Communist Party history. Even in Britain, where the party's achievements and ambitions stand in somewhat distant relationship to each other, the last decade has seen a stream of writings of the most varied character and level of achievement. Failing to achieve its own larger goals, the party nevertheless provides a radical counterpoint to conventional political histories and opens up wider issues and comparative methodologies that are often obscured by a sort of historiographical channel fog. Communism, for good or ill, was one of the major forces shaping the twentieth century, and its faith and zeal, sometimes combined with numbers, offer distinct and challenging perspectives on issues of social protest and political identity. At a personal level, it comprises a host of stories of commitment, betrayal, credulity, conflicts of loyalties and of conscience, and the interplay of the local, national and international in the shaping of such allegiances. 'Interesting but irrelevant', has been one sceptical response, as if relevance were a sort of absolute, axiomatically defining the limits of 'proper' history. If Communist history helps to undermine such notions, then so much the better for Communist history.[1]

Admittedly, much of the existing historiography is, if not exactly irrelevant, then somewhat self-referential. If the subject has a wider interest, it is in the party's faith, zeal and union rather than blow-by-blow accounts of its corporate development, and certainly in Britain it is not as an institutional actor that it most effectively holds our attention. Instead, among a variety of social and cultural approaches, one of the most promising developments in the recent literature is the appearance almost for the first time of a credible sub-genre of Communist lives. In the overall weakness of traditional Communist historiography, no form of writing was feebler than this. Internationally, it is only in the 1990s that figures of the stature of Palmiro Togliatti, Earl Browder, Eugen Fried, and Aksel Larsen have received scholarly biographical treatment. In Britain, biographies of Harry Pollitt and R. Palme Dutt were almost the first such works on leading British Communists. Currently work is in progress on several other figures including Clara Zetkin, Alexander Losovsky, Karl Radek, Otto Kuusinen, and William Gallacher. But in the bibliography of a scholarly Comintern history published as late as 1996, it is notable that scarcely a single biography is listed.[2]

That can hardly be accidental. Biography has always sat a little uneasily alongside other forms of historical writing, existing in what the French historian Claude Pennetier has called a sort of 'purgatory'.[3] Popular with readers and publishers, it has seemed to its critics a naïve, banal or distracting approach to the past, at once abstracting the individual from the social and imbuing this discrete 'life' with a wholeness, coherence and narrative logic that are illusory. Conversely, its practitioners have argued that biography recovers social actors and areas of experience lost in grander narratives, and for this reason life stories have become as much identified with history from below as they traditionally were with the exploits of 'great men'.

Whatever the emphasis, to approach a social or political movement from the standpoint of its disaggregated members is not the same as viewing the same organisational textures through a microscope, but allows a distinct and formative role to individual human agency and motivation. Moreover, the focus on that single movement is qualified or contextualised by the other influences, sequential or concurrent, which go to make up any particular life. Subtly disintegrative of more structured causation, the implications are nowhere more contentious than in the case of a Communist movement whose proverbial conformism, intrusiveness and monolithicity were backed up by the strictest codes of party discipline. That, as much as the lack of sources, has led to the comparative dearth of Communist biographies. If the deficiency is now to be rectified, not only the archives themselves but the methodological assumptions we bring to them need to be scrutinised.

Some of them are addressed in this opening chapter. Its particular concern is to assess the biographer's implicit affirmation of individual agency as against the institutional emphases of most existing Communist Party history, and the bearing this might have on the centre-periphery debates which have dominated recent Communist historiography.[4] It also addresses the particular complexity of Communist lives, at once complicit, however remotely, in some of the greatest crimes of the century, and yet displaying a commitment to social justice which in many cases was disinterested to the point of death.[5] The opinions offered are tentative, but do suggest that the adoption of biographical methods provides a way of moving on from traditional party historiographies, not to a facile inversion of their superficial conclusions, but to an altogether more complex, nuanced and unsettling account. By a thousand personal ties, biography attaches communism to the history around it, and the first issue for its historians is simply whether insights and methodologies can be applied to it that have become very largely uncontentious in this wider context. Conversely, the adoption of such methods may be thought a denial of the exceptional character of Communist politics, set politically and historiographically apart and denied internal differentiation precisely because this was denied by the party itself. Whatever the merits of such assumptions, which have been central to so-called 'totalitarian' approaches to Communist Party history, they do not seem conducive to the writing of Communist biography.

II

The question of how far one can or should individualise the phenomenon of communism takes us to the heart of these debates. Implicitly, the construction of Communist biographies affirms both the possibility and validity of approaching the individual Communist as a tangle of relationships and ambitions irreducible to a single line of determination. That is a trite assumption but it nevertheless jars with a vast academic literature almost never biographical in form, but predicated upon a group identity so intense and pervasive as to leave little room for distinctive life histories. Whatever the details of association or habitat, the sole or central meaning of these lives was 'political', in an especially circumscribed definition, and politics was a matter of party orders. Where sociological detail was provided, it had a descriptive and not explanatory value, and though specificities of origin, function and preferment were sometimes acknowledged, these were always subordinate to the totalitarian logic of party discipline. The defining metaphor was the transmission belt, always running from the centre outwards, and the main variation allowed was of distance from the centre, as in the hidden linearity of Annie Kriegel's concentric circles. Sometimes described as a 'Cold War' approach to Communist history, the durability of such conceptions is attested by the recent success of the *Black Book of Communism*, published to great sensation in France and currently circulating in some 700,000 copies world-wide. Less important here than the scale of the *Black Book*'s indictment of Communism is its sheer smothering comprehensiveness.[6]

Such interpretations have a powerful support and rationale in the party's own habits of self-representation. Although ostensibly it was given to cults of leadership, even the figures at the apex were avowedly creatures of the organisation, and in Britain at least, commemorative accounts of the party's history struck a curiously impersonal note.[7] Harry Pollitt himself could be lionised but never vindicated, and neither strength nor failing was admissible that would have set him apart from the party. The result was a lifeless and statuesque tradition in which comradely regard was mandatory, anonymous and sometimes unintentionally comical. 'Comrades in sorrow deep tho' mute, for this our leader in battle fell': thus wrote Gallacher of his colleague Bill Rust, when he died of a stroke during a King Street business meeting. Disregarding if we can the Augustan mock heroics, it is equally remarkable that Gallacher's dislike for Rust had behind closed doors been anything but mute. Not Rust in any individual sense, but Rust the functionary, Rust the battling editor of the *Daily Worker*, Rust the embodiment of Communist virtue, was now the occasion for his doggerel, and there was not one of his colleagues for whom he would not similarly have drooped his flag. Of the personal animosities which Andrew Flinn mentions in his contribution here, not a breath was allowed to seep beyond the Communists' ranks.[8]

For the same reasons, the idea of an honest or absorbing party memoir could not be entertained. That was not for reasons of incapacity. Britain's first-generation Communist leaders were compulsive autodidacts, steeped in an idiomatic literary culture and well-versed in the demands of biographical narrative. In the early lives of Pollitt, Bell and Tommy Jackson, they arguably provided some of the finest working-class memoirs of the period, each evoking his origins with a demotic verve that echoed their reading of Dickens, Wells or

Blatchford. The continuation of such narratives into the years of the party itself was nevertheless unthinkable, and all such accounts either petered out, supplanted the autobiographical 'I' with the party, or remained unpublished. Differences, let alone antagonisms, were more or less inadmissible. The most that was allowable was a sort of functional specialisation, exemplified by Pollitt the worker and Dutt the intellectual, ostensibly representing the unity of revolutionary theory and practice. Constrained as it was, it is telling that almost the party's only major biographical enterprise was Dona Torr's life of Tom Mann, never getting within thirty years of the party itself.[9]

Not only issues of strategy and leadership were taboo, but so was the mildest deprecation of self or party. So harmless a confession was disallowed as Pollitt's anxiety not to miss last orders when working evenings with Dutt on the *Workers' Weekly*. So too was his forgetting the few words of Spanish drummed into him, as he travelled incognito to the civil war. Not human frailty or temptation but a steely self-control was expected, and party lives had to be exemplary in the mass, and at the peak bore an almost symbolic significance. Learning that his image had been borne through Moscow alongside other great comrades, living and departed, Pollitt noted equably that 'I prefer to walk about on two legs, and not in the form of In Memoriam placards'. Nevertheless, his own encomiums, often delivered in the form of ceremonial birthday messages, were scarcely less disembodied. Pollitt was also the first and only Communist leader to receive substantial biographical treatment from within the party, a volume by John Mahon published in 1976. Unabashedly a work of dedication, it rests beneath an epitaph – 'All his days he was on fire' – engraved on the book as if on a tombstone.[10]

While recalling the official biographies of Soviet Russia, Mahon's biography also belongs to a native tradition that produced so similar a work as William Stewart's life of Keir Hardie. Hardie too was presented with apostolic fervour as the 'Great Exemplar', humane, incorruptible and dauntless in adversity, and a careful regard for party proprieties was evinced in the entrustment of Stewart's manuscript to Ramsay MacDonald for editorial revisions. Hardie's image too, it may be added, was carried aloft by his supporters, and grotesquely the tradition was sufficiently maintained to bestow even on Harold Wilson the same distinction. Nevertheless, the analogy should not be stretched too far, at least with respect to its legacy for the biographer. Such were the Communist Party's loyalties and collective discipline that, even long after the event, the raw materials were not available for potential biographers unconstrained by such ties. Not only memoirs, obituaries and funeral odes, but periodicals, speeches, even the interviews given years later to oral historians, usually adhered to a convention of collective responsibility. In unity was strength, and in a sort of self-abnegation one discerns a parallel with the extraordinary paucity of trade union biographies and personal archives surviving from the same period.

Pollitt, for one, was immersed in the cultures of both union and party, and his self-restraint even in matters of personal pride and humiliation was remarkable. When in 1959 he wished to record his own version of the events which led to his removal as general secretary in 1939, it was intended even after his death for his family's eyes alone, and gave no hint of the fierce antagonisms the episode generated. Traditionally exhorted to 'show the face of the party', Communists thus made sure that they showed even to posterity nothing but the face. In France, Philippe Robrieux did get behind the facade of Maurice Thorez, sniffing out the 'secret life' of this self-designated *Fils du Peuple*, and indebted to defectors whose loosened tongues and papers now escaped the jurisdiction of the party. But in Britain, the literature of disillusionment was comparatively meagre and uncorroborated, and not one major Communist archive, whatever its provenance, was exhaustively accessible to researchers. An alternative approach, pioneered in Britain by Joan Smith and Harry McShane, was the reconstruction of Communist lives on the basis of extensive oral interviews. Such collaborations, and some increasingly frank and expansive party memoirs, provided a growing body of vivid testimony in the 1970s and 1980s. Literary and cultural figures, whom none could reduce to their party persona, gave rise to scholarly biographies based on personal archives. History from below, and from the party's margins, flourished. But to reconstruct the so-called 'party people' of the Comintern period could hardly even be attempted.[11]

The archives now available are thus in many cases a necessary condition for such works, but not perhaps a sufficient one. After all, there are different ways of using these materials, and the choice between them reflects or determines the sort of Communist history one is trying to write. Just as grassroots and oral histories have been largely disregarded by some traditionalists, so the relative autonomy of biography itself may be thought inappropriate to the overpowering disciplines and moral enormity of Stalinism. Relentless institutional constraints, such as inform much of the academic literature on communism, seemingly require narration at the level of the institution, not the individual, unless it is the individual as instrument or victim.

Patrick O'Brien, in dismissing biography from the standpoint of the conventional political historian, has suggested that 'the only significant illumination to be gleaned from political biography is how and why a particular individual came to occupy high office'. In this perspective, the demands of office always outweigh any possible contribution by its incumbents, and the incidental markings of the latter offer no substantial insight into the political process.[12] For the Communist biographer, assuming the same centrality of political function, the one significant question would be the how and why of joining the party, for even the not uncommon sequel of leaving it suggests corrosively that this commitment often proved rather less than total. Sometimes the experience was of an intense deconversion process, the more dramatic, perhaps, the more fully a party person one had become.[13] More commonly, however, defection revealed persistent pressures of function, association or political judgement, never wholly overcome and finally appearing incompatible with party membership. The very fact that this was a party so many people left – especially during the high membership turnover of the Comintern period – tells us something about the sort of party it was. If fully a quarter of its members were capable of quitting it in 1956-7, that says something not only of the tremendous shock caused by those events but of the brittleness, organisational or ideological, that rendered the party so vulnerable to them.

Not only social but temporal differentiation is at issue, for unless within the basic commitments of being a Communist it was possible to make significant individual choices – which may or may not have been 'political' in the party sense – then the scope for a personalised narrative is narrow indeed. 'Stalinism', in its cruder colloquial uses, becomes an inert as well as monolithic concept, which does not contain the possibility of its own reform – including those countless individual reforms by which the Communist became the ex-Communist. A more historicised approach does not just mean accentuating the individual, still less a denial of the social. Rather, it avers that the complexity of social identity cannot be reduced or subordinated to a single party affiliation, however intense. The individual is located, not in a self-referential world of her own, but in a series of temporal, spatial, social and institutional contexts whose precise inter-relationships distinguish that individual and help explain the dramas and dilemmas of that particular life.

Perhaps in a country like Britain Communists were particularly susceptible to external pressures. Certainly, due as much to the party's size as to a relatively secularised associational culture, there was never much prospect of the sort of insulated 'world' or 'social and moral order' to which the Communists aspired in post-war Italy.[14] At one extreme, embedded within the party apparatus, there were the total party people represented in this collection by Rust. 'Christ! It was like a copy of *Inprecorr* coming to life and reciting its own contents!', T.A. Jackson remarked of him in his own – necessarily unpublished – memoirs.[15] However, as Andrew Flinn demonstrates, even Rust was not without his complexities, and the very feelings he aroused suggest that both within and beyond the party he was regarded as a distinctive 'type'. Others, even among the nationally prominent cross-section presented here, were clearly involved in potentially awkward relationships with the party. In the case of the four Communist mining leaders – three of them sometime central committee members – an alertness to the industrial realities of the coalfields produced uneasy and sometimes conflictual relations with the party's political imperatives. Rose Smith, a formidable activist also from the industrial heartlands, faced distinct problems as one of a handful of leading women members of a party less subversive of traditional gender relations than its rhetoric indicated. Randall Swingler, moving freely in the very different purlieus of literary London, was involved in a continual battle for space with the party's cultural apparatchiks, and it was Randall's gold and not Moscow's which gave him the opportunity for his prolific publishing ventures. Arthur Reade, in more bohemian fashion, also experienced the difficulties of the intellectually restless and socially conspicuous, while Dora Montefiore was shaped by networks, experiences and a coherent political philosophy which long predated the Communist Party and cut across its relentless prioritisation of class. Jack Gaster, recruited after ten years in the ILP, attributed to its training his own resistance to the 'obedient take it without question' mentality he detected in other Communists. The explanation is plausible, but the existence of such a hinterland, predating or coexisting with party membership, was more common than Gaster may have realised.

Hardly any of these figures had consistently straightforward relations with the party. Most eventually broke with it or might have done so, and that tells us something about the character of their party membership itself. Typically in Britain, adhesion involved a more or less voluntary process of becoming and remaining a Communist, without ever entirely shedding the 'outside' family and social networks, work relations, political and professional associations, and the class and gender relationships which inevitably were replicated even within the party. Communist lives turn out to have been other things than a

Communist life, and these other things helped determine what sort of Communist life – and there were many – it was. Moreover, it is precisely these other things which have tended to explain the attraction of particular party lives to their biographers. Usually these are socialists too, but it is as feminist, black or cultural historians that biographers have been drawn to figures like Stella Browne, Sylvia Pankhurst, J.D. Bernal, Sylvia Townsend Warner, Shapurji Saklatvala and the black Manchester boxer Len Johnson. Were these only Communist lives, they would attract only 'Communist' biographers, and this is far from being the case.[16]

Not all writings about Communist lives share these emphases, however, nor can all such writing be described as fully biographical according to the usage adopted here. Prosopographical studies have dwelt in a more impersonal way on social origins and career paths, and Harvey Klehr, who certainly did not intend emphasising the autonomy of Communist Party members, has produced an invaluable such analysis of the American Communist elite. Branko Lazitch, whose intentions were likewise anything but revisionist, co-edited a pioneering biographical dictionary of the Comintern. Even individual studies have sometimes had the character of 'instrumental' rather than 'intrinsic' case-studies, to which the subject's privacy or a lack of sources have sometimes been contributory factors. In Britain, John Callaghan's book on Dutt, aptly subtitled 'a study in British Stalinism', is as much concerned with exploring Stalinism through Dutt's ideas as with Dutt himself. Ralph Darlington, who writes on J.T. Murphy as a study in British Leninism gone astray, expressly confines himself to Murphy's 'political trajectory' and eschews the 'irrelevant ... personal idiosyncrasies' he associates with conventional biography. In a different type of study, the individual case is presented as exceptional, usually with the aim of dissociating that person from the full implications of their party membership. Thus Bryan Palmer writes that Edward Thompson was 'never the "pure-and-simple" Communist', thereby at once extricating his subject from his rather energetic involvement in the party and reaffirming the crude collective backdrop which Palmer designates 'Stalinism'. No doubt all biography involves that uneven focus, although it does in such cases seem a rather obvious device – not incidentally one employed by Thompson himself – for minimising a commitment that had come to seem embarrassing or compromising.[17] Juxtapose these party lives, as in the present volume, and it is difficult to make out which ones the pure-and-simple Communists were.

Possibly that is why the effect of biography within Communist historiography has often been to suggest more nuanced or variegated interpretations than totalitarian-derived models readily accommodate. Even in a Russian context one thinks of Stephen Cohen's biography of Bukharin and the oblique light it cast on the Stalin-Trotsky dichotomy which until then had largely framed early Soviet history. Elsewhere, the lives and reminiscences of figures like Steve Nelson and Paddy Troy were among the quintessential products of the 'new' Communist history, using oral history to recover the quality of individual experience. More recently, it is fitting that a de facto response to the *Black Book* has been assembled by a group of French historians long associated with the prosopographical study of labour movements and responsible among other things for a forthcoming *Dictionnaire biographique des Kominterniens*. Its title, with a significant plural emphasis, is *Le siècle des communismes*. On a modest scale, the sheer diversity of the lives presented in the present collection might seem to tend in the same direction.[18]

III

Such interpretations have sometimes been described as 'revisionist': an unfortunate word suggesting the mere inversion of 'Cold War' approaches. But as the different treatments in this volume show, biography no more lends itself to so obvious a counter-orthodoxy than to any other schematic treatment. If the idea of communisms, plural, rightly conveys the diversity of experiences the word encompasses, biographies keep reminding us of the linkages between these communisms, which in the period of the Comintern were visible, continuous and systematic. That is obviously true of the leadership cohort whose relations with Moscow can be found fully documented in the archives there. But it also takes us right into the party's districts and localities, finding there, as the party did, some 150-200 British recruits for the International Lenin School and several times that number to fight fascism in Spain. Even without setting foot outside the country, images of Russia, Spain, of Nazi Germany or of the exploited British colonies, had a formative influence on generations of Communist activists. Asked what single thing in the universe gave him most satisfaction, the young Cambridge graduate John Cornford replied, after due reflection, 'the existence of the Communist International'. Cornford was to give his own proof that this was more than just rhetoric as one of the first Britons to die in Spain.[19]

The Spanish volunteers are not represented in this volume, unless one includes the non-combatant Rust, but Barry McLoughlin has an important contribution on the less numerous but not less significant category of British functionaries or emigrés in Soviet Russia. Figures of this type provided some of the most disturbing memoirs of the Stalinist period, the outstanding British example – discussed in the same essay – being Freda Utley's *Lost Illusion*. Poised or torn between different 'communisms', these are exceptional lives in a British context, but their significance is not confined to those directly affected. At a factual level, they provided a body of information available to and disregarded by British Communists, though offering insights into Soviet experience which cut through the easy generalities of socialist construction. Circulated in books like Utley's, this information was available to any party member, not just the leadership, and none had to wait until 1956 for enlightenment. But also, like the Spanish volunteers in a more positive sense, those caught up in the Soviet experience seemed to represent the potentialities of other Communist lives, not this time as example or inspiration, but as warning. It is a common assumption in the literature of the camps – Hitler's as well as Stalin's – that responses to such extreme situations are not just of intrinsic significance but provide an insight into 'ordinary' mentalities and relationships stretched to their limits.[20] Perhaps in more modest fashion these uprooted British lives also provide us with 'eloquent episodes' – the phrase is Primo Levi's – illuminating the deeper attributes of British communism, both for better, as in Spain, and for worse. The challenge is to register their significance without reducing communism to a single universal narrative, differing only in degrees of realisation, such as we find in 'Cold War' writings of both Communist and anti-Communist persuasions.

Unquestionably, such issues have been addressed with far greater frankness and human insight in writings on the Holocaust. To invoke such a parallel does not mean conflating the Nazi and Stalinist dictatorships under a 'totalitarian' rubric, still less confusing the practitioners of genocide with the widely scattered adherents of the world Communist movement. Nevertheless, common to both cases was a diffused responsibility for the perpetration, toleration or disregarding of acts which offended not just abstract human values but, in this instance, those vigorously proclaimed by the Communists themselves. Moreover, similar explanations have been offered in both cases, of an indiscriminate collective guilt defined either racially, as befitting the racist ideology of fascism, or politically in the case of the Communists. The parallels are unmistakeable. The year before the *Black Book*, there appeared that other controversial bestseller, Daniel Goldhagen's *Hitler's Willing*

Executioners. Goldhagen's method was to apply a similar sweeping reductionism not in this case to a political grouping, the Communists, but to successive generations of Germans. Beginning with the unarguable truth that 'ordinary Germans' carried through the Holocaust, he endeavoured to show that all Germans, at all times, and of all political or religious persuasions, were thus potential perpetrators. The most obvious caveats – for instance, the comparative racial tolerance of the socialist and Communist movements – were simply brushed aside. Biography, at however rudimentary a level, was irrelevant. Differentiation between Germans, for example of active Nazis, was explicitly ruled out, and so was any sense of process by which ordinary Germans became perpetrators. As an attempt at historical explanation, the book's limitations were widely recognised by serious reviewers.[21]

Communism raises somewhat different issues as a freely chosen affiliation, but the poverty of so indiscriminate a methodology is equally applicable to it. 'Trotsky is only Mr Gallacher with the power to murder those whom he cannot convince', Winston Churchill once declaimed during an election contest, polemically encapsulating what would become the defining assumption of a certain approach to Communist history. Informally we make these leaps all the time, and it is part of the fascination of biography. Particular lives are imagined, not as the interaction of personality and circumstance which they really are, but as if representing some intrinsic human quality, a person, transportable in time and place – like the fantastic interludes in Peter Ackroyd's *Dickens*. Often the exercise has a salutary moral purpose, as in those reflections in Holocaust literature as to how far and in what circumstances other human beings, ourselves included, could have acted in these ways. More prosaically, a sort of counter-factuality is no doubt implicit in a narrative form propelled by decisions and contingencies, where every action is an alternative denied. In this case, however, the limits of the counter-factual are coterminous with the institution, as in Goldhagen's they are with nationality, serving at once to focus and delimit responsibility and establish guilt not so much by association as by affiliation. Collectively, the heat generated by the histories of even quite marginal Communist parties has for this reason reflected a sense of complicity and virtual interchangeability in an overwhelming common responsibility. *The Soviet World of American Communism* is the telling title of one recent publication, while the avowed intention behind the *Black Book* was that Communists in countries like France be judged not only on their own record, but that of all Communists, at all times, everywhere.[22]

No doubt there is another danger: that in our empathy with the underdog, especially one as remote from power as the British Communist Party, we forget the temper it might have displayed had the world been turned upside down according to its prescriptions. As Linda Colley has observed in relation to the Jacobites, perhaps the very remoteness of such a prospect in middling Britain can mean 'approaching these phenomena too wistfully and idealistically, of looking avidly for signs of turmoil and convulsion without considering what they would have meant for the men and women living at the time'.[23] That is a valid reflection, as long as we remember that in this case it was a party of protest, not of power, which British Communists joined, and that in every transition from one to the other, the identity of the party was transformed. As Inga Glendinnen notes in relation to Goldhagen's work: 'Sequence matters'. Not only did the interaction with different circumstances give rise to different patterns of behaviour, as wars, revolutions and the exercise of power always have, but prosopographically the actual personnel of these parties often changed dramatically. Notoriously, that was the case with the 'old' Bolsheviks, for it was the peculiar character of Communist persecutions, unlike those of Europe's fascist regimes, that they were typically and sometimes pre-eminently directed at the system's founders and supporters. Churchill was not to know in 1922 that Trotsky was himself to be murdered, although neither can Trotsky be absolved from responsibility for the system which perpetrated such crimes. Bolshevism was the progenitor of Stalinism, but the Bolsheviks – or many of them – were its victims.

So too, in a handful of cases, were British Bolsheviks, for whom transportation to a revolutionary order was not a dream or literary device but a reality. Untypical in their Russian experiences, it is the typicality of what led up to them that is ultimately disquieting. There is a letter in Allen Hutt's papers in which one of these victims, Freda Utley, refers to another of them, Rose Cohen. 'Generally I find the English crowd here divided into cliques, which make one feel rather uncomfortable & afraid of butting in even when they seem to be very amiable & friendly', Utley wrote from Moscow, where her Russian husband was to perish in the purges. 'Rose Cohen I have taken rather an objection to – she is so very smooth & insincere and also so terribly conceited. She really implies herself to be *the* power in the Eng[lish] section of the Comintern'.[24]

It is far from earth-shattering, and there are hundreds of such unsentimental reflections on fellow comrades to be found in the Moscow archives. What makes this one unsettling is that Rose Cohen, more than any other British Communist, is known to us mainly as a 'victim' of Stalinism, one who but for that fact we would barely be able to name. Utley's remark reminds us how arbitrary that fate was, how little related to any known criticisms of Soviet rule, and how nothing else but circumstance singled out the victim from scores of other potential victims. Utterly unlike the German case in this respect, supporters and victims were not neatly categorised but knew each other, sometimes denied each other, and typically represented different possible stages of the same lives. The 'ordinariness' of both victims and bystanders is thus grimly confirmed. Ironically, it was not those who perished but those who publicly acquiesced in their fate – Pollitt being an obvious British example – who possibly excited greater political suspicions, and were themselves lined up as victims in projected trials and interrogations. All that protected them – and they could hardly have been unaware of this – was their public standing in open societies.[25]

One wonders at such complicity and in part may ascribe it to a surpassing political cynicism – what Primo Levi in a different context described as a 'willed ignorance' – here diffused throughout the Communists' ranks.[26] That alone, however, cannot explain the complex correlations between knowledge, commitment and denial which the conjoined fates of bystander, accomplice and real or potential victim engendered. Notoriously, there were those who went to their death still believing their particular case to be a 'mistake'. But there were also those, harbouring no such illusions, who nevertheless retained their faith in a communism which to them represented something deeper than its betrayal by Stalinism. In Britain we have the testimony of Marian Šlingová, a British Communist who married the Czech party leader and former International Brigader, Otto Šling, during his wartime exile in London. Some ten years later, Šling, now party chief in Brno, was charged and condemned at the infamous Slansky show trial, and his British wife was herself subjected to a brutal imprisonment over a period of some two-and-a-half years. The sequel is in some ways more remarkable. Not only did Marian Šlingová never-theless remain a Communist, but on being deprived of her Czech citizenship for 'anti-state activity', rejoined the Communist Party in Britain, where she played a major role in the pro-dissident Committee to Defend Czech Socialists. Hers is a shocking story, marked by an extraordinary absence of bitterness towards those British Communists who, though subject to no coercion, had pushed her very existence to the recesses of their minds. Some of them indeed remained among her closest friends. On reflection, one ponders, as Marian Šlingová must have, how easily – but for the tragic contingencies of love and marriage – the positions of such comrades might have been reversed.[27]

IV

If relating such stories constitutes revisionism, it is simply in the sense of a populated history, fragmented enough to embrace the extraordinary diversity of experiences it encompassed over some three-quarters of a century. It is less an argument about autonomy than complexity, and if it is right that communism cannot be reduced to a single set of problems or relationships, it may be that one of the strengths of biography is to offer a possible route out of the recent impasse of the centre-periphery dichotomy. Despite much spilt ink, these debates are nowhere nearer a resolution than when they began – shortly after 1917 – and the archives now accessible are just as amenable to varied interpretations as were those already in the public domain. Extremes of control or autonomy are disproved, having already lacked credibility, but between these extremes there is scope for endless inconclusive calibration of centre-periphery relations, rotating on a single axis. Biography, potentially, offers an alternative approach, exploring relationships more historically and expansively, including those with different centres, or no centre at all. While centre-periphery is perhaps intrinsically an institutional metaphor, as befits its Soviet derivation, biography conversely is a reminder that we are all of us our own centres and that these personal centres are culturally, politically and geographically mobile. Described institutionally, a Communist Party is like a great goods train lumbering along, with a distant controller who every so often changes the points. Described prosopographically, it is more like a passenger service, with people constantly getting on and off, and bringing their baggage with them. Of course, they include many who travel 'to the end of the route' – as David Caute comments of fellow-traveller Hewlett Johnson – and some who travel not as passengers but as functionaries. The commitments the journey involves, in either case, are not usually negligible ones. But they are, nearly always, in Britain, freely undertaken.[28]

But if biography thus reaffirms the indigenous factors involved in the making of Communists, it is not by the exclusion of 'Russian' or other international factors, or the insistence that these were necessarily cosmetic or ritualistic allegiances. Indigenous in this context does not connote a particular place or ethnicity, and British-indigenous, as demonstrated in this volume, begins or ends in many different parts of the world. Rather, it may be taken as a modest, relative concept which simply means that in explaining why people became, remained and defined themselves as Communists, we need to be exploring realities and mentalities indigenous to them and not simply offloading the problem to an exteriority described as Bolshevism, Stalinism or 'orders from Moscow'. Perhaps this is all that the vaunted 'revisionism' adds up to. Of course the mechanics of democratic centralism, Moscow subsidies and party patronage networks helped, in certain cases, in certain periods, to decide people's actions. But a colloquial vocabulary of orders and compulsion needs to be used with especial care in what in its main aspects was essentially a voluntary movement. No serious historian would adopt such an approach to fellow-travellers like the Webbs whose fascination with Stalinism was in many cases every bit as compelling as that of most Communists. Communist Party membership, though conditional in its disciplines, doubtless provided a structured vehicle for such enthusiasms whose significance for many of its adherents was incalculable. Nevertheless, the fixation with the *machinery* of allegiance, which dominates a certain type of Communist Party history, is both politically and psychologically inadequate.

It has also made for some notably complacent accounts. It is by acknowledging that Bolshevism-Stalinism was not something that simply happened to the British left, but something that a significant segment of that left actively embraced, that one confronts the ultimately more challenging question of what patterns of thought or forms of association might have led to such an identification. Such a question takes us beyond the ranks of the Communists themselves, for in the Comintern period an identification with Soviet Russia was surprisingly pervasive among what one might call 'qualitative socialists', and many of these associated with or passed through the party.[29]

Explaining this phenomenon in conspiratorial or exogenous terms has usually meant the careful avoidance of its native preconditions, often with a view to sentimentalising some real or imagined alternative to Communism. But it is precisely that emphasis which breaks down at an individual level, where so often one discovers not so much the abstraction of 'suppressed alternatives', often lacking any plausible agent of suppression, but a process of self-suppression or – less tendentiously – simply a choice of alternatives. One does not have to endorse these choices, or overlook the material factors, career and patronage networks – offset or reinforced by countervailing forms of discrimination – which helped determine them. One simply has to recognise the human agency and rationality of the individuals involved.

Perhaps we ought to think of them, not in this case as ordinary Germans or even Britons, but as 'ordinary socialists' who found the most plausible vehicle for their socialism in the Communist Party. For what one presumes can now safely be called a 'post-Stalinist' generation, this means approaching Stalinism not as a sealed historical capsule of largely antiquarian interest, but as something in which the tradition to which socialists themselves belong is deeply implicated. It does not imply Goldhagen's rigid teleology, or the suggestion that all British socialists warmed to Stalinism, but it does remind us that this is the tradition that British communists mostly came from and belonged to.[30] To paraphrase Foucault, we need to explore that tradition, and these lives, not just for a condemnation in advance of the Gulag, but also for what made the Gulag – or in this case a toleration of the Gulag – possible.[31] That indeed is precisely why the problems signified by Stalinism still need to exercise our minds and consciences. Tzvetan Todorov has rightly cast doubt on the moral or political significance of simply denouncing slavery or totalitarianism when this is merely the lip-service of our times. 'On the other hand', he writes, 'if I discover that I myself or people with whom I identify have participated in acts like those I have condemned, then the conditions do exist for me to take a moral position'; to which it might be added that it is precisely such an identification that demands that such a reckoning be made.[32]

'Stalinism', it is true, has not usually been used by socialists for the identification of problems within the socialist tradition, but on the contrary has often served as a form of dissociation that has been particularly pronounced among those appearing to share many of its basic ideological and organisational postulates.[33] On the other hand, to acknowledge these commonalities in writing of the Communists means emphasising the responsibility of the historian, particularly the socialist historian, as well as the participant. Charles Maier has observed of the Holocaust that Jewish historians ought to emphasise its ordinariness, and German historians its uniqueness: exactly in the way that while other Europeans need to confront the Holocaust as an episode in European history, for Germans themselves such an emphasis can come dangerously close to apologia. Perhaps in relation to Stalinism, one can trace a similar issue as to whether the whole Soviet 'experiment' should be seen as something which the western socialist tradition inflicted on Russia – or the other way round. Russian historians will obviously make their own decisions, but if the 'post-Stalinist' left is to pay heed to Maier's precepts, then it is as adherents and historians of the western socialist tradition that we need to acknowledge and make what sense we can of its darker chapters.[34]

But of course, for those who continue to identify with that tradition, it is because this is not only a history of dark chapters. Most 'ordinary socialists' had only the faintest regard for Stalinism – though they may have had their own occlusions – while in the lives of the majority of 'ordinary' Communists the Soviet dimension was, by all empirical indices, demonstrably a subsidiary element. We need to know which structural and ideological determinants helped lead to one course of action and which another. But we also need not just history as 'lesson' but history as 'example': both the sorrier episodes in which British Communists were involved, but also Edward Thompson's 'hundred other things' that Communists did – those things which were 'important and within an alternative, authentic socialist tradition, some were heroic, and some of them no-one else would do'.[35] We also need to acknowledge that both aspects were often combined in the same lives, for, like the Communists themselves, historians have perhaps been a little prone to compartmentalisation in reclaiming these more inspiring moments without the complicating factor of Stalinism (or of course vice versa).[36]

It is an antidote both to such forms of compartmentalisation and to the tendency to homogenisation that the present collection may be regarded. If there is anything in the arguments presented here, then the depiction of British communism through these particular lives will differ materially from that which any alternative selection might have offered. In general, however, one notes the absence of the sort of oh-no-they-didn't exchanges which were once the very lifeblood of Communist Party history. The development of a critical Communist historiography, with biography one of its principal tools of analysis, continues.

NOTES

1. E. Gibbon, *Decline and Fall of the Roman Empire*, 1776-88, ch15; E.J. Hobsbawm, 'The Fabians reconsidered', in *Labouring Men*, London 1968, p250; S. Fielding, 'Interesting but irrelevant?', *Labour History Review*, 60, 2, 1995, pp120-3.
2. A. Agosti, *Palmiro Togliatti*, Turin 1996; J.G. Ryan, *Earl Browder: the failure of American communism*, Tuscaloose and London 1997; A. Kriegel and S. Courtois, *Eugen Fried: le grand secret du PCF*, Paris, 1997; K. Jacobsen, *Aksel Larsen: en politisk biografi*, Copenhagen 1993; K. Morgan, *Harry Pollitt*, Manchester 1993; J. Callaghan, *Rajani Palme Dutt: a study in British Stalinism*, London 1993; K. McDermott and J. Agnew, *The Comintern: a history of international communism from Lenin to Stalin*, Aldershot 1996. The author is familiar only with the works cited in English and French.
3. C. Pennetier, 'Singulier-pluriel: la biographie se cherche' in S. Wolikow

(ed), *Ecrire des vies: biographie et mouvement ouvrier, XIX-XX siècles*, Dijon 1994, p32.

4. See M. Narinsky and J. Rojahn (eds), *Centre and Periphery: the history of the Comintern in the light of new documents*, Amsterdam 1996. The centre-periphery relationship is that between Moscow and the national Communist parties.

5. I am thinking of the remarkable number of Spanish volunteers – perhaps a thousand – from a party itself only a few thousand strong at the start of the Spanish war.

6. A. Kriegel, *The French Communists: profile of a people*, 1972; S. Courtois et al, *Le livre noir du communisme*, Paris 1997.

7. See R.P. Arnot, *Twenty Years*, London 1940; J. Gollan, *30 Years of Struggle*, London 1950.

8. W. Gallacher, *Relaxation*, London 1950, p16.

9. H. Pollitt, *Serving My Time*, London 1940; T. Bell, *Pioneering Days*, London 1941; T.A. Jackson, *Solo Trumpet*, London 1953; D. Torr, *Tom Mann and his Times*, London 1956.

10. National Museum of Labour History (NMLH) CP/Ind/Poll/9/1; Russian State Archive of Socio-Political History (RGASPI) 495/100/1006, Pollitt to 'Dick', 2 May 1935; J. Mahon, *Harry Pollitt*, London 1976.

11. W. Stewart, *J. Keir Hardie: a biography*, London 1923, p347; P. Robrieux, *Maurice Thorez: vie secrète et vie publique*, Paris 1975; H. McShane and J. Smith, *No Mean Fighter*, London 1978.

12. P. O'Brien, 'Is political biography a good thing?', *Contemporary British History*, 10, 4, 1996, pp60-6.

13. See D. Hyde, *I Believed*, London 1951; A. Macleod, *The Death of Uncle Joe*, London 1996.

14. D.I. Kertzer, *Comrades and Christians: religion and political struggle in Communist Italy*, Cambridge, Massachusetts1980.

15. NMLH CP/Ind/Misc/10/3, T.A. Jackson, 'Interim Report', p260.

16. S. Rowbotham, *A New World for Women: Stella Browne, socialist feminist*, London 1977; B. Winslow, *Sylvia Pankhurst: sexual politics and political activism*, London 1996; M. Goldsmith, *Sage: a life of J.D. Bernal*, London 1980; W. Mulford, *This Narrow Place. Sylvia Townsend Warner and Valentine Acland: lives, letters and politics 1932-1951*, London 1988; M. Wadsworth, *Comrade Sak*, London 1998; M. Herbert, *Never Counted Out*, Manchester 1993.

17. B.D. Palmer, *E.P. Thompson: objections and oppositions*, London 1994, p57.

18. H. Klehr, *Communist Cadre: the social background of the American Communist elite*, Stanford, California 1978; B. Lazitch, *Biographical Dictionary of the Comintern*, Stanford, California 1986; R. Darlington, *The Political Trajectory of J.T. Murphy*, Liverpool 1998, ppxxii-xxv; S.F. Cohen, *Bukharin and the Bolshevik Revolution: a political biography*, Oxford 1973; S. Nelson, J.R. Barrett and R. Ruck, *Steve Nelson: American radical* (Urbana, 1982); C. Pennetier, 'À propos du dictionnaire biographique des Kominterniens', in S. Wolikow (ed), *Une histoire en révolution? Du bon usage des archives, de Moscou et d'ailleurs*, Dijon 1996, pp141-150; see also *Le Monde*, 21.09.2000.

19. V. Kiernan, 'Recollections', in P. Sloan (ed), *John Cornford: a memoir*, London 1938, p120.
20. See T. Todorov, *Facing the Extreme: moral life in the concentration camps*, London 1999, pp27-30.
21. D. Goldhagen, *Hitler's Willing Executioners: ordinary Germans and the Holocaust*, London 1997, pp6-7, 27-31 and passim. See the comments of I. Glendinnen, *Reading the Holocaust*, Cambridge 1999, pp116-33.
22. Churchill cited C.A. Cline, *E.D. Morel 1873-1924: the strategies of protest*, Belfast 1980, p132; P. Ackroyd, *Dickens*, London 1990; J.E. Haynes and H. Klehr (eds), *The Soviet World of American Communism*, New Haven and London 1997.
23. L. Colley, *Britons: forging the nation 1707-1837*, New Haven, Connecticut 1992, p72.
24. NMLH CP/Ind/Hutt/1/3, Utley to Hutt, 29.08.1928.
25. See also A. Vaksberg, *Hôtel Lux: les partis frères au service de l'Internationale communiste*, Paris 1993, pp209-42.
26. Levi cited Glendinnen, *op. cit.*, p42.
27. Marian Fagan, interview with author, 12 November 1999; M. Šlingová, *Truth Will Prevail*, London 1968.
28. D. Caute, *The Fellow Travellers*, London 1973, p1.
29. I take the phrase 'qualitative socialists' from N. Ellison, *Egalitarian Thought and Labour Politics: retreating visions*, London 1994.
30. Preliminary findings from the Manchester prospographical project show that nearly all of those British Communists for whom prior political affiliations are recorded had been members of Labour or socialist organisations (and hardly any of the right).
31. In 1978, when Stalinist institutions and practices still seemed very much in evidence, Edward Thompson cast strong doubt on the idea of a post-Stalinist generation; see *The Poverty of Theory*, London 1978, pp328-9.
32. Foucault cited A.J. Polan, *Lenin and the End of Politics*, London 1984, pp182-3; Todorov, *op. cit.*, pp116-17.
33. As Sheila Rowbotham has written, one winces at the 'self-satisfied tone' with which socialists sharing rather similar attributes, have sometimes referred to 'Stalinists'. 'I felt Cold War anti-communism became mixed up in the stridency of anti-Stalinism. Somehow by overshooting the mark Trotskyism blocked many aspects of the New Left resistance to Stalinism proper, which was not only a political system but a particular stance towards being a socialist'. Sheila Rowbotham, 'The women's movement and organising for socialism', in Sheila Rowbotham, Lynne Segal and Hilary Wainwright, *Beyond the Fragments. Feminism and the making of socialism*, London 1979, p9.
34. C. Maier, *The Unmasterable Past: history, Holocaust and German national identity*, Cambridge, Massachusetts 1988, pp160-72.
35. Thompson, *op. cit.*, p330.
36. That might be the one criticism of James K. Hopkins's excellent account, *Into the Heart of the Fire: the British in the Spanish Civil War*, Stanford, California 1998, which, while finely balancing the idealism of the volunteers and the negative influences of Stalinism, does arguably separate and counterpose them in rather too stark a fashion.

Dora Montefiore:
a different Communist

KAREN HUNT

Dora Montefiore's party life only lasted a few years, although she was a communist long before the formation of the Communist Party of Great Britain (CPGB). She was untypical of party members, even foundation members, and was unrepresentative of the few female Communist activists of the 1920s. So why should she be included in this collection? In the earliest days (when conferences were more open than they were to become), Dora Montefiore was elected twice in twelve months to the Party's executive – its sole female member on both occasions. This was a mark of the respect in which this elderly (she was seventy in 1921) middle-class woman was held by the left wing groups who formed the CPGB. She was one of a handful of British women Communists who travelled to Moscow in the early years of the revolution and was one of the few to address a Comintern Congress. She was a friend of the veteran German socialist Clara Zetkin and the Bolshevik leader Alexandra Kollontai and an experienced propagandist for a woman-centred socialism. On these grounds, she deserves to be remembered not only in women's histories of Communist politics but also in rigorous accounts of the CPGB.[1]

But because she was not to be part of that small group of men who came to dominate the Party leadership, her role and significance, if recognised at all, has been assumed to be marginal. Yet this chapter is not simply an exercise in reclamation – placing Dora Montefiore back among the pantheon of British Communists. I want to argue that it is at least as important to understand the significance of Montefiore's *difference*. By difference I not only mean her gender, her class origins and her generation but also her distinctive, long sustained and wide-ranging political experience. This was expressed through a practice which was hard to translate into the language of democratic centralism.

Studying her 'difference' helps to broaden our understanding of the early Party and the range of journeys its founders took to CP membership. Moreover it is suggestive of other possibilities for Communist politics in those early years after the First World War.

EARLY LIFE

Dora Montefiore did not have a 'classic' Communist background. She was born in 1851 into a large English middle-class family. Her father, Francis Fuller, worked closely with Prince Albert to plan the Great Exhibition which opened earlier in the year in which she was born.[2] Fuller was a successful surveyor and railway entrepreneur who, with his wife, brought up thirteen children at Kenley Manor in Surrey. Although Dora's upbringing was fairly typical of the mid-Victorian middle classes, there were aspects of it which she was able to draw on later when she began to lead a life which her early training had not anticipated. For a mid-Victorian girl she received a good education, becoming fluent in French and German. On leaving school she took on a practical, rather than the traditionally ornamental, role of women of her class by becoming her father's amanuensis.[3] Later she was to recall the importance of this time, for: 'It was when looking up statistics for the papers he read at the British Association, or writing at his dictation, or listening to excellent talk between men of the day and himself, that I absorbed, half consciously, the knowledge of, and interest in, those economic and social problems which form the basis of our Socialist propaganda'.[4] Of the generation of young women for whom a university education was not a possibility, Dora nevertheless acquired an exceptionally wide-ranging formal and informal education. In this she differed not only from many contemporaries but also from some of the more famous of the later generation of socialist women, such as Katherine St John Conway and Enid Stacy, who were graduates and who had had jobs as teachers before becoming full-time propagandists. Perhaps as important for the transformation of this relatively privileged young Victorian woman into a founder member of the CPGB was that, although she recalled a happy childhood, she also remembered herself as the darkhaired tomboy who felt different. This sense of difference combined with her extensive education provided fertile soil from which her later political activities would spring.

In 1874 Dora went to Australia to keep house for her eldest brother and there met George Barrow Montefiore, a merchant. After their marriage – seen as something of a rebellious act because he was Jewish – in 1881, they lived prosperously in Sydney where their two children were born. In 1889 her husband died at sea and Dora subsequently discovered that she had no rights of guardianship towards her own children unless her husband had willed them to her. This experience led her to meet other women in the same position and to make the connection with the most obvious sex-disability of all, the lack of a vote.[5] As a result, the first meeting of the Womanhood Suffrage League of New South Wales was held at her home in March 1891. In its earliest days she acted as the group's Honorary Secretary but by 1892 she had returned to Europe.[6] She settled for a time in Paris so that her children could learn French and finally returned to England so that her son could attend preparatory school.

There are many ways to narrate the life and politics of Dora Montefiore from this point on, for example by headlining her suffragism or her socialism, or by focusing on her experience of being represented as 'a difficult woman', a woman who does not fit into the traditional stories told of her time by contemporaries or by historians. Although my purpose here is to identify her genesis as a Communist, it is important to recognise that alternative narratives are possible.[7] Dora's understanding of politics meant that her practice was dynamic and self-consciously wove together many apparently separate interests, prioritising one particular identity over another depending on her judgement of the needs of the moment. If we are to understand her journey towards the CPGB's executive, certain aspects of her political life are necessarily foregrounded. But it is equally important to not lose sight of the landscape as a whole – her evolving broader politics set within the context of the changing possibilities of the time.

Dora had returned from Australia as a relatively inexperienced suffrage activist. The limitations of being a single-parent, albeit a middle-class one, and lack of experience of British politics – she had been living outside the country for nearly two decades – did not deter her. In the 1890s Dora moved through a range of political organisations, particularly various suffrage pressure groups. She was part of an attempt to change the Liberal Party's position on women's suffrage, lobbying from 1896 as part of the Union of Practical Suffragists to make suffrage a 'test question'.[8] She also campaigned with the Women's Local Government Society to promote women candidates and to ensure that women voted where they could.[9] By the end of the 1890s, in pursuit of her suffragism Dora Montefiore had acquired key political skills. She had become a more assured public speaker, was publishing as a journalist and was also a committee woman. It is also clear that Dora would not find her political home in the Liberal Party.

THE MAKING OF A SOCIALIST

In the latter part of the 1890s Dora Montefiore was stretching beyond liberalism and what she saw as the 'male policy' of the Liberal Party, seeking an organisation which reflected her evolving politics. Reading labour history, corresponding with Julia Dawson of the socialist newspaper the *Clarion* from 1897, two weeks as an itinerant propagandist with the Clarion Van in 1898, and attendance at the Independent Labour Party (ILP) Annual Conference in 1899, were all part of her journey to socialism.[10] For her there was no moment of conversion, to use the language so familiar from the 'religion of socialism' of the period.[11] Later she recalled the effect of her experience as a Clarion Vanner:

> I returned home feeling that there was much more than reading and study to be done in order to get the right angle from which to study social conditions and evolve a possibility of a cure for the horrors I had observed of bad housing and poverty. I must study at close quarters working-class conditions, and before I joined definitely any party either reformist or revolutionary in its outlook, I must (not being myself a member of the working class) train my imagination and intelligence to see eye to eye with the workers in their class struggle in which they were so severely handicapped.[12]

Dora Montefiore understood politicisation as a process anchored in experience but which was profoundly influenced by reading and studying, hence her involvement from an early stage in the propaganda work of 'making socialists'. She remembered that, for her, reading socialist literature and attending socialist meetings were part of a process 'till, finally, the intellectual appeal grew strong enough to make me desire to join a Socialist organisation'. In choosing between the ILP and the Social Democratic Federation (SDF), she said it was 'Social Democracy, with its international and revolutionary basis, [which] captured me'.[13] It is not clear when exactly she joined the SDF. But by 1901 she was a guest at the Central SDF's monthly dinners and was writing for the organisation's papers.[14] By 1903 she was on the executive, and was elected on three subsequent occasions, in 1904, 1908 and 1909. She remained an energetic although often dissident worker for the SDF and its successor the British Socialist Party (BSP) until the end of 1912.

Dora Montefiore developed her socialist ideas as a journalist and propagandist and explored the possibility of creating a woman-focused socialism. In the early years of the century, she developed ways of contributing to the cause whilst at the same time balancing her domestic responsibilities, her sometimes uncertain health and her continuing commitment to suffragism. Patterns were set then which continued to mark her activism long after her children had grown up. Her writing took several forms. She had published a volume of poetry, *Singing Through the Dark* (1898), and was to continue to produce poetry throughout her political career; some of which would be published in the CPGB's weekly *The Communist*. Like many contemporary socialists and suffragists she used poetry as a form of propaganda. Didactic and often burdened with emotion, Dora's poetry expressed her anger at the system and her aspirations for a future world. She also published two selections of quotations, *The Woman's Calendar* (1906) and *The People's Calendar* (1919), which demonstrated wide reading and her belief that creativity and politics were not necessarily counterposed. Glancing through the socialist and even the early Communist press, the presence of poetry and fiction suggests that her instincts were shared by others.

Nevertheless, the bulk of Dora's writing was journalism which drew on the networks she developed with suffragists and socialists as well as her wide reading of the press, including the international socialist press.[15] From 1897 she was part of a correspondence network centred on the radical suffragist Elizabeth Wolstenholme Elmy, until their friendship abruptly ended when Dora left the Women's Social and Political Union (WSPU) at the end of 1906.[16] The practice of sending cuttings and notes to each other was then continued informally by Dora with other correspondents such as Clara Zetkin. Dora was able to use this material as the stimulus for weekly columns. From 1902 to 1906 she wrote the 'Women's Interests' column for the radical paper *New Age* while in 1909 and 1910 she wrote 'Our Women's Circle' in the SDF's weekly paper *Justice*.[17] Here she was able to draw attention to, and reflect upon, day-to-day developments, respond to readers' queries and report on the international socialist and women's movements. It was in these spaces within the press that Dora was able to consider what a woman-focused socialism might be and articulate with little editorial interference some of the concerns marginalised in the body of the paper. She also submitted articles and reports to *Justice* and *Social Democrat* and, after leaving the BSP in 1912, wrote for and to papers as various as the *Daily Herald* and *The Vote*. In addition she published in foreign presses, such as the American *Progressive Woman*, the South African *Voice of Labour*, New Zealand's *The Maoriland*

Worker and Australia's *Socialist* and *International Socialist*. It was the latter, the paper of the Sydney branch of the Socialist Federation of Australasia, which Dora edited during 1911 when its editor Harry Holland became seriously ill. She also established and edited her own shortlived paper in England immediately before the First World War – *The Adult Suffragist*.

Although not living by her writing – her husband's will set up a trust fund which supported Dora and her children – Montefiore became an experienced journalist and editor in the service of the movement. In addition her speeches, campaigns and actions were themselves the subject of many column inches. Dora Montefiore was also a pamphleteer. She wrote two important pamphlets for the SDF's women's organisation – *Some Words to Socialist Women* (1907) and *The Position of Women in the Socialist Movement* (1909).[18] Part of Dora's reputation was based on her writing, so when she was introduced to socialists in Australia she was described as 'one of the party's ablest lecturers, and at the same time a cultured and forceful writer. Her contributions to "Justice" have been read and quoted from throughout the world. We welcome our talented comrade'.[19]

Unlike some of her fellow SDFers, who wrote but were unable to make public speeches and rarely participated in the cut and thrust of debate, Dora developed her ideas through public speaking, through attending conferences and even through international travel. These occasions continued through her life and provided an opportunity to meet a wide range of people, make connections across classes and encounter experiences very different to her own. In 1898 with the Clarion Van she had toured the colliery villages around Mansfield while twenty years later, speaking in Abertillery, she had stayed with a miner's family and learnt about mining conditions in the Welsh valleys. When in May 1921, the police raided the CPGB offices and arrested prominent leaders, Dora was instructed to disappear for a time; it was to Abertillery that she turned. Adopting her mother's maiden name and wearing a nurse's uniform, she went into hiding. She lived with a worker's family in their council house, working with the committees being organised to feed miners' children during the lockout of that year.[20] This was no 'political tourism', for Dora had already established strong working relationships with working-class women. In the early years of the WSPU, Dora had been an organiser in the East End, working with the Canning Town WSPU. Branch minutes show she was viewed with respect and affection and a particular bond was established with Adelaide Knight, a working-class mother imprisoned as a suffragette and later a foundation member of the CPGB.[21]

It was not only through voyages into the domestic 'unknown' that Dora fed her evolving socialist ideas. Aside from attending international conferences, she travelled extensively in Europe in the first decades of the century, particularly in Scandanavia in 1905 and 1906 where she learnt much about the effect of the enfranchisement of women on local socialist movements. From 1910 to 1912 she toured the USA, spent a year in Australia and visited South Africa, returning there in 1914. She spent 1923 in Australia although by then she was a Communist and many more restrictions were placed on her actions. In her travels before the war she spoke at meetings, attended conferences and met local comrades and radicals. She seems to have been an effective, even a 'robust' speaker, described on one occasion as holding 'the rapt attention of her delighted and appreciative listeners. Applause was frequent and the speaker's points sharp and telling'.[22] On another occasion in Australia she was described as 'international, charming and lovable, filling the eye with a fine personality, and charming the ear with a musical voice and noble language and sentiments'.[23] For a woman in her sixtieth year to prompt such a response, she must have had charisma. Throughout her political career socialist women speakers were still unusual; but to sustain a reputation as a propagandist novelty was insufficient. Skills and argument were required: and the latter was honed not only on the public platform and in the pages of the socialist press but by work in the party's organisation. Here too Dora Montefiore developed her socialist practice over the years, inside and outside the SDF and its successors.

When Dora took part in the annual conferences of her own party, she was a rare female voice, as in 1904 when she called for a 'different atmosphere in the branches' in order to recruit women and for socialist support for women's enfranchisement, citing the positive example of Australia.[24] These two themes were central to her politics. She did not attend SDF/SDP conferences regularly but when she did, as in 1908 and 1909, she also spoke; for passivity was not her strong suit, indeed participation was all.[25] Similarly when she attended the 1907 and 1910 International Congresses of the Second International and the meetings of the Socialist Women's International, few could ignore her presence. Certainly the ILP women in the British delegation were irritated by her, as Margaret MacDonald, campaigner for women's rights and wife of the future Labour Party leader, Ramsay MacDonald, made clear in 1910. She reported that 'for the sake of letting things go smoothly, [we] put up quietly with much more of Mrs Montefiore than is justified by her influence or representative character in the British movement'.

MacDonald complained that 'Mrs Montefiore [had] smilingly assured me, when I appealed to her to have the common courtesy to let one of us move our own ... resolutions, that she would speak about them for us in the course of her speech, [so] we felt it was time to make a public protest, and we walked out of the hall in a body'.[26]

Dora could prompt walk-outs and lead them too, as at the 1909 International Woman Suffrage Alliance (IWSA) Congress.[27] Such occasions produced the opportunity to dramatise your case. This was particularly so when yours was the minority position, as it was for Dora as an adult suffragist in the IWSA. Dora's final experience of a congress of the Socialist International was the Basle Peace Congress of 1912, when she was the only female member of the British delegation. She reported that delegates, including herself, had been muzzled and she protested at the officialdom and bureaucracy of the English group. She felt that the delegates were only present as 'window-dressing' and that the key vote had been stage-managed. In protest she was one of the only people present who refused to vote for the International's manifesto on peace.[28] For this she was censured by her party and subsequently resigned from the BSP. For her the International's manifesto on peace was a 'lengthy climbdown, signifying nothing'.[29] Dora was not happy about, and was generally not used to, conferences where delegates could not make an intervention and where there was little space for debate. It is not clear what she would have made of the conferences of the CPGB, once the party was fully 'Bolshevised'.

If there is a temptation to diminish Dora's contribution to socialist politics as attention-seeking, this should be tempered by the fact that she was perfectly willing to work where no spotlight shone. Over the years she undertook a number of tasks over and above her work as an SDF executive member. She acted as Reporter for the Socialist Women's Bureau (the British arm of the Socialist Women's International) from 1907, became Honorary Secretary of the Adult Suffrage Society in 1909, and was Chairman of the Women's League of the Central Labour College in 1913; while during the first year of the war she sat on the executive of the Women's Suffrage National Aid Corps. She clearly could undertake the less glamorous but equally necessary work of holding office and participating in committee work. As a socialist journalist, propagandist and committee woman, she had much to offer a new party like the CPGB. But why should Dora Montefiore want to take that step when so many other socialist women, particularly of her generation, did not?

COMING TO COMMUNISM

A number of experiences took Dora along the road to foundation membership of the CPGB. Fundamentally, as she noted in 1910, her experience in fighting as a suffragist for almost twenty years had changed her view of the political system and what was needed to change it:

> I may add that it was in fighting for the vote as a passive resister (when my furniture was sold for three successive years, because I refused as an outlander to pay income tax), and as a militant (when I went to Holloway among the first batch of suffragist prisoners for speaking in the lobby of the House of Commons) that I learnt of how little real value is the political vote in the upward struggle of the workers ... without proper representation the present electoral system, with its brute majority rule, is of little use, and without Industrial Unionism, to speed up political action there is but little hope for the revolutionary, whose aim is to over-throw Capitalism and all its works.[30]

Anchored as these comments are in direct political experience, it is hard to dismiss them as rhetoric. Certainly by this time she characterised her politics in revolutionary terms. For example, in a discussion with Archie Crawford, editor of the Johannesburg *Voice of Labour*, over their mutual desire for what Dora termed a 'Red International', she said, 'our motto must be that of William Morris – "Educate towards revolution!".'[31] But there were to be two other issues with which Dora became involved while she was in Australia in 1911 that crystallised this emphasis in her politics and which were to be central to the thinking of the Third International.

The first was the issue of imperialism, particularly how 'coloured workers' were to be integrated as equal partners into the class struggle along with white working men and, of course, working women. This was an issue which Dora was to continue to struggle with. But it was this round-the-world trip in 1910-12 which allowed her to see for herself how divisive race was within the working class and hence for socialist politics. She was only in America for two months, largely in the north east. There is little reflection in her journalism at the time on race as an issue in American society although an aside in her autobiography, *From a Victorian to a Modern* (1927), comparing her experience of train travel in Soviet Russia with America reveals something of the discomfort she still felt about the issue. Dora recalled her journey to Moscow in 1924:

I found the Russian sleeping arrangements far more comfortable for my sex than are those obtaining in America, where one has a berth in a long sleeping car, shared by both men and women, and where the attendants are coloured men. To reach the ladies' toilet room for dressing and undressing, one has to walk down a long corridor of curtained berths, and run the gauntlet of these coloured men.[32]

Yet when Dora encountered 'White Australia', she instinctively pushed at the sensitivities of her socialist audiences.

In one of her earliest speeches in Australia she emphasised that 'the workers of the world, including the coloured workers, had to be organised in order to down Capitalism'.[33] On another occasion she warned Australian Labour, 'When they tap at the door of the International Bureau, they will have to drop their provincial impediments of a "White Australia" and "compulsory military service" because International Socialism unites on the basis of THE CLASS STRUGGLE, NOT COLOR OR SEX STRUGGLE'.[34] It was in arguing this case that she suggested:

The picture that should be held up to the workers of Australia is not that of the yellow man thirsting to wed or outrage the white woman on a wholesale scale, which is the favourite bogey of the Australian yellow press, but that of the cosmopolitan trader, using the teeming millions of the East IN THEIR OWN COUNTRY to compete against the more highly paid workers in Australia and America. That is the Yellow Peril of the near future, and it behoves the leaders of the white wage slaves, besides organising them, to EDUCATE them not in ignorant prejudices, not in the vocabulary of senseless abuse, but in the economic facts of the case, so that the solidarity among the exploited in every country, may become an accomplished and a menacing fact for the exploiters.[35]

These were arguments that Dora developed largely against the grain of both the Australian labour movement and the local socialist movement. Yet like her socialist contemporary Tom Mann who had lived in Australia from 1901 to 1910, Dora found her internationalism was clarified and strengthened. Now she would emphatically argue for an internationalism that was exclusive of neither race nor gender. This was not an emphasis which all those who called themselves socialist internationalists would have shared in the years before the First World War.

When Dora left Australia for South Africa, her views on the centrality of race to the class struggle were reinforced. She marvelled at the cosmopolitan society that South African capitalists were creating. Their purpose, she argued, was exploitation but this also provided for the possibility of a very different outcome from such diversity. She was optimistic:

> The Socialists could not have accomplished this miracle which economic forces are driving the capitalists to undertake; but we can interpret for the workers how the stars in their courses are fighting for us, and we can link up throughout the world that comradeship which makes first for revolt against organised exploitation, and then for construction of the new economic and social order.[36]

Like Tom Mann, who also visited South Africa, Dora was to carry forward these ideas into her communism. Indeed when she and Mann spoke at the Fifth Comintern Congress in 1924, both emphasised the importance of solidarity between black and white workers in the context of a ferocious and exploitative imperialism.

The other question which was influential in Dora's journey to communism was militarism, particularly the implementation of compulsory military service for young men and boys in Australia and the issue of a white citizen defence force in South Africa – a militia which was soon used by the government against striking workers. These issues were in the news between 1910 and 1912. In Australia, she outlined an internationalism which was defiantly anti-militarist – 'Workers of the world unite. It is you, and you only, who can make war on war'.[37] When editing the *International Socialist* she argued strongly against compulsory military training for school-age boys, writing 'seditious' leaders calling on the boys to boycott the training and refuse to take the military oath. In an article on 'The Baby Army', she appealed to mothers, in particular, not to let their sons undergo the training and be swallowed up in the militarist machine – 'no "love of country" can justify mothers in inciting their sons to maim and destroy the sons of other mothers'.[38] When she arrived in South Africa she found the Labour Party intensely divided over the issue. While in the country Dora worked behind the scenes to encourage the substitution of anti-militarism for peace propaganda.[39] She continued to publicise these campaigns and the socialist anti-militarist arguments that underpinned them both in the British press and at international meetings. For example, after the meeting of the Basle Peace Congress, she spoke with Zetkin and the German socialist leader Rosa Luxemburg about her experiences of anti-militarist campaigning and as a consequence a meeting was hastily convened so that Dora could put before an international audience the facts about the military preparations being made in the British Empire. The meeting was 'packed to the doors'.[40]

These themes of anti-imperialism, particularly racial solidarity, and of anti-militarism linked together by a fervent internationalism, dominated the politics of Dora Montefiore in the years after she left the BSP. 1913 and 1914 saw her working with a range of groups and publications on the Left, particularly publishing in the *Daily Herald* and speaking for the Herald League. She had always juggled membership of a range of organisations, socialist and suffragist, and been active in cross-party campaigning. This was to continue to characterise her politics, even after she rejoined the BSP in 1916. It may explain the familiarity with her name and reputation displayed by those who attended the founding conference of the CPGB in 1920, as well as her ability, particularly as she grew older and less identified with a single party, to somehow rise above the sectarian battle.

But it was the war years, as for other foundation Communists, which were to be crucial in bringing her to define herself as a communist. Unlike other leading women of the first generation of British Communists, such as the Scottish ILP leader Helen Crawfurd, it was not anti-war campaigning which radicalised Dora and brought her into the orbit of the wartime rebel networks.[41] For her the war brought novel public and personal experiences and reinforced the urgency of sustaining a broad-based socialist politics – broad in its concerns as well as in its organisational forms. In the first months of the war she was arguing at the Suffrage Club, 'In all their struggle women must never lose sight of the fact that they must secure economic independence, and it was for women themselves to grapple with this problem; they must not allow it to be settled by men'.[42] She was particularly keen to draw attention to the issue of 'Women and the Food Supply' while maintaining a persistent demand for adult suffrage.

The war itself was not an abstract issue for Dora Montefiore. Despite her opposition to the war, her son enlisted. Her anxieties about the well-being of Gilbert, who as part of the Australian Imperial Forces served in France, might be shared by other mothers but by fewer of her socialist comrades. But unlike many mothers of soldiers she also chose to visit and work in the war-zone. She ran the hospital kitchens at a depot for sick French soldiers just behind the Arras trenches. She had chosen to help the French because they were an invaded nation. This episode demonstrates many of the paradoxes which underlie any sustained political practice, particularly the balance that is continually having to be struck between the demands of the public and the private. At the suggestion of a member of her club, the Lyceum (for after all she was still very much a middle-class woman), she contacted the Croix Rouge Francaise and, after having provided guarantors from personal friends in the Privy Council and the army, obtained a passport. Part of the arrangement was that she would provide fresh food at her own expense for the soldiers to supplement the rations. In the months from the end of 1915 when she worked at the Cantines des Dames Anglaises, she learned at first hand the reality of a militarism she had long opposed.[43] When she heard her son was due to arrive with the Australian forces in Britain, she felt she had to return to England to provide a home for him when he was granted leave. As she observed: 'This story strictly speaking, should not come into my reminiscences of a suffragist and socialist; it was an interlude, but one that steeled my heart to fight ever more insistently for a social and economic change which should place fellowship above competitive imperialism'.[44] At the time it also seemed to strengthen her determination to argue for a revolutionary socialism. She rejoined the BSP, now affiliated to the Labour Party, and wrote regularly for its paper, *The Call* – one of the few female voices to be found in it.

Soon the other wartime catalyst to her becoming a Communist was galvanising Dora as speaker, journalist and activist – the Russian Revolution. She spoke at the BSP meeting called to greet the February Revolution, emphasising the anti-imperialist and socialist character of the struggle in Russia and calling on the British working-class movement to rally against capitalist imperialism and the war.[45] She now described herself as a 'revolutionary socialist'. A key speaker at the Leeds Convention in June 1917, when the Left united briefly to hail the Revolution, she chose again to concentrate on imperialism in her speech, linking the fight against Russian imperialism to the necessary fight against the English variety: 'They had got to do what the Russians had done'.[46] On a speaking tour in early 1918, when she had just said goodbye to her son as he left for the front 'without letting him see too much what I was suffering', she lectured under the title 'Get on with the class war'.[47] During the trip she took time to visit the son of a friend who had been imprisoned as a conscientious objector in Walton Gaol. Due to speak at Openshaw BSP to a special women's meeting, the strain of the emotional and political demands on her began to tell and she collapsed with bronchitis. Nevertheless, that year her political activity continued: she was the only woman elected to the BSP executive in 1918; as a delegate to the Labour Party Conference that year she protested at the conference being addressed by the foremost opponent of the 1917 revolution, Alexander Kerensky, without also hearing a Bolshevik speaker; she took part in the discussion within the BSP on whether to remain affiliated to the Labour Party, which was to prefigure later discussions in the CPGB; she attended the Labour Party Women's Conference; and was there in Glasgow to greet the revolutionary socialist and anti-war campaigner John Maclean when he was finally released from prison.[48] Busily she spoke and wrote, energised by her understanding of what was happening in Russia so that she could overcome her own worries about Gilbert and her health.

A DIFFERENT COMMUNIST

With the end of the war she kept the momentum up, fighting unsuccessfully a London County Council election for Hammersmith Labour Party, attending conferences and addressing meetings. Still the same themes galvanised her, as when in 1919 she and Sylvia Pankhurst addressed a meeting in Sheerness on 'Class struggle from the international standpoint'. Drawing explicitly on the experiences she had gained from her travels, she argued, 'there must be no aristocracy of Labour and no conscious or unconscious understanding between Labour and Capital to exploit backward and coloured races'.[49] Soon after this her son returned to Australia.

She was never to see him again. In June 1921, four days after his own son was born, Gilbert died of a haemorrhage, his lungs having been damaged by mustard gas in the war. As Dora remembered, bringing together in her words the public and the private: 'On joining up he had been passed as a first-class life, but he was one of the millions of victims of imperial rivalries, and his death turned for me the light of day into darkness'.[50] But this event was still to come, a few politically-engaged years later. Nevertheless her son's and her own experiences in the war affected her journey to communism. His death was a spur to a final burst of activity by Dora in Australia on behalf of the CPGB. It also provided one of the reasons for the breakdown in her health in the 1920s, for she was both physically and emotionally less resilient. More speculatively, it may also explain her distance from the day-to-day life of the party once Bolshevised.

Like many others who continued to work on the Left after the war, who were inspired by 1917 and who desired unity between the disparate socialist groups and factions, the logic of her political practice led Dora Montefiore to attend the unity convention which formed the CPGB in the summer of 1920. Only twelve and a half per cent of the delegates over the two day conference were women and of them, four stood for the executive. Only Dora was successful – she was considerably older than the other three women, Melvina Walker, Norah Smythe and Cedar Paul, and unlike them was not an ex-member of the Workers' Socialist Federation.[51] At the conference Dora spoke in the debate on affiliation to the Labour Party, arguing that 'Important as the industrial method was, important as was the stopping of making munitions, at the same time we must go into Parliament and work there'.[52] To clinch her argument she cited the example of her friend Clara Zetkin, who as a revolutionary had been elected to the Reichstag.

Dora served on the executive for a year, wrote regularly for *The Communist* and sustained her networks with other socialist-now-Communist women such as Alexandra Kollontai.[53] She represented the British party at the founding congress of the French Communist Party, where she witnessed Zetkin's dramatic speech as she was spirited in and out of the conference to avoid the attentions of the police.[54] Police surveillance was becoming more and more constricting. Indeed one of the reasons she had spoken to the French conference was that the chairman of the CPGB, Arthur MacManus, was denied a passport. This was a problem that Dora was to face herself in 1922 when she applied to visit her son's grave in Australia. Only by signing an agreement to refrain from Communist activities was she finally given a visa. Even after the French meeting the police followed her to her hotel and questioned her. Meanwhile in 1921 she was kept busy by executive business, until forced to go into hiding in Abertillery in May.

She returned to hear of her son's death and after that point she seems to have been less active in CPGB activities. As she wrote: 'This was a crushing blow, from the effects of which I have never recovered, and my health which was already compromised by frequent attacks of bronchitis, began seriously to fail'.[55] She nevertheless took an active interest in the Russian Famine Fund, into which much female Communist activity was channelled, donating funds, opening the Grand Bazaar and Fair and becoming a member of the fund's Children's Homes Committee.[56] But she was not recorded as being involved in the tentative work among women members in these years despite her wealth of experience and she did not stand again for the executive in 1922. Indeed no woman was elected that year although Helen Crawfurd was co-opted as the women's representative.[57] Once Dora recovered from an operation for appendicitis in February 1922, she was determined to get to Australia even if that meant she had to be seen to be more distanced from the Party and King Street.

When letters travelled back and forth between the Australian Investigation Branch and the British authorities, it became clear that the authorities were convinced that Dora Montefiore was 'dangerous and undesirable'. According to them: 'In recent years Mrs Montefiore has been prominently identified with the Communist movement in this country and is a well-known anti-militarist and advocate of world-wide revolution and anarchy'.[58] Although there was an acceptance that Dora wanted to go to Australia to visit her daughter-in-law and grandchildren and for health reasons, it was felt necessary to get her to promise to abstain from political activities. And to ensure that she did, she and her mail were closely scrutinised for contacts with the Communist Party of Australia (CPA). Those watching her concluded that 'this elderly lady' has 'to all outward appearances ... lived as a person of comfortable means and good standing'. But they continued:

> Her connection with Communist leaders in England is well known, and she has been in communication with them from Australia and has rendered an account of the Labour movement here; she has discouraged immigration, and she has approved JS Garden[a CPA leader]'s statements. In Sydney she has not directly concerned herself in Communist Hall activities and has evidently been in touch privately with the leaders only ... Her correspondence from abroad marks her as a Communist. When applying for a passport to Australia, Mrs Montefiore gave a written assurance that she would not engage in Communist work out here, but she is evidently disregarding her undertaking. It is likely that she may leave on her return to England this year. She can only be regarded as an important intermediary, despite her years and upbringing.[59]

Dora did indeed eschew public meetings while in Australia, no doubt partly to meet the conditions of her visa, but also because her doctor had told her after the 1920 May Day demonstration to refrain from outdoor public speaking as her throat was giving trouble.[60] Nevertheless, as 1923 wore on, Dora did at least feel able to publish a series of articles in the CPA's new paper, *Workers' Weekly*, giving sketches of various socialist leaders she had known such as the American trade unionist Eugene Debs, Rosa Luxemburg and the Irish leader Jim Larkin, while also producing a digest of views on 'Foreign Affairs' for *New Outlook*.[61] She also went to some lengths to meet Communist groups informally in order to gain an impression of the prospects of the CPA, which formed the basis of her report to the Comintern the following summer. Unfortunately the journey back to

England left her dangerously ill and she was advised to winter in Bournemouth. By now her public activities on behalf of the CPGB were almost at an end but there was one last task for this seventy-two year old.

In June 1924, Dora Montefiore travelled to Moscow in order to attend the Fifth Congress of the Comintern, representing the CPA. There she met again with her old comrade Zetkin. It was a 'great joy to talk over our work in the past, and our hopes for the future'.[62] In the draft of her report for the Comintern on the CPA she claimed to have visited key branches in Brisbane, Sydney, Adelaide and Perth. She had done her homework. But she also felt the need to explain herself. Why was a middle-class woman representing the Communist workers of Australia? She said that for the last twenty-five years and more she had identified herself with the cause of the workers in various parts of the world. In addition in 1911 and 1912 she had edited with Harry Holland the *International Socialist* in which they had attacked the work of the Australian Labor Party. She reiterated their role in opposing the military training of boys. She acknowledged that this work followed on from that undertaken by Tom Mann in Melbourne. Indeed when she returned to Australia in 1922, she said that the Australian workers gave her a cordial welcome 'and acknowledged that if they had understood the world situation in the years before the war, as we International Socialists understood it, they would not have wasted lives and wealth in the wars of rival Imperialisms'. Giving a great deal of detail of the economic and political developments in post-war Australia, she reported that the Communists 'are succeeding to some extent in their task of permeating the Unions'. She then considered the prospects for the CPA.[63] Not all of this speech was eventually delivered to the Congress. But it gives a good indication of her sensitivities – her class position in particular – as well as the crucial importance of Australia in the development of her politics, specifically the intertwined themes of anti-imperialism and anti-militarism.

When Dora Montefiore addressed the Fifth Congress she asserted that the tasks of the Australian party were in many respects similar to those of the British party, by which she meant the question of affiliation to the Labour Party, developing a United Front and attempting to become 'real live parties'. She addressed the problem of the 'White Australia' policy and pointed out that 'when Marx said "workers of the world, unite", he did not mean to say, "white workers of the world, unite".' She conveyed a message from the CPA to their comrades of the Pacific rim 'assuring them that no Communist supported the colour line'. She suggested, rather pointedly, that 'if the Communist Party of Great Britain would take an interest in the Pacific and in Australia, the way would be open towards the formation of a true mass party and the workers would understand what revolution meant and rally to its cause'.[64] Tom Mann was one of the only other speakers to raise the issue of race, outside the debate on 'The Negro Question'. Soon after Dora delivered her report she fell ill once more and was granted permission by the Comintern to return home. She had been excited by what she had seen and said that if she had been a younger woman and in better health she would have wanted nothing more than to spend two or three years studying conditions in Soviet Russia. The CPA remained important to her and one of her last letters on party matters was to CPGB general secretary, Albert Inkpin, in 1925, commenting on the muddled situation of Communism in Australia. It was her view that 'with the Pacific situation developing as it is doing, it is of extreme importance that a strong and well organised Communist Party, with a real international outlook, should be started in Australia, with an organiser sent out from Moscow'.[65]

Gradually losing her sight and suffering from severe bronchial asthma, Dora Montefiore now had 'to live much indoors with my books and my thoughts'. So she wrote her autobiography, which ends with the words, 'it is in the faith that the workers will eventually accomplish their mission that I have lived and done my days' work in the world'.[66] On her death at the end of 1933, Dora's obituaries commemorated a socialist, a militant suffragist, a pioneer of social democracy, an old friend of Clara Zetkin and a founder member of the Communist Party. *The Times* also noted not only that she bore her blindness with great courage but that she even spoke from a public platform when quite blind. She was held in such esteem that on her eightieth birthday her friends, both political and personal, had entertained her at dinner. The *Daily Herald* noted that at nearly eighty-three years of age, Dora Montefiore had dictated a message denouncing the reactionary view of women adopted by Mussolini and Hitler. Only the *Daily Worker* failed to conjure up such a tenacious figure, noting instead that ill health and loss of sight had prevented her from taking an active part in the movement in recent years.[67]

So in what ways was Dora Montefiore a different Communist? Women rank and file members of the early CPGB were a distinct minority and leading women activists were few. Dora as the sole female member of the executive was therefore unique and thus quintessentially different. All the other leading Communist women of this early period were of a different generation to Dora, although a number shared her pre-war commitment to suffragism, such as Helen Crawfurd and Ellen Wilkinson. Crawfurd, like Montefiore, was a widow and came from a better-off background, although her father's job as a master baker was hardly equivalent to that of Francis Fuller. Widowhood also often brings a curious declassé position, although more unusually Montefiore was surprisingly well-provided for. Although never rich and often worried about money, she nevertheless did not need to earn a living. Dora's class origin made her unusual compared with the young male leaders of the new party. Her long political experience was not common and was partly a function of her age; but she also stood out because many who shared her SDF background had been lost to the movement by 1920 or had relocated to the Labour Party. In some ways an equivalent figure was Tom Mann, venerated and yet not viewed as entirely reliable in the new disciplined party. Both had learnt from their experience of political work within the White Dominions of the British Empire and tried to take seriously the issue of race. Yet in other ways their politics differed, with Mann's primary focus being the industrial scene while Montefiore always recognised that politics are gendered.

So there was no-one quite like Dora Montefiore. What is not clear is whether, if her health had not broken, she would have continued to find the CPGB a congenial home as the 1920s wore on. As it was, neither the Party nor she were tested in this respect and she can safely be included among the ranks of the early Communists – a different Communist, but still a Communist!

I am grateful for an Australian Bicentennial Fellowship and British Academy support which enabled me to explore the Australian sources for the life and politics of Dora Montefiore.

NOTES

1. See S. Bruley, *Lenininism, Stalinism and the Women's Movement in Britain 1920-39*, New York 1986; J. Damousi, *Women Come Rally: socialism, communism and gender in Australia 1890-1955*, Melbourne 1994.
2. See J.A. Auerbach, *The Great Exhibition of 1851: a nation on display*, New Haven 1999.
3. D.B Montefiore, *From a Victorian to a Modern*, 1927, pp26-8.
4. D.B. Montefiore, 'How I became a socialist. A human document', *Socialist*, Melbourne, 13 January 1911.
5. Montefiore, 1927, *op.cit.*, pp30-31.
6. Mitchell Library, Sydney, Rose Scott Papers, ML MSS 38/33/1, Minute Book of Womanhood Suffrage League, pp2, 8.

7. See K. Hunt, 'Journeying through suffrage: the politics of Dora Montefiore', in C. Eustance, J. Ryan and L. Ugolini (eds), *A Suffrage Reader: charting directions in British suffrage history*, 2000; K. Hunt, 'Internationalism in practice: the politics of a British socialist and feminist before the First World War', paper to European Social Science History Conference, Amsterdam, March 1998.
8. See, for example, *Summary of Federation News*, 1897-1899.
9. British Library, Correspondence of Mrs E.C. Wolstenholme Elmy, Add Ms 47,451, Elmy to Mrs McIlquham, 14 November 1897.
10. Montefiore, 1927, *op.cit.*, pp61-3. See also *Clarion*, 20 February, 23 October 1897; 4 June, 25 June, 9 July, 8 October 1898.
11. See S. Yeo, 'A new life: the religion of socialism in Britain, 1883-1896', *History Workshop Journal*, 4, 1977.
12. Montefiore, 1927, *op.cit.*, pp63, 62.
13. *Socialist*, 13 January 1911.
14. *Justice*, 9 November 1901. A profile in the Sydney-based *International Socialist*, 9 March 1912, suggested that she joined the SDF in 1899.
15. For example, in the *Socialist* Montefiore thanked the editor for regularly sending the paper to her in England, 11 November 1910.
16. Elmy Correspondence, Add Ms 47,449-55. Montefiore is first referred to in Elmy to Mrs McIlquham, 4 July 1897
17. For these and other women's columns, see K. Hunt and J. Hannam, 'Propagandising as socialist women: the case of the women's columns in British socialist newspapers, 1884-1914', in B. Taithe and T. Thornton (eds), *Propaganda. Political Rhetoric and Identity, 1300-2000*, Stroud 1999.
18. Dora also wrote: *Prison Reform from a Social Democratic Point of View*, 1909; *Our Fight to Save the Kiddies: Smouldering Fires of the Inquisition*, 1913; *Race Motherhood. Is Woman the Race?*, 1920.
19. *Socialist*, 11 November 1910.
20. Montefiore, 1927, *op.cit.*, pp99, 208-9.
21. Museum of London, Suffragette Fellowship Collection, 50.82/1133, Minutes, Canning Town WSPU. Private Collection (copies held by Fay Jacobsen), D.B. Montefiore to Mrs Knight, 15 December 1906, 13 February 1907. See also Montefiore, *op.cit.*, pp52, 122-3.
22. W. Gallacher, *Last Memoirs*, 1966, p32; *Socialist*, 16 December 1910.
23. *International Socialist*, 24 June 1911.
24. *SDF Annual Conference Report*, 1904, pp19, 20-21.
25. Ibid. (1908), pp9, 27; *SDP Annual Conference Report*, 1909, p28.
26. *Clarion*, 23 August 1907. For the context, see K. Hunt, 'The immense meaning of it all: the challenges of internationalism for British socialist women before the First World War', *Socialist History*, 17, 2000.
27. *Justice*, 8 May 1909.
28. *Daily Herald*, 27 November, 29 November 1912.
29. Montefiore, 1927, *op.cit.*, p153; *Justice*, 7 December 1912.
30. *Socialist*, 13 January 1911.
31. *International Socialist*, 6 May 1911.
32. Montefiore, 1927, *op.cit.*, p213.
33. *Socialist*, 16 December 1910. For the Australian socialist movement, race

and the 'White Australia' policy, see G. Osborne, 'A socialist dilemma' in
A. Curthoys and A. Markus (eds), *Who Are Our Enemies? Racism and the
Australian working class*, Sydney 1978; V. Burgmann, 'Revolutionaries and
racists: Australian socialism and the problem of racism, 1887-1917', PhD,
Australian National University, 1980.

34. *International Socialist*, 30 December 1911. Capitals in the original.
35. *Ibid.*, 23 September 1911. Capitals in the original.
36. *Ibid.*, 13 April 1912.
37. *Ibid.*, 24 June 1911.
38. *Ibid.*, 2 September 1911.
39. *Ibid.*, 13 April 1912.
40. Montefiore, 1927, *op.cit.*, pp153-4.
41. For Crawfurd, see National Museum of Labour History,
CP/IND/MISC/10, H. Crawfurd, 'Autobiography', unpublished type-
script. For the rebel networks, see S. Rowbotham, *Friends of Alice
Wheeldon*, 1986.
42. *Vote*, 27 November 1914.
43. See Montefiore,1927, *op.cit.*, ch.13.
44. *Ibid.*, p192.
45. *Call*, 29 March 1917.
46. *Ibid.*, 7 June 1917.
47. Montefiore, *op.cit.*, p198; *Call*, 14 February 1918.
48. *Call*, 4 April 1918; Montefiore, 1927, *op.cit.*, p200; *Call*, 11 July, 24
October, 12 December 1918.
49. Montefiore, 1927, *op.cit.*, p202.
50. *Ibid.*, p203.
51. Bruley, *op.cit.*, p63.
52. *Official Report of Communist Unity Convention*, 1920, p17.
53. *Communist*, 21 October 1920.
54. Montefiore, 1927, *op.cit.*, pp 207-8; *Communist*, 6 January 1921.
55. Montefiore, 1927, *op.cit.*, p209.
56. *Communist*, 24 September 1921, 18 March 1922; *Forward*, 17 February
1923.
57. J. Klugmann, *History of the Communist Party of Great Britain*, Vol.1,
1969, pp212-3.
58. Australian Archives, Victoria, B741/3 V/408, Director, Investigation
Branch to All Representatives Melbourne, 12 January 1923.
59. Australian Archives, Canberra, A6122/40 111 file WA 1024A, 'Summary
of Communism, June 1922 to December 1923', pp281-2.
60. Montefiore, 1927, *op.cit.*, p206.
61. *Workers' Weekly* (Australia), 22 June, 29 June, 6 July, 27 July 1923; *New
Outlook*, fortnightly from 7 July until 27 October 1923.
62. Montefiore, 1927, *op.cit.*, p215.
63. Mitchell Library, Sydney, Comintern Archives, ML MSS 5575
FM4/10416/ 495/94/26, D.B. Montefiore, 'Report on Communist Party in
Australia'. I would like to thank the Search Foundation for permission to
consult this material.
64. *Abridged Report of Fifth Congress of the Communist International*, 1924,
pp89-90.

65. ML MSS 5575 FM4/10416/ 495/94/26, pp18a-b, D.B. Montefiore to Comrade Inkpin, February 1925.
66. Montefiore, 1927, *op. cit.*, pp220, 222.
67. *The Times*, 1 January 1934; *Daily Herald*, 28 December 1933; *Daily Worker*, 27 December 1933.

The Young Manhood of
Arthur Reade

JOHN McILROY

Meditating on avoidable absences in Communist history and the lack of curiosity of some of its practitioners, Royden Harrison alighted on the intriguing figure of Arthur Reade, surmising 'surely there is more to be discovered here'.[1] His verdict was a fair one. Reade has attracted minimal attention in work on the Communist Party of Great Britain (CPGB) and while he is frequently referred to in Trotskyist history, information on his life and political career is slight.[2] I have therefore taken up Harrison's challenge and some of the results are presented in this chapter. As usual, the process of discovery dissolves received impressions: the complex, flawed, attractive character I encountered in my research was very different from the images conjured up in my mind when I first read of 'the lawyer A.E. Reade' or 'Palme Dutt's right-hand man'.[3] The picture it discloses of a man who was neither simply the renegade dabbler in Communism nor the icon of Trotskyist legend remains partial and provisional. If we now know a lot more about Reade, he must remain, like his mentor, the leading CPGB intellectual Rajani Palme Dutt, ultimately elusive.

One of those tantalising but neglected minor actors who crowd Communist history, Reade demands attention for a number of reasons. He was one of that minuscule group of bourgeois youth who joined the CPGB around its foundation, without any direct experience of exploitation and working class struggle, attracted by the power of its ideas. He stands out from most of the 'post-war generation' of bourgeois Communists who joined the party later, in the aftermath of the crisis of 1929-31. Reade, in contrast, was a man of 1917. 'A Communist of the old school', he experienced a CPGB still exhilarated by the élan and romanticism of revolution. His CPGB was very different from the pink party whose Popular Front politics appealed to bourgeois radicals in the 1930s.

Reade was Britain's first nationally-known student Communist. He stood near the start of the line of Oxford University Communists that stretched through such diverse and unlikely figures as Tom Driberg, A.J.P. Taylor and Graham Greene to Dennis Healey, Kingsley Amis and Iris Murdoch. He was Britain's first Trotskyist, a member of Evelyn Waugh's circle, and the first homosexual we know of in the ostensibly rugged and proletarian ranks of the CPGB. Reconstruction of his early career sheds light on overlooked aspects of Communist activity in the 1920s. His story demonstrates the difficulties young converts from the ruling class encountered and underlines the gigantic problems a democratic centralist party confronted in wrenching members from their roots and reconstituting them as Bolshevik cadres.

BECOMING A COMMUNIST

The Reades were an Anglo-Irish family, Catholics who arrived in London with a lot of money in the 1840s. William Reade, Arthur's grandfather, eloped with Georgina Kitchener, the daughter of a rich Protestant family also with Irish connections. He converted to Protestantism and moved on to the United States. Losses on the stock market and relative impoverishment ensured the family remained in America. But the son Essex, named in affirmation of the family's new English Protestant identity after Elizabeth's I's Earl of Essex and Lord Lieutenant in Ireland, was brought up in London by his grandmother, Georgiana Edgeworth. He emerged a model Victorian gentleman, a financier and aesthete, educated at Eton and the Slade School of Art. Between periods of leisure financed by his Edgeworth inheritance, he worked in South America for Baring's Bank. In 1901, at the age of 45, Essex married Sheelah Chichester, the 23-year-old granddaughter of the Earl of Galloway. They lived at Wrotham Rectory in Kent and 14 Bolton Street, Piccadilly where Arthur Essex Edgeworth Reade was born on 22 January 1902.[4]

The Edwardian certainties of his early life were disrupted by crisis when his father died in 1908. Sheelah Reade was an independent woman and Essex's financial good fortune had enabled him to bring his family back from America. Much of Arthur's infancy was spent with his aunts in Suffolk. Here he was the centre of attention and they provided him with a confidence and interest in different kinds of life that were to mark his future. The family was socially concerned and artistically inclined but neither religion, conventional Church of England, nor politics loomed large in his upbringing. In 1911, he was sent to Gibbs Preparatory School in Sloane Street, where he was happy and later to Stonehouse Preparatory School in Broadstairs, where he was beaten and unhappy. In January 1915, he followed Essex to Eton. His career under that Spartan regime was largely uneventful. He excelled at French, was interested in history and, despite his athleticism, hated sports.

With society disrupted by war, the class struggle in Britain reached a new pitch between 1917 and 1920. Driven by the 'war to end all wars', the Russian revolution and new working-class confidence, the ripples from what James Cronin has called 'the moment of insurgency' touched the ruling class.[5] And it radicalised sections of its youth, among them Arthur Reade. Echoes of the storm reached Britain's premier public school. George Orwell, an Etonian at the time, recollected that by 1918, ' … the revolutionary mood extended to those who had been too young to fight, even to public schoolboys'.[6] Early that year, the young Earl De La Warr, who would remain a political associate of Reade into the 1930s, was at the head of a group of socialists permitted to form a radical but respectable Eton Political Society. They were even allowed to invite the anti-war George Lansbury to address them, although a complementary paper, the *Eton Review*, soon encountered problems with the college authorities. This episode awakened in Reade an interest in politics and journalism. Armed with good French from his governess, Reade, powerfully built and 6 ft 3 inches in height, left Eton in January 1919 for Strasbourg University. In the cafés and bars of the newly French city, the radical wave sweeping Europe and the resonance of the short-lived flowering of workers' and soldiers' councils in Alsace-Lorraine intensified his political awareness while he won his journalistic spurs with articles for the *Daily Mail*.[7]

Reade arrived at Worcester College, Oxford to study History in October 1920. A million miners were on strike, the Triple Alliance of mining and transport unions was flexing its muscles and, fresh from the success of the Council of Action in curbing British intervention in Russia, the August Unity Convention decided to found the CPGB. Although he stood at some distance from the new party, Reade was already a confirmed if unformed and eclectic socialist. He admired G.D.H. Cole, the left-wing thinker then advocating Guild Socialism, and the Labour leader Ramsay MacDonald. He affirmed his support for 'direct action if constitutional means failed' and declared: 'I believe in the programme of the National Labour Party only as a stepping-stone. My sympathies tend to the Independent Labour Party.'[8]

His journey from Eton to socialism was not unique but it was unusual. His background was technically but not typically *rentier,* run through with *arrivisme,* the Irish connection – Reade was a passionate supporter of Sinn Fein – and inherited experience of financial calamity. For the historian, making connections between Reade's early experience and his later allegiances, or assigning priority to different influences in his political formation, must be precarious. But by contrasting his own good fortune with the predicament of the London and rural poor and his own family servants, he undoubtedly developed a sense of unfairness, sympathy for the underdog and guilt, sharpened by the intrusion of growing class conflict, the excitements of the Russian revolution and events in Ireland. In keeping with Palme Dutt's requirements for the proper formation of the revolutionary intellectual, he had had a chance to stand outside his own privileged milieu, look at Britain from the outside and cultivate the critical 'alien eye' which saw far beyond the ornate imperialist façade to the brutal realities of exploitation and oppression in British society.

Like so many bourgeois socialists of the period, Reade was in rebellion against his mother. As to the role played by his youthful homosexuality, common at the Eton and Oxford of this time, and his desire to shock, we can likewise only speculate.[9] Sixty years later, Reade's closest comrade at Oxford, Charles Gray, recalled as key to their radicalisation the combination of release and responsibility which the war they had so narrowly missed induced and the consequent impulse to make a better society it engendered: 'Moreover, I suppose both Arthur and I were in revolt against an over-privileged upbringing. In my boyhood, we had at least seven living-in servants, including a nanny and an under-nanny for the two of us, my brother Basil and myself. Bolshy ideas were around and we absorbed them readily.'[10]

Reade's allegiance to Labour, stimulated by attending political meetings in London and visits to the 1917 Club in Soho before he went up to Oxford, was strengthened by his induction into the newly established University Labour Club; he was influenced by its leading lights, the future M.P. Kenneth Lindsay who had fought in France and who was at Reade's college, and Malcolm MacDonald, the Labour leader's son who was at Queen's. Lindsay and MacDonald, representing the new modernising socialism, were eager to link the new clubs more intimately with the transformed, burgeoning Labour Party and were instrumental, together with the Labour MP Arthur Greenwood, in creating the new University Labour Federation (ULF), viewed contemptuously by the Communists as a vehicle for Parliamentary careerists.

But the Labour Club constituted a broad coalition and was linked to the older Oxford University Socialist Society, in its turn affiliated to the University Socialist Federation (USF). Founded by Cole and the gifted Independent Labour Party supporter Clifford Allen in 1912, the USF had now come under the control of the Communists. The secretary of the Socialist Society and its representative on the USF was Charles Gray who had arrived at Balliol the previous year, where he encountered the proselytising of a fervent young Communist Andrew Rothstein, who had also fought in France. Gray was influential in turning Reade left. So was the Vice-Chancellor (VC), the unbending Victorian Lewis Richard Farnell, whose attempts to suppress the Labour Club led to the banning of meetings by the philosopher Bertrand Russell and George Lansbury, then a powerful voice on Labour's left and editor of the *Daily Herald*.[11]

Reade's emergence as a student activist was recognised in January 1921 when he was appointed editor of *The New Oxford*, the journal linked to the Labour Club. A new mood was signalled when a motion that socialism 'can best be attained by a violent break with the present system' was lost by only one vote. Reade recorded the rise of 'an energetic left wing movement inside the Labour Club'.[12] The left, dubbed by *ISIS* 'the Giler politicians', held open air meetings on St Giles and, in the face of right-wing disruption, a Free-Speech Movement developed. Through the USF and his consequent links with the future Cambridge economist and lifelong CPGB member, Maurice Dobb, undergraduate editor of the Cambridge University paper *Youth*, to which he contributed an 'Oxford Letter', and Palme Dutt, still at the epicentre of socialist student politics, Reade was coming closer to the CPGB.[13]

If the CPGB constituted an increasingly uncomfortable home for intellectuals as the 1920s developed, it would be wrong to paint too bleak a picture of the party's undoubtedly weak intellectual base in its early years. Composition and ideology bred tension and suspicion but Robin Page Arnot, the ascendant force in the Labour Research Department (LRD) now dominated by the CPGB, and Andrew Rothstein were in the leadership, Dutt was a commanding mind and the large votes which returned them to the executive testify to their *political* popularity with the members. Similarly, the view of a later Communist student that the 1920s constituted 'a blank period in the history of University socialism' is exaggerated.[14] Certainly the infant party's proletarian orientation meant that, despite occasional references to the importance of capturing the next generation of the intelligentsia and white-collar workers, similar to the policy statements of the 1930s, and appearances at USF gatherings, the leadership took only a limited interest.

The students' own public self-deprecation and sense of marginality was evoked by Dobb's introduction of himself to a meeting as 'that pathetic spectacle, a Cambridge undergraduate'. But public deference was often mixed with private arrogance, certainly in relation to their proletarian peers: 'Why not go along to the YCL office at 36 Lambs Conduit Street and inform them you've come to edit their mouldy paper', his Cambridge friend, the future CPGB journalist Allen Hutt loftily suggested to Reade.[15] Centred on the USF, with most students giving the Young Communist League (YCL) a wide berth, the work does not seem to have been integrated into party strategy but left to the voluntary efforts of students and graduates. If they were prepared to fund expensive journals from their own resources, so much the better.

By 1920-21, the USF's longstanding leaders, Page Arnot, his fellow former Guild Communist and Comintern courier Mary Moorhouse, the Cambridge scientist Alfred Bacharach and Dutt, had long since left University and were increasingly preoccupied with weightier matters. In search of broad support, they had avoided committing the USF to the Third International, contenting themselves with commitment to 'the class war'. But the Federation's slender base in the Universities was underlined by the growth of the ULF, which circumspectly opposed merger – an issue which divided the USF – in favour of co-operation. Nonetheless, the USF brought a small number of younger students, including Reade, into the Communist orbit. The April 1921 Conference in Oxford, where Dutt was seen as triumphing over the reformist Hugh Dalton, and Gray was appointed secretary of the Federation, was a key incident in Reade's passage to the party. Some five years older, the charismatic Dutt became Reade's model and political mentor.[16]

Reade's development was reinforced by wider events. The post-war struggle reached crisis point with the lockout of the miners in early 1921 and the threat of solidarity strikes by the Triple Alliance. The government began to recruit a Defence Force and the USF mobilised to prevent enrolment from the Universities, 'its HQ at Moorhouse's flat being a constant furore of telephoning, typewriting and heated controversies'. An eve of strike rally against 'attempts to form a White Guard' drew an audience of 2,000 addressed by R.H. Tawney, Cole, Lansbury and future Labour Party Minister Ellen Wilkinson, then a leading light in the CPGB. Convinced by the austere ratiocination of

Dutt, Reade was now bedazzled by 'the extraordinary energy and organising abilities of Mary Moorhouse'.[17]

Black Friday, 15 April 1921, when the Triple Alliance failed to support the miners, was attributed by the CPGB to the machiavellian machinations of the railway workers' leader, Jimmy Thomas. It completed Reade's conversion to Communism. Impatience and desire to kick over the traces – 'it was plainly time for a left wing revolt to startle the Club out of its self satisfied smugness' – was combined with concern at what he saw as Labour's right-wing drift and the sense Communist analysis made of it.[18] At the Oxford Union, he spoke as 'a revolutionary' in support of the miners, and in the Labour Club proposed a motion condemning the Alliance leaders and demanding Thomas's removal as vice-president. It was lost by only four votes. He recorded: 'Excitement increased when a few days later *The New Oxford* produced its first definitely "Red" number'. Reade's editorial, 'The Great Betrayal', excoriated 'the lying little Welshman's latest victory' and the role played by the Labour Party leaders Arthur Henderson and J.R. Clynes: 'CONSTITUTIONALISM HAS FAILED ... DIRECT ACTION ALONE REMAINS ... COMMU-NISM ALONE REMAINS'.[19]

Self-affirmation as a revolutionary through this formative incident was reinforced by the response of the Labour Club moderates, 'the surprised and agitated bevy of associate editors and Club officials writing letters to the press disclaiming all responsibility'. His identity as a Communist was strengthened by the celebrity or notoriety he now attracted: 'Extremists such as your correspondent', he remarked with satisfaction, 'are looked on askance by the moderate section of the Club'. After 'a fortnight of intrigue', Reade agreed to step down as editor.[20] But he had no intention of forfeiting the spotlight. His brain-child, *The Free Oxford*, was launched in June 1921, as an impressively-produced 38-page journal. Four issues appeared between October and December 1921 and two further issues in early 1922.

The journal emulated the conventional review of the period: it included political commentary and controversy, literary criticism, poems and short stories, anchored by discussion of Oxford affairs levelled largely at Farnell, and a 'Cambridge Letter' from Dobb. There were contributions from Comintern leaders Karl Radek, Alexander Lozovsky and Eugen Varga, Conrad Noel, the Red Vicar of Thaxted, and the pioneer of sexual politics, Edward Carpenter. There were debates with Labour MP Arthur Ponsonby and Gerald Gould of the *Daily Herald*, while the journal featured poems and reviews by long-term Communist sympathiser Antony Bertram, future member, critic and poet Edgell Rickword and the Australian Irish radical Bertram Higgins.

The magazine proudly declared itself 'A Communist journal of youth'. Its crowded masthead demanded 'Workers by Hand and Brain Unite!' and proclaimed that it was 'Founded and Edited by Arthur E.E. Reade (formerly Managing Editor of *The New Oxford* ...)'. The political coverage, as Gray later recalled, was 'party line'. Reade's writing resounds with the exuberance and leftist élan of the CPGB's first period, infatuation with the romance of 1917, the genius of Lenin, the grandeur of Trotsky, the immanence of world revolution. Heavily dashed with the excesses of student journalism, it made a heady brew.

> We do not question his sincerity, we merely pity his ignorance ... We have attacked in this leading article three men, all of whom are personal friends of the Editors and we have exposed the intellectual cowardice or incapability that inspires their opinions ... By TERROR we shall destroy the domination of the bourgeoisie; by TERROR we shall destroy the counter-revolution; by TERROR we shall establish the RULE of the workers.[21]

Charles Gray, the Associate Editor, another intriguing character long forgotten in Communist history, was an able student politician widely praised for his speeches in the Union. Educated at Winchester and Bradfield, he was a Brackenbury Exhibitioner at Balliol where he was reading History, and had already published a book on reform of the public schools. His critics acidly observed that Gray's sentiments, 'I am a traitor to my class and proud of it', did not 'prevent him from keeping his private income'.[22] Oxford's first post-war generation mingled ex-schoolboys with ex-soldiers. Alan Porter, the literary editor, a self-described 'long term Communist', was a grammar school boy who had fought in France, and an editor of *Oxford Poetry 1921*. He stood at the heart of literary Oxford and was pronounced by *ISIS* as likely to have 'the finest and most exciting future' of all the contemporary Oxford poets.[23] The recently demobbed 25-year-old Louis Golding, already published as poet and novelist, and a contemporary of Porter's at Manchester Grammar School and Queen's College, made up the board of *The Free Oxford*.

The first issue was judged, even by critics, a surprising success. Despite invective and wit – 'Reade writes it and Gray reads it' – the journal became a fixture of the Oxford scene. It was on sale at most British

Universities, reached France, Germany and Scandinavia, attained a circulation of 2,000 and was boosted as the future journal of a revitalised USF. The magazine was available from the CPGB and the YCL and was favourably reviewed in the *Communist*, the CPGB's weekly paper, by its editor Raymond Postgate; he praised its politics but was censorious about its literary coverage. But there was no formal CPGB organisation in the University, indeed the only active member other than Gray and Reade seems to have been Graham Pollard, son of the Professor of History at London University, who came up to Jesus College in 1921 and in succeeding years was the mainstay of Communist activity in the Labour Club. Despite allegations of Russian gold, the paper appears to have been extravagantly financed by Reade, largely by running up debts, and directed by him, with Dutt as his guide.[24]

Confident, outspoken, restless, spending whatever money he could lay hands on hand over fist, making friends and enemies with equal facility, Reade, resplendent in new red beard and the corduroy trousers of 1920s Bohemia, haunted Fleet Street and the *Daily Herald* office, improving his knowledge of journalism and his capacity for beer. In London, he was a fixture at the 1917 Club whose premises in Gerrard Street, Soho achieved 'all the squalor and dinginess associated in the popular imagination with a conspiratorial den of Bolsheviks and thieves'. There he rubbed shoulders with 'heavy drinkers, Folk Song experts ... Union officials, journalists, poets, actors, Communists, theosophists'.[25] In Oxford, discarding an early interest in the mainstream social clubs, he resorted to The Hypocrites Club – motto 'water is best' – a 'noisy alcohol-soaked rat warren' in St Aldates, its habitués sporting 'unshaven chins and beer-stained corduroys ... inclined to a communism which expressed itself in (illicit) pub crawls'.[26]

He also wrote poetry – the aptly entitled 'The Banished Rebel' was published in *Oxford Poetry 1922* – and aspired to novels. While there is no evidence of deep immersion in the Marxist classics, he devoured the party press in Britain and journals such as the *Liberator* from the USA and *Clarté* from France. Absorption in journalism and the student life ensured Reade failed his exams and was 'rusticated' for the Michaelmas term 1921. Despite a poetical effusion from Antony Bertram in *ISIS*, likening the unlikely Reade to a silenced nightingale, this simply presented him with more time to indulge his preoccupations.[27]

But Oxford in the 1920s was far from indulging Bolshevism as an aberration of youth. The authorities now attempted to break Reade, ensuring in the process that he passed from local to national recognition as a Communist. The VC Lewis Farnell was a mid-Victorian martinet who had been in Oxford since the early 1870s. He had written to *The Times* a few years earlier to denounce communism and now declared: 'we will not have Bolsheviks in the University'.[28] Farnell rested his case on Reade's advocacy of terror and Porter's irreligious poetry. There was no question of warnings or a second chance. In December 1921, Reade was informed by the Provost of Worcester: 'The College has received a communication from the Vice-Chancellor and Proctors to the effect that they have before them *The Free Oxford* for which you are responsible and that they have this day removed your name from the books of the University.'[29] Gray received two terms' rustication and was forced to give assurances of future good behaviour, while Porter who had already taken his degree escaped with an apology.

The forgotten episode of *The Free Oxford* demonstrates that, if in a small way, Communist students before the 1930s were not simply occupied in study circles and agitation among the workers.[30] There was activity inside the University but, in keeping with the ethos of the early CPGB, the orientation was propagandistic and there was little attempt to develop a critique of the University or mobilise over students' problems. Few converts were made and these were largely ephemeral, literary Communists such as Porter and the future historical novelist Alfred Duggan. Few inroads were made into 'the proletarian scholars who scrambled fiercely for facts in the lodging houses of the Iffley Road', while Ruskin students seem to have taken little part in student politics at this time.[31]

Yet the perceived unfairness of Farnell ensured Reade received extensive support from the student body. The Labour Club turned to succour their prodigal son and representatives of all the student papers and political clubs, with the exception of *ISIS*, wrote to the press condemning his expulsion. The affair provoked widespread and surprisingly sympathetic coverage in the national press, with the *Daily Express* and the *Evening Standard* joining the *Herald* in staunch support and even those critical of Reade praising his sincerity and commitment.[32] For a moment, he was more famous than the party chairman, the mercurial Irish Scot, Arthur MacManus. With journalists at his feet in the 1917 Club, 'the genial young giant ... this amazing young fellow' propounded his views on revolution and intellectuals.

We have had a certain amount of training at the expense of the workers and we want to put our training at their service. The capitalist system will break down then the workers must take over. It is highly probable that the capitalists will use force to resist. The workers will then have to use force to destroy the existing members of the capitalist class. Of course, I hope there would not be any need for bloodshed. But judging from the capitalist psychology, I think there will be.[33]

Demonstrating 'how thoroughly he enjoys the role of rebel', Reade concluded with the portentous inflation of youth: 'We leave Oxford and its hypocrisies behind us to embark on the real task of our life, content to remember one Lenin whose University career was broken by political imprisonment.'[34]

BECOMING A DISSIDENT

Farnell metaphorically excommunicated Reade from bourgeois society and commenced his induction into the realities of class politics: if you preached revolution you were made to pay. He now had the choice of retreating, returning to his own class after 'a student escapade', or of pressing on with his Communist career. He does not seem to have hesitated, extending his estrangement from his class by becoming a trade unionist and cogitating about whether he could best serve the party by seeking '(i) either a capitalist job at NUJ rates or (ii) a revolutionary job into which I could throw my heart'.[35] In following the revolutionary path he had the commendation of the party leader MacManus, although his peers, such as Dobb, were worried that fame had gone to his head, and the approbation of other leaders was more studied. The sober-sided CPGB leader Bob Stewart, once of the Prohibition Party remarked:

> [observing] that aged assurance that belies his youthful appearance, I kept wondering how much might be genius and how much mixed coffee. Nevertheless, Arthur is a good lad, inclined to think that a taste in beer, clay pipes and dirty faces is proletarian. Doubtless when he fares North he will learn that it ain't so. Nevertheless, the boy has the journalistic flair and may be heard of.[36]

For the next year, he was not. Reade spent most of 1922 seeking a sponsor to pay off the debts *The Free Oxford* had incurred as a result of his aristocratic disdain for the details of finance – inhospitable ports of call included the Communist Youth International, the YCL and the USF – studying Marxism, working at freelance journalism and writing a novel. By early 1923, Hutt was urging the 'degenerate beer-bibber', still 'disgracefully unemployed', to offer his services as editor of 'that bloody awful paper' the *Young Communist*. In defiance of 'the cult of the worker', Reade shared Hutt's disdain for the 'revolutionary boy scouts' and was having problems coming to terms with emerging party discipline: 'I, of course, accept the policy as laid down by the International but as to the whole of the journalism, I must be an absolute autocrat.'[37] Nothing came of the liaison with the YCL and the Communist student milieu was collapsing. By 1923, at its final conference, the USF was lamenting the final exit of 'that brilliant older generation of Page Arnot, Dutt and Moorhouse' and there was little to replace it. The following year, with membership down to 200, Hutt resigned as secretary, declaring, 'I don't believe the organisation has the remotest significance in the class struggle.'[38]

The role of young intellectuals who aspired to become full-time revolutionaries was now, more than ever, to utilise their skills in writing for and producing the party press and servicing the wider movement through the Labour Research Department. Reade worked at a series of temporary, poorly paid, jobs on the CPGB's *Labour Monthly* and *Workers' Weekly* through 1923. Overcoming his reputation as 'a university student' in a workers' party in which he only had to open his mouth to show the difference, and living largely on his own resources, he became well known in London as a junior member of 'the nucleus' around Dutt which was challenging the MacManus-Bell-Inkpin leadership on the basis of a purer Bolshevism.

Dutt and Page Arnot attempted to fashion Reade into their image of the revolutionary intellectual. In 1924, he was appointed Business Manager, in succession to the anti-war journalist Joan Beauchamp, of the *Labour Monthly*, the journal Dutt, Page Arnot and the foreign editor of the *Daily Herald*, W.N. Ewer, had established in 1921 as an instrument of CPGB intellectual hegemony in the United Front. In 1924, they were trying to come to terms with the reflux of world revolution, the problems of Bolshevisation and the efflux from the party of much of its slender intellectual base. Morgan Phillips Price, a gifted journalist and future Labour MP, Postgate, the capricious J. Walton Newbold, the party's first MP to be elected on a Communist ticket, Frank and Winifred Horrabin, mainstays of the Plebs League and the National Council of Labour Colleges (NCLC), the *Daily Herald* journalist William Mellor and Ellen Wilkinson, had all left, in response to the changed political situation and the rigours of organisational imperatives requiring subordination of individualism and freethinking. A further factor was finance. In 1924, the CPGB remained dependent on the

Comintern for maintenance of its apparatus and press. The Comintern's attenuation of financial subsidies to the CPGB, their channelling away from the control of party leaders, their earmarking by Moscow for specific purpose and the consequent pressure on resources stimulated tensions.[39]

Reade was a member of the South West London Local and was elected to the London District Committee, becoming its Training Officer. Contemporaries in 'the nucleus' saw him as 'possessing qualities of daring and initiative ... a forceful and likeable personality'.[40] He was now for the first time encountering workers intensively. He was sobered by their patience and moderation; they were impressed by his commitment and chaotic working environment.[41] Acceptance as a full time revolutionary was important to his sense of identity and he was happy to be part of the great adventure of Communism in the 'heroic age' of the Russian revolution. The energy he invested and the excitement he found permeates his account of the episode in April 1924 when police spies were discovered at the London District Congress:

> After the incident I was busy in work in connection with it from 2.30 pm all the afternoon and evening until 10 pm when I went down to see George Lansbury at Bow to arrange for him to raise it in the House next day. Thence I called on two newspapers in Fleet Street; back at midnight to the Party headquarters where after an all night confabulation I went with two others to see Lansbury again at 7 am and then back to headquarters again; slept from 11 am till 6 pm Monday; work at HQ continuously from 6 pm Monday night until 4 pm Tuesday afternoon. One hour's sleep in the sun in St James' Park and then back to write the story for the *Workers' Weekly* which I finished just before sunrise on Wednesday. And since then I have SLEPT, SLEPT, SLEPT. I had two bottles of champagne which I think I had earned.[42]

The champagne suggests that the apprentice Bolshevik did not break completely with other existences even in the face of proletarian leaders who railed against 'a certain kind of intellectual ... the type that believes one has to wear hobnailed boots and corduroys to be a good Bolshevik'.[43] His contradictory personality reflected the conflict between different Reades. He remained part of the night world which dawned at dusk at the 1917 Club, radiating out to Mrs Meyrick's 43 Club across the 'tart-infested street' and Elsa Lanchester's cabaret, The Cave of Harmony in Charlotte Street, a demi-monde of *boulevardiers* which intersected with Evelyn Waugh's Bright Young, often homosexual, Things. If Reade's sexual orientation was submerged in the party, the thrill of the illicit could be found in the safe territory between Bloomsbury and Mayfair, centred on Great Ormond Street where, as if in acknowledgement of Reade's divided allegiances, Gray and Waugh had flats and the party its District office.[44]

Reade's Bohemianism, and the undisciplined attitude to work he saw it fostering, drew criticism from Dutt. More specifically, I have found no evidence about attitudes to homosexuality inside the CPGB in the 1920s. We can surmise that it would be better understood amongst the intellectuals than among Calvinist proletarians such as the Scottish CPGB leaders Stewart and Tom Bell, but that it would remain subterranean. We also need to know more about attitudes to alcohol in a party in which the Scottish puritanism of Stewart and Willie Gallacher co-existed with the Irish indulgence of MacManus and the more measured intake of the English tradesman Harry Pollitt.[45] But it was not Bohemianism, rather it was his love of freedom from political constraint, support for internationalism and attachment to 1917, which led to the unravelling of Reade's allegiance to the CPGB.

The controversy over the Left Opposition which raged between 1923 and 1925 was not the first time British Communists had been called upon to follow Russian leadership or consider the internal affairs of the Russian party. The continuity from 1921 of the CPGB's scrupulous, if at times fumbling, adherence to Russian initiative sits uneasily with accounts which analyse Stalinism as a complete rupture, or argue that the party's health depended on the former Socialist Labour Party leaders, or an emphasis on the party's exercise of relative political autonomy.[46] The British scarcely saw themselves as initiators of policy in the world party but as recipients or refiners: in comparison with other national parties, the CPGB was doggedly conformist. Its lack of debate and dissent over this issue stands out, not only in contrast with more theoretically sophisticated 'mass' parties, but with the similarly small and weak Belgian section. There is no evidence that the programme of the Opposition was seriously discussed. Bukharin recorded in May 1924 that 'there had been many members in the sections and in some cases entire central committees which leaned towards the opposition'.[47] The CPGB was not among them.

Initially its leadership contented itself with a balanced presentation of Trotsky's criticism of the growth of bureaucracy in the Russian party and state. But they fell into line against the background of the Comintern leader Grigory Zinoviev's purges of the leadership of the Polish, French and German parties. The matter was not discussed at the

CPGB Congress in May 1924. Nothing daunted, the British delegation led by MacManus and Petrovsky, the Comintern representative in Britain, moved 'whole hearted support' for the Russian majority at the ensuing Fifth Congress of the Comintern, the Congress of 'socialism in one country'. The Opposition, they claimed, 'imperilled the dictatorship of the proletariat' and 'brought into contempt the authority of the Russian leadership which is the leader not only of the Soviet state but also of the Comintern'.[48]

When later that year Trotsky suggested, in *The Lessons of October*, that it was advantageous to ponder the less than glorious role Zinoviev and Lev Kamenev had played in 1917, and was judged to have reopened the discussion which had been closed by the World Congress, the die was, for the CPGB, already cast. In the face of Comintern prompting, the issue was finally put before the members at the Party Council of 30 November 1924: a Political Bureau resolution condemned *The Lessons* and recorded 'solidarity with and implicit faith in the Communist Party of Russia'. We now know that this statement was drafted, not by CPGB leaders but by Comintern representatives then in London, the Austrian Richard Schüller and the German Arthur Ewert, who expressed concern at the British leaders' lack of grasp of the situation.[49]

Lack of understanding of what was happening in Russia and its international implications did not constrain the British leaders. That the triumvirate of Zinoviev, Kamenev and Stalin controlled the Russian Party and the Comintern on which the CPGB was both ideologically and materially dependent, and that dissent played into the hands of Russia's enemies, sufficed. The novel Marxist notion of 'implicit faith' demanded, according to Bell who led the discussion, the necessity to combat 'the large element of the democratic mind who do not like to come to decisions before they have got all the facts before them'.[50] Despite honourable reservations from the YCL leader Jack Cohen and the veteran organiser and ex ILP activist Jock Wilson, the gathering unanimously condemned Trotsky's preface without having read a word of it. The psychology of opportunist conformism, which mocked the best, if it strengthened the worst, of the Bolshevik tradition, had taken root. The CPGB leaders saw in this small but significant compromise of truth only routine business.

Perhaps not completely. A recently discovered letter discloses Bell as head of the CPGB's Agitprop department remonstrating with the Comintern over the failure to provide a promised translation of Trotsky's preface and, on this account, significant doubts among the membership. But his concern is ultimately managerialist and self-protective: because of the Comintern's prevarications 'quite a number' of members, albeit many intellectuals, were reluctant to commit themselves.[51] On the whole, documents from the Moscow archives add only detail to the picture of a party which grasped the issues superficially and was willing to boil matters down to discipline and the pre-eminence of the Russian leadership.

If this characterises the position of the worker leaders MacManus and Bell, what of the party intellectuals and their *doyen*? Did Dutt, as some historians suggest, 'experience the temptations of Trotskyism'?[52] His writings between 1924 and 1926 indicate a strong attraction to Trotsky's political method and in some cases his arguments. This was arrested by Dutt's governing conception that without an authoritative International there would be no revolutionary progress. His correspondence with Trotsky's American supporter Max Eastman in 1925 demonstrates his belief – which he passed on to his protegés Reade and later the London CPGB members on their way to Trotskyism, Reg Groves and Stewart Purkis – in iconoclastic intellectual exploration and free-ranging debate. But, centrally, the correspondence is stamped with his incredulity that Communists should pursue this to the extent of coming into conflict with the International and risking exclusion from the movement, outside which there was no salvation. For Dutt, the Comintern finally and legitimately set the bounds of the permissible.

Thus, significant interest in Trotskyism on the part of intellectuals occurred outside the CPGB; it was the preserve of the Horrabins, Phillips Prices and Postgates and found its outlet in *Plebs*, the journal of the NCLC. Had the controversy flared a little earlier, they may, briefly, have been the bearers of Trotskyism inside the CPGB. As it was, their individualistic and politically incoherent defection from the CPGB earlier in the vital year of 1924 further demonstrated for many the unreliable romanticism of bourgeois elements. As intellectuals were in caricature identified with Trotsky (himself recast as rootless intellectual rather than ruthless General), their defection acted as a further barrier against his ideas.[53]

Some of the reasons behind the 1924 haemorrhage of intellectuals worked against the growth of dissident communism. The introduction of the Russian model of combat organisation – whatever the necessities and advantages then perceived – with its fragmented task groups, culture of hyperactivism, subordination to leadership and prohibition of organised dissent, meant there was little political discussion, particularly of international issues. There was a problem of priorities in a small over-extended group of around 4,000 members trying to mimic a revolutionary party and facing attacks from the state, the Labour Party and the trade union leaders.[54] But one member who did take a critical interest was Arthur Reade. We have little access to his interior dialogue over this issue but hitherto he had recorded no political differences with the party. Indeed in 1921 he had extravagantly condemned the dissident Communist Sylvia Pankhurst's 'hysterical and sentimental' support for the Workers' Opposition in Russia, loftily and imperiously pronouncing,

> Disobedience to the central authority cannot possibly be tolerated for one moment. For this reason, *The Free Oxford* has felt compelled to refuse an advert for the organ of the rebellious left. Communism influenced by sentiment would be a *reductio ad absurdum*. We should all be back in the old ILP or the Fabian Society.[55]

In the unlikely event that Reade ever pondered these words, and reflected that he and Trotsky were being attacked with the sword they had themselves wielded against dissent, his only defence would be that Trotsky was a different matter than the leaders of the Workers' Opposition A.G. Shliapnikov and Alexandra Kollontai. For Reade's politics turned on the romance of 1917 and its personification in Lev Davidovitch. For Reade, Trotsky was 'brilliant ... magnificent ... the inspiration of the revolution ... inseparable from Lenin'.[56] He represented Reade's ideal: the unity of the man of action and the artist. Without Trotsky, 1917 could have no meaning. Moreover, he had followed the controversy in Comintern publications and in the French and German press. He was convinced by the arguments of the Opposition and had taken the issues up in the classes he conducted. One YCL member recalled

> Tall, with a fine physique and ginger beard, he was admired by us members of the YCL in Battersea for the talks he gave us on Marxism. He could read German so it was from him that we first heard of the differences of Trotsky with the Russian party. To young Communists, Trotsky was the big hero. I remember in the early days of the YCL one of our popular pamphlets that was published in Moscow by the Young Communist International was *My Flight From Siberia* by Trotsky. Arthur Reade to us youngsters fitted into that pattern of the young revolutionary, audacious and committed to the Cause.[57]

Hitherto, Reade had curbed his rebelliousness and it is fascinating to conjecture what difference Dutt's absence in Brussels from mid-1924 made to this. As it was, when in 1923-4 Trotsky elaborated a distinctive political programme, it was easy for Reade to become a Trotskyist. When the Comintern attacked Trotsky, it was easy for Reade to identify with the imperious underdog. When the CPGB endorsed the anathema, Reade's tenuous attachment to discipline fractured and he was impelled to speak out. This was facilitated by the unease felt in some quarters and the protest by the London District Committee over the way the decision had been taken. It was constrained by the fact that this was an argument conducted within the framework of Bolshevism in power and its conceptions of morality and the infallible monolithic party, which Reade, like Trotsky, had endorsed but which now militated against them.

Matters were resolved at the London Aggregate in January 1925. J.T. Murphy, bursting to demonstrate his zeal for the Comintern position, moved endorsement of the November Party Council resolution condemning Trotsky, and Reade countered by moving support for the District Committee position that the decision had been taken on inadequate information. But he went further and urged 'most emphatic support for the Left Wing Minority's fight in the Russian Party against bureaucracy'. Reade defended the Opposition's platform and 'referring copiously to extracts from international journals' and to Lenin's Testament, justified his criticisms of the triumvirate, arguing that the national parties had received only a partisan account of the issues. For the leadership, Murphy continued the erection of the new mythology – Lenin and Trotsky had been 'in continuous opposition [to each other] for 25 years'. Rothstein, another indefatigable Cominternist and like Murphy, 'radiating authority', denounced Reade's 'anti-party attitude' and the Glasgow University graduate, Page Arnot, put it all down to Reade's romantic infatuation with Trotsky, whose supporters were to be found only among University students. Reade found himself once more among lost causes. The real anxieties in the party were attested by the relatively narrow vote, 81 – 65, against a motion that debate be adjourned until members possessed more information. But his amendment mustered only ten votes and only fifteen members refused to accept the final substantive motion.[58]

Dutt had failed to inculcate in Reade the Bolshevik virtues of obedience and silence. His romanticism was unarguable, but what separated Reade from Dutt and Page Arnot was their different, but equally romantic, visions of recent Russian history and the fact that Reade put forward a principled political argument, in contrast to Page Arnot's paternalist sociology. Reade's *savoir-faire* was highly questionable: he was simultaneously asserting that members did not have sufficient information to make a decision and that they should take a decision in favour of Trotsky. But Reade stood alone and under pressure. And nothing should detract from his persistence and courage in discovering what was happening in the Soviet Union and speaking out. It is, moreover, a measure of the CPGB that a junior member, scarcely 23 years of age, rather than, as in other parties, experienced components of the leadership, should have to take on the responsibility of warning against what was happening in Russia.

The response of the leadership could only intensify Reade's alienation. He was swiftly removed from the London District Committee by the Political Bureau who, he now bitterly asserted, could be divided into those 'who did not think at all' and 'office seekers and careerists'. The party leaders stepped up their attack, persistently but unsuccessfully demanding that he reveal the identity of a member whom he had referred to in his 'reprehensible speech' as providing him with information. The South West London Local's invitation to Reade to address them was branded 'tantamount to factionalism within the Party' and Murphy and Rothstein were deputed to oppose his appeal. In dismissing it, the Control Commission stated that his defiance 'justified his removal from any responsible position in the party, if not indeed from the party itself'.[59]

If not from the party then, in the estimation of Page Arnot – defender of the faith in the absence of Dutt – expulsion from the depleted, embattled party group of intellectuals, unless contrition was speedily exhibited. Scrupulously fraternal if stern, Page Arnot addressed his and Dutt's past dissatisfaction with Reade's management of *Labour Monthly,* which he saw as related to his inability to adopt the regime demanded of a Communist. Reade's good qualities, 'cleverness and quickness and power of rapid assimilation', militated against his acquisition of 'the severe mental self-discipline' demanded of a cadre. This was inextricably bound up with Reade's heretical support for Trotsky.

> Now whilst this was urgent before it has become in the last ten days something to be decided immediately. Your resolution went right against the decisions printed in the last number of the *Communist International.* You know what I said about it – that it should be considered as romanticism and that a romantic might become a very good Communist. (That

is, I treated it as irresponsible.) But just from the one or two fragmentary talks I have had with you since, I feel you must begin immediately to grow out of romanticism in a Communist direction or you will find yourself going straight in a non-Communist direction ... Why do I put these two things together – the LM and the resolution? Because they arise from the same cause. You are one of the University youth who have come into a workers' party. Birth, Eton and Oxford are a hell of a heritage to get rid of. You have felt that I think. But you have tried to get rid of them by becoming a Bohemian not a Bolshevik.[60]

Reade, Page Arnot urged, had come to the crossroads: he must cease to be a student, a Bohemian, a Trotskyist, a heretic, and accept party discipline – or cease to be a Communist. He was treating the proletarian leadership 'as a sort of corporate Farnell'. If Reade persisted in his current heresy 'there is no reason to think you will escape the developments of some others ... Sylvia, for instance, if not worse'.[61] It was a bitter comparison for Reade to swallow and Page Arnot went unheeded. In April, Reade was dismissed from his post on *Labour Monthly* over a dispute about the journal's debts and the late printing of that month's issue.[62]

The journal and the group around it constituted the centre of gravity anchoring Reade in the CPGB. His identity as a full-time revolutionary was important to him and he was now an outsider. He did not leave but he drifted out of activity. Although he had followed the Russian controversy in France, he seems to have made no attempt to test party patience further by contacting Trotsky's French supporters around Boris Souvarine, or Eastman, who was in Europe at this time. But we do encounter tantalising traces of discussions he conducted inside the CPGB. Hundreds of miles away in Methil, in the Fife coalfield, a young miners' leader wrote:

The impression I got from Reade re his position was to the effect that Trotsky's Preface was his defence which justified him in Reade's eyes. I, at that time, pointed out that although not having read the Preface, still Trotsky's previous erratic actions were sufficient in themselves to condemn him, although at the time I hadn't exactly made up my mind as to how I stood owing to the fact that I had read very little of the discussion. Since then I have definitely taken my position against Trotsky. The movement is greater than any individual, immaterial who he is or what he has been, and the fact that Trotsky's attitude is a defiant and deliberate act of indiscipline puts him 'out of court'. It is certainly good for the party, from the point of view of another test, that there are Reades who try to kick up a noise and by doing so focus party members' attention on those things and afterwards those who remain are certainly to be reckoned as of some use. A somewhat similar but more important and far-reaching test than that of Newbold's resignation. It is part of the process (in the words of a circular issued by the Party on Leninism) 'of hammering out a Party which must be of steel and all of one piece, incapable of splitting into sections and groups in the current of the *intellectual* and petit bourgeois stream'.[63]

This passage, suggestive of the psychology of working-class CPGB activists, exemplifies the process by which Scots 'learned to speak Russian' and Moscow elicited consent from the 'Little Moscow' of Methil. The writer, David Proudfoot, a future leader of the United Mineworkers of Scotland, inclined to reject Reade's argument on the grounds of his vague impressions about Trotsky's 'erraticism'. Not having read Trotsky's Preface (it was not published in English until a month after Proudfoot wrote), he condemns Trotsky on the basis of a circular adapted from Russian statements. Proudfoot had little time for reading and he puts forward no views on the Russian situation but simply bases his position on the need for discipline and anti-intellectualism. Proudfoot in Methil appropriates and personalises rhetoric minted in Moscow and customised in London. He declares that totalitarianism and subordination, a party like an army fighting for a great cause, are relevant to his predicament, for it helps to make real the party he sometimes feels 'only exists in one's imagination'. His letter refracts back Russian rhetoric for embellishment in Bell's subsequent speech to the Comintern Executive in which he elaborated British workers' hostility to Trotsky.

Reade decided upon a last throw of the dice. He would go to the heart of the matter, to Moscow, his spiritual home and the source of his difficulties. The response was a crushing and final rebuff. The central committee 'were not prepared to afford him the facilities to visit Russia ... there was no work the CEC desired him to undertake'.[64] Reade was isolated. There was silence as Bell reported the action against Reade and pronounced Trotskyism a political disease at the 1925 Congress. The leadership's further attempts at condemnation drew critical response only from the Comintern, which felt the CPGB was insufficiently vigorous in combating Trotskyism and from activists, who felt the issue was a distraction.[65] The CPGB was not particularly interested and certainly not, as Reade's continued membership demonstrated, possessed of the zealotry on this issue it mustered in the 1930s.

The only defence of Reade on record came in February 1925 from Group 11 of the St Pancras Local in which the energetic Tom and Amy Colyer, finding their feet after deportation from the USA, were active. They demanded that 'Comrade Reade should be reinstated in his position on the DPC [District Committee] and the Party Training Department thereof, conditional, of course, in his being willing to accept all party decisions'.[66] They were informed that the matter was closed. Reade was transferred to St Pancras and at the local Aggregate in May, a group resolution calling for education to 'combat the dangers of Trotskyism' was narrowly defeated as a disguised attempt to reopen the discussion.[67]

In the face of rejection, Reade chose exile. In May 1925, he and Charles Gray left for the Balkans and Greece, where for the next three years Reade exercised his interest in Hellenism. His final contribution to the debate on Trotskyism in the 1920s was a letter from Athens in July, in which he affirmed that as a Communist he had nothing in common with Trotsky's literary supporters, grouped around the NCLC journal *Plebs*. 'Trotskyists', he averred, 'scorn and repudiate the encouragement of the Postgates who are perhaps the most treacherous of all the enemies of a party founded by a Trotskyist greater than Trotsky himself – Lenin'.[68]

Reade settled temporarily in Athens with Waugh's former *inamorata* Alastair Graham, in an exotic ménage which inspired Sebastian Flyte's Moroccan apartment in *Brideshead Revisited*.[69] His Bohemian identity had, at least temporarily, triumphed. We last hear from Reade as a Communist in 1927. Early that year, he was still criticising 'Bad conventional Communism' and lamenting:

> My services would have been at the free disposal of the party unpaid if anyone had thought them of any use in the last two years. Anyway my mind's irrevocably made up now. I shall feel answerable to the Party for little but my sub unless I feel I am strong enough to contribute something really fresh and useful to the English revolution. And, meanwhile, may all fortune be with those who are killing themselves or becoming nervous wrecks in the Party service.[70]

ENVOI

Little came of the CPGB's work among students in the 1920s and when a fresh start was made, *The Free Oxford* was a long buried embarrassment. Reade's stand lingered only in the mind of the YCLer and future Trotskyist, Harry Wicks. After the turbulence of working in the Left

Wing Movement, an alliance of the CPGB and the Labour left inside the Labour Party, and a spell as secretary of the breakaway Holborn Labour Party, Gray resigned from the CPGB in 1928 and Reade seems to have bowed out the same year, for he returned to history as a Labour Parliamentary Candidate in the 1929 General Election. This story of his youth discloses many Arthur Reades, the Bolshevik, the Bohemian, the gay, the gentleman, the Communist renegade, the Trotskyist hero, the Reade that slips between our fingers. His story illuminates the totalitarian party, the CPGB's attitude to revolutionary morality and political debate, its emerging way with dissenters, its relations with the Comintern and, to focus on one aspect, the problems of democratic centralism. In the 1930s, Bolshevism frayed, democratic centralism became more elastic and many were able to make communism part of the texture of their lives. In the 1920s, Moscow's totalitarian model was in the ascendant and many encountered intense difficulty in reconciling party membership with life.

In singular fashion, Reade reflected the experience many had with the CPGB. His revolutionary politics were authentic and deeply felt. This was insufficient. Bourgeois recruits, Dutt insisted, had to 'unlearn from the roots, to break all ties with their old associations'.[71] Their fate was to embrace discipline and subordination. Reade formally accepted this but he was incapable of practising it in a sustained way. Recalling his experience in 1927, he reflected: 'I'm really too contemptuous of all authority by nature ever to work well in harness in a subordinate position'.[72] After further outsider engagements with Mosley's New Party and MacDonald's National Labour, he returned to his class and until his death in December 1971 proudly wore his Eton tie.

Reade represented *in extremis* many others who tried disciplining the virtues of freethinking, audacity and rebelliousness which had brought them to the party, in the service of a system which increasingly embodied the vices they had revolted against in the first place. Their commitment was sometimes total, more typically incomplete: they held something back, kept open an avenue of retreat and eventually used it. This is hardly surprising. Revolutionary asceticism in a non-revolutionary epoch, democratic centralism without organised dissent, political thinking constrained in the final instance by the requirements of the Soviet Union – in the end it couldn't and didn't work.

Some in the CPGB saw the consequent defections as illustrating the unreliability, even treachery, of intellectuals. But, of course, many workers did the same thing. And those who persisted were guilty of their own form of treachery. Those like Dutt sacrificed their lives, and their commitment to truth and human liberation, to constructing in Russia a harsh bureaucratic industrial despotism where workers were powerless. Reade had one final brush with his alternative life. Make of it what you will. One golden morning in July 1968, when the summer wind was once more tinged with the false promise of revolution, and students and Trotskyists were again on the march, he was amazed to receive across the decades a warm personal letter from Dutt. His old friend, the septuagenarian Stalinist, urged him to get in touch. Reade began a reply: 'My Dear Raji, What a delightful and stimulating surprise to get your letter after all these years, forty three to be precise …'.[73] He began to tell Raji about the rest of his life. But he never finished the letter and he never sent it.

This work has been carried out as part of the Communist Party Biographical Project at the Universities of Manchester and Liverpool financed by E.S.R.C. Grant No. R000 23 7924. I would like to thank Julian and Viola Reade, Kevin Morgan, Alan Campbell, Linda Lawton, Andy Flinn and Andy Croft.

NOTES

1. R. Harrison, 'Communists', *Labour History Review*, 59, 1, 1994, p41.
2. The only reference in party histories is in J. Klugmann, *History of the Communist Party of Great Britain, volume 2: the General Strike 1925-1926*, 1969, p327. Most of what was known about Reade until now is in H. Wicks, *Keeping My Head: the memoirs of a British Bolshevik*, 1992, pp38, 42-5.
3. S. Bornstein and A. Richardson, *Against the Stream: a history of the Trotskyist movement in Britain 1924-38*, 1986, p1; A.S. (Arthur Siffleet) to the *Newsletter*, 7 January 1964.
4. This section, and where unreferenced what follows, is based on information and papers provided by Julian and Viola Reade.
5. J. Cronin, *Labour and Society in Britain 1918-1979*, 1984, p19.
6. G. Orwell, *The Road to Wigan Pier*, 1937, pp129-130.
7. See note 4; interview with Reade, *News Review*, 20 May 1937; G. Smith (ed), *The Letters of Aldous Huxley*, 1969, pp137-9; C. Hollis, *Along the Road to Frome*, 1958, pp27-8; P. Tamerlan, 'Il y a 80 ans, en Alsace, La Révolution', *Rouge*, 10 December 1998.
8. A. Reade to S. Reade, n.d., November 1920.
9. There are only brief references in the literature to homosexuality in the CPGB in the 1930s and after; see W. Mulford, *This Narrow Place: Sylvia Townsend Warner and Valentine Ackland*, 1988, pp99-100; M. Joannou, 'Sylvia Townsend Warner in the 1930s', in A. Croft (ed), *A Weapon in The Struggle*, 1998, p94; and, very insightfully, A. McLeod, *The Death of Uncle Joe*, 1997, pp97-8.

10. C. Gray to V. and J. Reade, 28 September 1980; to V. Reade, 4 June 1981; University of Hull DAR 1/6/70, Page Arnot Papers, Notes on Origins of University Socialist Federation; USF, *Bulletin*, May 1921.
11. J. Mabro, *'I Ban Everything': free speech and censorship in Oxford between the Wars*, Oxford 1985.
12. *New Oxford*, February 1921; A.E.E. Reade, 'Oxford letter', *Youth*, March 1921.
13. *Ibid.*; *ISIS*, 1 June 1921; Reade, *op.cit.*
14. R. Nahum, 'Twenty-one years of the ULF', *University Forward*, February 1941.
15. USF, *Bulletin*, May 1921, p5; National Museum of Labour History, Manchester, CP/IND/HUTT/1/2, Hutt to Reade, 19 January 1923.
16. *Bulletin*, May 1920, March, May 1921.
17. *Bulletin*, May 1921, p9; B. Pearce, 'The last years of the University Socialist Federation', *Bulletin of the Society for the Study of Labour History*, 4, 1962, pp45-6.
18. *Youth*, May 1921.
19. Oxford University Archives (OUA) MS Top Oxon. d296, Labour Club Minutes, 27 April 1921; *Youth*, May 1921; 'Leading article: The Great Betrayal', *New Oxford*, May 1921.
20. *Youth*, May 1921; Labour Club Minutes, 10 May 1921.
21. *Free Oxford*, 12 November 1921 and n.10.
22. C. Hollis, *Oxford in The Twenties*, 1976, p25.
23. *ISIS*, 5 June 1921; A.E. Coppard, *It's Me O Lord!*, 1957.
24. *Communist*, 19 November 1923; n. 10; CP/IND/DUTT/1/1, Reade to Dutt 7 December 1921; Rothstein and Tom Wintringham having left in 1920, the only other CPGB members at Oxford at this time were Ralph Fox who was at Magdalen and Esmonde Higgins at Balliol. Fox spent some time in the Soviet Union and, like Higgins, has left no trace of activity; E. Porter to author, 9 February 2000.
25. D. Goldring, *The Nineteen-Twenties*, 1945, pp145-77; n. 4.
26. See n.1; C. Cockburn, *In Time of Trouble*, 1956, p64; H. Acton, *Memoirs of an Aesthete*, 1948, pp122-3.
27. *Free Oxford*, 22 October 1921; CP/IND/HUTT/1/2, Hutt to Reade 7 March 1923; A. Bertram, 'The everlasting nightingale (for AER)', *ISIS*, 11 May 1921.
28. *The Times*, 15 August 1919; M.P. Ashley and C.T. Saunders, *Red Oxford*, Oxford, 1933, p36.
29. OUA PR/1/23/9/4, Papers and Correspondence; L.R. Farnell, *An Oxonian Looks Back*, 1934.
30. M. Dobb, 'After Versailles', *University Forward*, February 1941, p25.
31. E. Waugh, *Brideshead Revisited*, 1945, p28; Mabro, *op. cit.*, p7.
32. PR/1/23/9/4 Cuttings File; *Manchester Guardian*, 18, 24 January 1922.
33. *Evening Standard*, 12 December 1921.
34. *Ibid.*; *Manchester Guardian*, 13 December 1921.
35. Reade to Hutt, 20 January 1923.
36. *University Socialist*, June 1922, p6.
37. Hutt to Reade, 19 January 1923; Reade to Hutt, 20 January 1923.
38. Hutt to A.L. Bacharach, 23 May 1924; *University Socialist*, June 1922, p3.

39. R. Palme Dutt, 'Students and the Labour Research Department', *New Oxford*, December 1920; M. Dobb, 'Labour Research', *Labour Monthly*, December 1925; DAR/6/3, Page Arnot to Reade, 8 April 1925; K. Morgan, *Harry Pollitt*, Manchester 1993, pp33ff.; Russian State Archive of Socio-Political History (RGASPI), 495/100/171, A. Inkpin to Comintern Secretariat, 6 March 1924. See also Reade's reviews in *Labour Monthly*, June 1923, March, May 1924; 'Idealism and history', *Labour Monthly*, June 1924; 'May Day I', *Workers' Weekly*, 11 April 1924; 'May Day II', *Workers' Weekly*, 18 April 1924.

40. Page Arnot to Reade, 8 April 1925; Bodleian Library, Pollard Papers Box 10, London District, Report of Training Department 1924; Report of District Organising Committee 1924.

41. Interview with J. Reade, 12 December 1999; 'You ought to see my bedroom. More confusion and blooming mess with papers than even *Monthly* office when Reade was in it', D. Proudfoot to Hutt, 13 August 1925, in I. MacDougall (ed.), *Militant Miners*, Edinburgh 1981, p199.

42. A. Reade to S. Reade, 18 April 1924; T'cheka, 'How the cops were caught', *Workers' Weekly*, 18 April 1924. T'cheka was Reade's pseudonym.

43. T. Bell, *Pioneering Days*, 1941, p263.

44. D. Goldring, *op.cit.*, pp145-8, 151; M. Davie (ed), *The Diaries of Evelyn Waugh*, 1976, entries for 8 July 1924, 1 January 1927.

45. For different views on alcohol, see *Workers' Weekly*, 28 December 1923, 18 January, 8, 29 February 1924.

46. For the CPGB's position on the Workers' Opposition, see C. Porter, *Alexandra Kollontai: a biography*, 1980, p288; for the SLP argument, see R. Challinor, *The Origins of British Bolshevism*, 1977, pp215-77; on CPGB autonomy, see A. Thorpe, 'Comintern "control" of the Communist Party of Great Britain, 1920-1943', *English Historical Review*, 452, 1998.

47. J. Degras (ed), *The Communist International 1919-1943: documents*, volume 2, 1923-1928, Oxford 1960, p141.

48. *Ibid.* For more detail, see M. Woodhouse and B. Pearce, *Essays on The History of Communism in Britain*, 1975; Bornstein and Richardson, *op. cit.*; J. McIlroy, 'New light on Arthur Reade', *Revolutionary History*, 8, 1, 2001.

49. 495/100/173, A. Inkpin to Bennett (Petrovsky) 3 December 1924; 495/100/156, Ramsay to Comintern, 3 December 1924. *The Lessons of October* was the preface to the latest volume of Trotsky's *Works 1917*, published in Russia.

50. 495/100/156, Party Council Meeting: Discussions in the Russian Party.

51. 495/100/249, Bell to Bela Kun, 17 January 1925.

52. Harrison, *op. cit.*, p41.

53. McIlroy, *op. cit.*

54. Woodhouse and Pearce, *op. cit.*, p158; Wicks, *op. cit.*, p43; the Pollard Papers attest to the problems the group system imposed in isolation of members and lack of political discussion; N. Wood, *Communism and British Intellectuals*, 1959, pp182-4. The only clear statement of the issues after 1924 came from Maurice Dobb, 'Lenin and Trotsky', *Plebs*, May 1925.

55. *Free Oxford*, 26 November 1921, p4.
56. *Free Oxford*, 10 December 1921, pp5, 8, 10.
57. Wicks, *op. cit.*, p43.
58. *Workers' Weekly,* 23, 30 January 1925; Wicks, *op. cit.*, p44.
59. 495/100/265, Report of Control Commission on the Case of A.E.E. Reade, 25 April 1925; 495/100/233, PB minutes, 21 January, 6, 17 February, 29 March 1925.
60. Page Arnot to Reade, 27 January 1925.
61. *Ibid.*
62. Page Arnot to Reade, 8 April 1925; 495/100/233, PB, 14 April 1925.
63. MacDougall, *op. cit.*, pp201-2, quoting Proudfoot to Hutt, 27 January 1925.
64. 495/100/231, CEC Minutes, 26 April 1925.
65. CPGB, *Report of the 7th National Congress 1925*, p117; Pollard Papers Box 12, K. Beauchamp to *Workers' Weekly*, n. d., 1925; *Inprecorr,* 9 April 1925.
66. Pollard Papers Box 12, A. Colyer to I. Clarke, 4 February; Clarke to Colyer 13 February 1925.
67. Pollard Papers Box 4, Aggregate, 24 May 1925.
68. *Plebs,* 8 August 1925, p323.
69. Davie, *op. cit.*, entry for 21 January 1927; Reade to Gray 5 January 1927.
70. Reade to Gray, 4 January 1927.
71. Quoted in J. Callaghan, *Rajani Palme Dutt: a study in British Stalinism*, 1993, p133.
72. Reade to Gray, 4 January 1927.
73. CP/IND/DUTT/1/1, Dutt to Reade, 19 July 1968; Reade to Dutt, 20 July 1968; J. Reade to Dutt, 7 January 1972.

William Rust: the Comintern's Blue Eyed Boy?

ANDREW FLINN

When William Rust died of a stroke on 3 February 1949 he was only forty-five. He had been one of the leading members of the Communist Party of Great Britain (CPGB) for over twenty-five years. Since the winter of 1939 he had been, for the second time, editor of the *Daily Worker*. The party that he joined at seventeen, soon after it was established, framed his entire adult life. When he died he was still a young man who hoped to lead the party. However his death was not widely mourned.

Rust was not popular. He was considered by some to be ruthless, disloyal and nakedly ambitious. Today, he has the reputation as the coldest Stalinist apparatchik that the British party produced. This chapter will examine whether Rust deserved this reputation. It will question the legitimacy of demonising just one or two individuals amongst the CPGB leadership. Critical political biography involves issues of individual responsibility and the question of whether we can view individuals as representatives of a type. It may be argued that Rust was simply representative of a generation of activists, unencumbered by experience in the labour movement, radicalised by the Bolshevik revolution and as a consequence utterly loyal to the Soviet leadership. One could argue that if the actions of Rust and those like him resulted from ideology, then judgement should focus on the ideology rather than the individual. Bolshevism stressed ruthlessness in the service of proletarian emancipation as a virtue. Few leaders, even in a party as powerless as the CPGB, could claim to lack that virtue. However, individual responsibility and complex personal motivations cannot be excluded from any rigorous assessment. If it is clear that personal ambition and the enjoyment of the trappings of power were amongst Rust's primary motivations, then they must be included in the judgement on the individual.

CHARACTER

Rust was amply built, with a round, plump face which his *Daily Worker* colleague Claud Cockburn likened to a 'rising sun' with 'the skin of it seeming to be stretched as tight as a balloon'. Obituary writers commented on his Pickwickian appearance. Others noted his pride in being well-dressed, referring to him as a 'dapper, soft-spoken, rather chummy man'.[1] Opinion on Rust's personality divided sharply between those who believed him to be without humanity and those who remembered him as humorous and good company. An extreme example of the former can be found in biographical notes on CPGB leaders compiled by the TUC Research department (presumably by its expert on Communism and future general secretary of the TUC,Vic Feather). Drawing on party sources, the note states that Rust was disliked intensely by other Communist leaders. He is described as being without warmth or humour, as arrogant, bullying towards his subordinates and obsequious to those more powerful. The memo concludes that Rust 'always gives me the same sort of feeling that I get when I look at photographs of Hess, the Nazi'. The disillusioned Communist Margaret McCarthy thought him 'ill-bred, conceited and a bully' whose influence was responsible for the drunken and juvenile behaviour of British delegations in Moscow. Party loyalist Walter Holmes, on the other hand, wrote of a companionable man, rigorous in his work but always approachable and open to suggestions.[2]

Rust does appear to have had difficulty in making close friends and there was a consensus that 'those that know him best, dislike him most'. The most favourable accounts were in the obituaries in the capitalist press by writers who had known him in a professional rather than a political capacity. These described Rust as friendly and benevolent rather than 'a cold professional revolutionary' and even as 'a very likeable, indeed loveable little chap'. These descriptions jar even with those offered by former party members who were sympathetic. The Communist journalists Malcolm MacEwen and Claud Cockburn both describe him as single-minded, even ruthless. In what may be an attempt to justify his own career, Cockburn portrayed Rust's lies and deceit as political virtues:

> He had, besides a good head on his shoulders, a streak of the urchin and a bigger streak of the pirate. In other words, while as sometimes happened, he was monstrously hypocritical, or lying horribly, he did those things with full consciousness, using the tricks as weapons. He had no 'lie in his soul' and ... one of the major differences in life is between

those people who lie on purpose and those who do not even know whether they are lying or not.

J. R. Campbell, another editor of the *Daily Worker*, confirmed that with Rust 'you could not separate the man from his politics'.[3]

Besides R. Palme Dutt and Holmes, the obituaries written by Rust's fellow party leaders contain few hints of personal warmth. The Scottish Communist Willie Gallacher and CPGB general secretary Harry Pollitt disliked him intensely. These personal animosities had their roots in the political disputes of 1929 and 1939. Sam Russell, a long time *Daily Worker* journalist, believed the divisions over the war between Pollitt, Gallacher and Campbell on one side and Dutt, Rust and the bearer of the Comintern's instructions, Dave Springhall on the other affected the party for years. Although Pollitt and the others were disciplined enough not to reveal their feelings publicly, they have been given voice by others. Pollitt's most recent biographer, Kevin Morgan, begins a sustained piece of invective by describing Rust as 'a man to whose memory it is hard to be kind' and 'everything that "Stalinist" means as a term of abuse'. The intended contrast with Pollitt's humanity is clear.[4]

The most vivid accounts of Rust are to be found in the memoirs of ex-Communists. The books by Douglas Hyde, Charlotte Haldane, Fred Copeman and Harry McShane are all written from an anti-CPGB perspective and, Haldane and Copeman especially, must be treated with caution. However, the picture they give of Rust is consistent enough to dispel most doubts. Both Haldane and Hyde knew Rust well and worked closely with him on the *Daily Worker* and Haldane described him as a close friend. Both agree on his ruthlessness and willingness to sacrifice others for political goals and personal advancement. Hyde argues that politics and careerism were intertwined: 'If he remained in the leadership, therefore it mattered little what indignities, what sacrifices, might be demanded of him. Sooner or later communism would triumph and he would be one of the mighty. He would have power. He would have the chance of retribution'. For Rust, political progress and his own advancement were to be achieved by complete obedience to the Soviet Union and the line advanced by the Communist International. McShane described him as 'the man who wanted every little thing done just as Moscow said'. Copeman likened Rust's behaviour in front of his Comintern masters to that of a 'mobile jelly ... begging alms from the great overlord'.[5] It is Rust's loyalty to Moscow and the extent to which this was motivated by career considerations that will be the main focus of this chapter.

BACKGROUND

William Charles Rust was born in Camberwell, south London on 24 April 1903.[6] His father, Frederick Rust, was a journeyman bookbinder. He told Charlotte Haldane that his family had been so poor that he had began work sweeping in a shop at the age of seven. Beckett describes Rust's upbringing as 'harsh' and 'under nourished' and Lee recalled being told 'mild stories of childhood atrocities'.[7] He grew up in a broadly working-class environment. In *Life and Labour in London* Charles Booth describes late-Victorian Camberwell as a working-class area with around a third of the population classified as poor. A large number of lower middle-class clerks and poorer City workers may have lived in the area. Rust found early employment as a clerk and perhaps other members of his family did also. Many descriptions of Rust characterise him as a typical Cockney, emphasising his working-class London roots. Cockburn describes him as 'the most cockney of cockneys'. However it is equally plausible to locate his family amongst the impoverished lower middle classes of the area.[8]

He left school at fourteen in 1917. His later career, particularly at the *Daily Worker*, demonstrated that Rust was certainly intelligent and had an aptitude for learning. However, like many of his contemporaries in the labour movement, he was by necessity an autodidact. He found his education in the Young Communist League (YCL), the CPGB and in prison. Some years later, Haldane was shocked to find that he could speak fluent German. He told her that he had learnt it in prison, though his long association with the Communist International was as likely a source. Rust was fiercely critical of state education. In his 1925 pamphlet, *What the Young Communist League Stands For*, he argued that capitalism offered two types of education. Formal education intended to produce docile wage slaves and an entertainment industry designed to convince working-class audiences of the glories of capitalism. He concluded that it was the role of the YCL to counteract this by providing revolutionary working-class education.[9]

Rust strove against disadvantages of background and schooling to improve himself, as a Marxist and as a journalist. He remained simultaneously dismissive and in awe of those whose class had allowed them access to a better education. In her memoirs *Daily Worker* journalist Alison Macleod recalls that he was unmoved by the arts and ridiculed those weak enough to 'sob at plays'. Nevertheless, he monopolised the privileges of attending the press nights at West End theatres and basked in the reflected glory of meeting actors backstage.[10]

Rust had several jobs before finding clerical work with the Hulton

Press Agency. He was sacked in 1920 after he revealed that the engineering union leader, J.T. Brownlie, was combining his union responsibilities with being the agency's paid Labour correspondent. He went 'on the run' and was given sanctuary in a government engineering works by the future *Daily Worker* correspondent, Jack Owen.[11] It is not clear what precise influences or events politicised Rust at such a young age. However, by the time he was sixteen he was active in the clerks' union and had joined the Labour Party. He seems to have been involved in the Workers' Socialist Federation and worked in some junior capacity on the *Workers' Dreadnought*. In 1920, only a few months after it was formed, Rust joined the CPGB. Radicals of Rust's age formed their beliefs against the backdrop of the slaughter of the First World War and the success of the Bolshevik revolution. Rust and many other young people who sought working-class emancipation gave their enthusiasm and unswerving loyalty to the USSR.

THE YCL AND POLITICAL APPRENTICESHIP

After 1920, Rust remained active in the Camberwell labour movement. He was a member of the Workers' Union. He stayed in the Labour Party for six years until Communists were expelled. He was an executive member of the local party and its delegate to the Camberwell Trades and Labour Council. Alert to changing political realities, as a delegate to the Communist International's Sixth World Congress in 1928, he denied previous membership of any other organisation. Association with social-democratic parties no longer found favour in the Comintern and presumably Rust felt it convenient to omit this detail of his past.[12]

After working for Hulton's, Rust spent long periods unemployed. He concentrated on full-time political activism, especially in the National Unemployed Workers' Committee Movement. There were many violent clashes between the police and unemployed demonstrators in Camberwell. In July 1922, Rust was sentenced to two months' imprisonment for wilful damage to property while resisting an eviction. Harry Adams (subsequently president of the Amalgamated Union of Building Trade Workers) recalled the 'tremendous energy' that Rust devoted to organising in Camberwell.[13]

At the same time, he began his rise through the party. He became secretary of his branch and served on the London district committee. His first major promotion was being co-opted into the leadership of the YCL. Before the YCL, revolutionary youth organisations had included the Young Socialist League and the Young Workers League.

Rust had been involved in the latter but was not initially active in the YCL. According to the Youth Communist International (YCI), the first version of the YCL was romantic and tactically naïve. It made little impact and was soon inactive. On YCI instructions, the British party re-organised the League and directed Rust and two other adult members into the YCL. At the League's second conference in October 1923, Rust was confirmed as YCL secretary.[14]

From the start, Rust owed his advancement to the Comintern. He began to regularly attend Comintern and YCI meetings in the USSR. Over the next twenty years, he would be one of the British party's most rigorous and inflexible advocates of Moscow's line. What is unclear is who, at this early stage, Rust had impressed in the leadership of the British party and upon whom he relied for his immediate advancement. One possibility would be another loyal supporter of Moscow, the party's theoretician, Rajani Palme Dutt. Referring to the inner-party conflict of 1929, Dutt's biographer describes Rust as Dutt's protégé. Certainly in most party controversies, the two were to be found promoting the Comintern orthodoxy. This alliance has led some writers to refer to 'Dutt and Rust' as if they were a single entity. However, Dutt stated that his 'close association' with Rust only began after the latter had been appointed as YCL secretary. Dutt was the Political Bureau (PB) representative at YCL executive meetings. He was immediately impressed with Rust's maturity and organisational ability but was probably not responsible for the initial promotion.[15]

Andrew Rothstein was another potential mentor. In the early 1920s, Rothstein had considerable influence in the relationship between the Comintern and the CPGB. He also had a supervisory role for youth organisation and may have used his position to advance Rust. His expression of disappointment at Rust's behaviour in 1929 indicates some sense of personal betrayal.[16] Whoever his patrons were, Rust had made an impact. In a party as small as the CPGB, an able comrade in London was bound to come to the notice of leaders hungry for talent. Once in position, Rust increasingly enjoyed the support of Dutt, Rothstein and others and was able to use the YCL to build his own base.

Under Rust and like-minded individuals such as Springhall and the live-wire Londoner Wally Tapsell, the YCL became disciplined and ultra-orthodox. As early as December 1924, Rust demonstrated the self-confidence of a youthful zealot in correcting what he viewed as the party leadership's mistaken assessment of the CPSU's and the Comintern's criticism of Trotsky and the left opposition. In 1927, Rust and the YCL were enthusiastic supporters of the action taken by the

Soviet leadership against Trotsky.[17] Although the YCL was committed to co-operation with youth groups in other political parties, its leaders were openly scathing about rivals. In contrast with other youth bodies and previous incarnations of the League, Rust wrote that the YCL was not 'an organisation of cultural faddists and intellectual idlers who spend their time building castles in the air' but a serious group dedicated to preparing youth to overthrow capitalism.[18]

Rust quickly became influential in the adult party. He was co-opted onto the Central Committee (CC) from 1923 and elected to it in 1926. From 1924, he began to attend PB meetings. His rise had personal drawbacks. In October 1925, he was among the twelve party leaders imprisoned on a charge of sedition as part of the state's preparations for the General Strike and, as he had already been in prison, he served a year.[19] Victimisation by the state boosted his credibility and enabled him to continue his political education in the company of experienced revolutionaries such as William Gallacher.

MOSCOW'S SPELL

As YCL secretary, Rust was intimately associated with the international movement. In July 1924 he attended the Fourth Youth International Congress and the Fifth Congress of the Comintern. Walter Holmes, who had a long association with Rust on the *Daily Worker*, first met his future editor on this trip. Holmes was impressed by the enthusiasm of the twenty-one year old. Despite Rust's youthful antics and snappy dressing, Holmes characterised him as the 'sort of working-class lad who is always neat and well turned out but no softy'.[20]

In his autobiography, J. T. Murphy, a senior figure in the CPGB and Comintern, describes the revolutionary fervour and intellectual excitement which existed amongst the international community around the Hotel Lux in Moscow in the early 1920s. One can only speculate about the inspirational effect of this on a mind as young and impressionable as Rust's. The young revolutionary carefully noted how the ruthless internal struggles of the Russian Communist Party were being conducted in the international arena. With little knowledge of the outside world, his loyalty to the Comintern can only have been strengthened by this experience. Another delegate to a YCI congress recalled how exciting it felt to be part of 'a great world movement of young people dedicated at all costs to changing the world', but also noted how youthful enthusiasm often made its members more fanatical than older party comrades.[21]

In the next four years, Rust travelled extensively in Europe and the USA and participated in various International meetings. He attended an enlarged meeting of the YCI executive and the Fifth Plenum of the Executive Committee of the Communist International (ECCI) in 1925. Although Klugmann maintains that Rust was present at the Sixth Plenum of ECCI, he was in prison at the time and it is more likely that he attended the Seventh Plenum and YCI executive following his release in September 1926.[22]

In 1928 he attended the Ninth ECCI Plenum and the Sixth World Congress where the new, sectarian, leftist line of Class Against Class, based on the theorisation of a new capitalist crisis and sharpening class conflict, was adopted. Previously, he had been part of the majority on the CPGB's Central Committee which voted to maintain links with the Labour Party but he quickly adopted the new orthodoxy. In the run up to the CPGB's Tenth Congress in January 1929, he became increasingly critical of the party's leadership. He accused them of 'opportunism' and 'right deviations' in failing to implement the new line. He argued that the new line had been applied purely as an electoral tactic rather than an independent revolutionary policy 'in all spheres of activity'. The failure to abandon co-operation with the 'pseudo-lefts' was hindering party growth. In particular, party leaders were guilty of 'trade union loyalism' by refusing to advocate the witholding of the political levy. In the mantra of the new times, the leadership had also failed to submit themselves to self-criticism.[23]

By the end of 1928, Rust had become pivotal to the relationship between the Comintern and the British party. He was working full-time in the YCI Secretariat and was subsequently elected YCI representative on the ECCI and ECCI Presidium. Given his loyalty to Moscow, he became one of the most dogmatic exponents of its sectarian and workerist politics in the British party. As a leading British official in the Comintern, Rust was in an unchallenged position to direct the International's anger against his rivals in the CPGB. 1929 saw Rust and other like-minded party activists use the failure to fully implement Class Against Class as their weapon in an assault on power.[24]

1929: 'IT WILL BE PERHAPS NECESSARY TO CHOP SOME HEADS OFF'[25]

1929 was a key year in Rust's career. Using loyalists like Rust and Murphy, the Comintern encouraged a bitter factional struggle within the British party. By the end of the year, Rust was seeking a purge of the 'leadership of the party from top to bottom'. He was not alone. Class Against Class was not simply imposed on a recalcitrant party. Although the new line was resisted by many, such as the level-headed anchorman of the party leadership J.R. Campbell, others positively welcomed a more militant, sectarian stance. Established figures such as Gallacher, Pollitt, Dutt and Murphy joined younger Communists based in the YCL in promoting the key aspects of Class Against Class, although some would soon express reservations at the consequences of the new approach in the unions.[26]

Nina Fishman identifies the 'Young Turks' who advanced the new lines as Rust, Tapsell, Springhall, John Mahon, Eric Woolley, Peter Zinkin as well as the more experienced transport worker George Renshaw and former miner George Allison. Many of these shared a similar lack of experience in the trade union movement to temper their revolutionary enthusiasms. The new line was particularly popular amongst London activists, with Reg Groves and Stewart Purkiss (later part of the Trotskyist Balham Group) taking the lead. Outside London, districts like Tyneside and Lancashire supported the change. In the background, advising the different elements was Dutt. Rust, spanning the Comintern and the British party, was an influential member of this movement.[27]

The CPGB's Tenth Congress in January 1929 brought the party into line with the Comintern. However, the conversion of many leaders was pragmatic rather than genuine. They used the Congress elections to gain revenge on their opponents and tried to exclude two of their most prominent critics, Rust and his fellow leftist Robin Page Arnot, from the CC. Though clearly a politically inspired move, they argued that there were practical considerations about the ability of Moscow-based comrades to participate in the committee.[28]

Rust returned to Moscow and portrayed his exclusion as a deliberate snub to the International. He called for continuing deviations from the Comintern line to be 'mercilessly opposed'. The ECCI Presidium meeting in Moscow heard reports on the Congress. While the veteran party leader Tom Bell and Pollitt praised the conduct and decisions of the Congress, Rust referred to the 'veiled resistance' of the CPGB leadership to the Comintern. The result was an ECCI letter to the British party that clearly echoed Rust's evidence. The closed letter was a detailed exposure of what the Comintern called 'serious deficiencies in the leadership'. The ECCI were particularly critical of the British CC's removal of Rust and Arnot which the ECCI interpreted as 'a certain demonstration against the Comintern'. Attempting to appeal directly to the membership, the ECCI demanded that the letter be distributed to district and local committees. The CPGB CC accepted the general criticisms but refuted the most serious accusations. The exclusions were not an attack on the International, because on certain issues 'comrade Rust adopted a line which was not the line of the Comintern'.[29]

The party's derisory vote at the May 1929 general election, when the electorate decisively rejected the call for a 'revolutionary workers' government', was used in the continuing dispute.[30] The position of the CPGB was re-examined at the Tenth Plenum of the ECCI in July 1929. In what Pollitt described as a 'prepared brief of all the shortcomings and deviations of our Party', Rust stressed the lack of self-criticism and called for a new leadership. Supported by Petrovsky, the Comintern representative in Britain, Rust named the miners' leader Arthur Horner, Campbell, the recently removed party secretary Albert Inkpin and Rothstein as among those responsible for sabotaging Comintern policies. The arguments continued over the exclusion of Gallacher, Murphy, Rust and Arnot from the party leadership. It was clear which side had Comintern support. The Comintern funcionary Dmitri Manuilsky epitomised the political methods that Rust sought to import into the British party. He expressly praised Rust's contribution. He criticised the CPGB's complacency and excessive politeness. Rather than the party as a 'society of great friends', he recommended 'courageous, frank, Bolshevist self-criticism' in which 'all the friendship in the world should not be a hindrance to telling the revolutionary truth'. Manuilsky singled out for praise the YCI, of which Rust was a leading member: 'We have a body of young workers lately brought to the fore in the Communist International who keep a vigilant eye on all points of difference in the Comintern. Is this good or bad? This is good. This vigilance is an element of the Party's Bolshevisation'. The speech left no doubt about the strategy that the Comintern expected the British party to operate.[31]

After this decisive outcome, a new CPGB Congress was called to purge the CC of those who had 'hampered' implementation of the Comintern line. Rust was placed in charge of a committee that recommended the names of the new executive. At the Eleventh Congress in December 1929, two thirds of the old committee were replaced. 1929 saw the short-term triumph of the politics espoused by the Young Turks. These events marked a lasting break between Rust and those like Pollitt, Campbell and Horner who sought to prevent the wholehearted importation of Russian political methods into the British party.

This dispute was personal as well as political. Pollitt, who owed his elevation to General Secretary to the Comintern's reorganisation of the party, was particularly angered by the cruel treatment meted out to long-serving party servants such as Albert Inkpin. He told Dutt that his opponents were 'impossible fools and mechanical parrots and gramophones'.[32]

Rust's self-proclaimed status as the 'standard bearer of the Comintern' was the subject of widespread cynicism. It was pointed out that Rust himself had at times deviated from the Comintern line. Other criticisms focussed on the inability of the YCL to successfully apply the new line. Horner noted that even when Congress delegates had been free to vote for Rust, he still failed to be elected to the CC. A recurring theme was Rust's lack of working-class credentials. A key element of the Comintern's left turn was workerist rhetoric and the focus on the factory. The British party was specifically criticised for being insufficiently proletarian. Rust's opponents referred repeatedly to his lack of factory experience, claiming he had 'never seen the working class except in pictures and from platforms'. Even those such as Idris Cox, who supported Class Against Class and the removal of the old party leadership, dismissed his credibility.[33]

A WORKERS' DAILY

Rust's reward was the editorship of the CPGB's new daily newspaper. The paper had been the subject of another controversy between the International and the British party. While the Comintern insisted on the appearance of a daily, many British leaders doubted whether the time was suitable, politically or financially. However, by the end of 1929 it was no longer possible to resist Comintern demands and on 1 January 1930 the first issue of the *Daily Worker* was published.[34]

Rust admitted that he was not chosen for professional expertise. Although he had edited the YCL's *Young Worker* and had been a member of the editorial board of the *International of Youth*, this was a political appointment and recognition of his 'persistent advocacy of the importance of a Communist daily'. The paper and Rust would eventually benefit from the journalistic experience of Allen Hutt and Walter Holmes, but initially little value was placed on these skills. The *Daily Worker* shunned the news and entertainment values of the capitalist press in favour of political education and worker correspondents. The paper was to be 'a daily weapon for the advancement of its [the party's] agitation and propaganda'. Rust was appointed because he was 'politically dependable and alert to deviations'.[35]

As a result the paper was largely unreadable. Stories illustrating the crisis of capitalism and impending revolutionary situation were set alongside unmediated columns of Comintern rhetoric. For one critic, Rust's appointment guaranteed that the paper 'would be drab and colourless, and inhibited from experiment and adventure by fear of deviation'. The fate of sport's coverage demonstrated the conscious rejection of any hint of populism. Sport, Rust recalled, was 'dropped after only three weeks on the grounds that it was a sink of corruption and a means of doping the working class'. He conceded, with under-statement, that 'in those days we were more than a little sectarian'.[36]

However, in his second spell at the *Daily Worker* (1939-1949), Rust developed into a talented editor. He gained approval from Fleet Street journalists for his willingness to compensate for lack of formal training by learning from those, such as Allen Hutt and Cockburn, who possessed greater experience. Under Cockburn's tutelage, Rust became 'a forceful, though not a subtle writer'. In earlier years however, his writings like his oratory were derivative and dogmatic, 'moulded almost completely by Moscow'. Pollitt's criticism of the obscure language in YCI and YCL publications neatly describes Rust's own style. Rust's pronouncements rarely sought to elucidate or justify the latest twists in party policy, rather he was content to repeat the Comintern line. As an organiser and bureaucrat, he was best suited to writing on practical problems; he was no theoretician or propagan-dist.[37]

Between 1930 and 1932, the victors of 1929 used their positions to promote Class Against Class. They were particularly critical of the 'trade union legalism' of Horner and the Communist leadership in the South Wales Miners' Federation. However, by 1931 the Comintern was moving away from ultra-leftism. At the Eleventh Plenum of the ECCI in July 1931, Pollitt criticised the sectarianism and inflexibility that accounted for the weakness of the party's trade union work. The fail-ure of Class Against Class to produce mass support for revolutionary trade unions allowed Pollitt to reverse aspects of the new line.[38]

In December 1931, an ECCI resolution on the 'Immediate Tasks of the CPGB' increased the pressure on supporters of Class Against Class. Although capable of different interpretations, the resolution emphasised the need for work within rather than outside reformist trade unions. It also criticised the content of the *Daily Worker*, which Rust was still editing. The following year, emboldened by the ECCI Twelfth Plenum's instruction to activists to seek to work in reformist trade unions rather than wreck them, Pollitt argued for an end to the party's isolation from the unions. Against the backdrop of cotton strikes in Lancashire, his articles in the *Daily Worker* sparked a bitter controversy about the party's failure to secure mass influence amongst the working class.[39]

Rust attempted to force Pollitt to justify himself but the latter refused to come to London to discuss the 'distortions on t.u. questions' contained in his articles. Rust also complained in correspondence that Pollitt had kept to himself 'knowledge of discussion' at the plenum. In turn Pollitt referred to Rust as 'contemptuous, high brow and mechanical'. Rust appeared to be prepared to accept these descriptions, though he did recoil at being portrayed as 'frivolous'. He replied that Pollitt's letter had been 'terrible' but that they should put their differences aside and 'get down to a real summing up of what faces the Party now'. A subsequent letter contained the unlikely claim that 'I have always worked loyally'.[40]

It was clear that Comintern support now lay with those who wished to curb sectarianism. Although the CPGB's Twelfth Congress formally approved the need to build the Revolutionary Trade Union Opposition, future party work was to be within unions not independent of them. The problem for those who wished to maintain the new line was that the Comintern had turned away from a leftist approach. The only voices still urging the old approach were Dutt's former proteges, the Trotskyists of the Balham group. For a Moscow loyalist like Rust, these were people with whom it was impossible to associate. Groves recalled Rust standing inside the hall at the Twelfth Congress confiscating the leaflets the Balham group were handing to delegates.[41]

Rust demonstrated his awareness of new realities by acknowledging 'neglect of work in the reformist trade unions'. However, he paid a price for his defeat. In November 1932, he was removed as editor of the *Daily Worker*. He was sent to Moscow, where for 1933 and part of 1934 he was the party's representative on the ECCI. This was an important position but it also removed him from immediate influence in the CPGB and was no doubt intended to ensure that he understood the Comintern's new perspectives.[42]

LANCASHIRE

In 1929 Horner accused some comrades of believing that 'work in the district is a degradation if you have once occupied a position in the Central Committee'. He argued that Rust, who had long been involved in the leadership of the YCL and subsequently the Comintern, had no experience of 'real working class life' and the 'difficulties that are involved in being a Party member in the ordinary sense'.[43] The implications of Horner's criticisms were not implemented until 1934 when it was decided to appoint Rust as the centre's representative in Lancashire.

In 1932, the party had designated the Lancashire and Cheshire district as deserving of special attention. Subsequent reports suggested a continuing pattern of under-performance. A Special Commission in 1933 condemned the party's weakness, particularly amongst cotton workers, and blamed the district leadership's complacency and obstruction of the new line. It was decided to send Rust to reorganise the district leadership. For the next three years, he was in charge in Lancashire, eventually becoming District Organiser. His initial impact was minimal. Shortly after arriving in Manchester, he was involved in a motor cycle accident which left him in plaster for nearly a year. At one point he returned to Moscow to recuperate. His responsibilities, which included preparations for the party's Thirteenth Congress held in Manchester in February 1935, were taken over by the Welsh leader Idris Cox. Rust did not return to Lancashire until later that year.[44]

Despite this, his tenure was viewed as a success. One local leader praised Rust for having 'rescued' the Lancashire party 'from a derelict state'. Once settled, he worked assiduously to build up the local organisation. He co-operated with the local members rather than simply imposing his authority. Eddie Frow, then a young supporter of Class Against Class, was impressed: 'Bill Rust was never a dogmatist. He was a very good organiser ... Everybody liked Bill to work with, because he did listen, and he did take account of what the problems were and was realistic in regard to everything'. Practical organisation made the best use of his talents. He functioned most effectively when removed from factional struggle and when he concentrated on the practical day-to-day issues. In Lancashire, he devoted himself to his work as an organiser, attending meetings, running campaigns and implementing a programme of political education. Rust's abilities lay as an administrator and organiser: he was more comfortable with bureaucracy than ideology.[45]

The most immediate problem was the crisis in the cotton industry which was in terminal decline. The CPGB had been unable to put forward an effective response; the 1932 cotton strikes had demonstrated the party's weakness amongst textile workers, especially in the spinning towns of south-east Lancashire. When the British Union of Fascists (BUF) launched a membership drive, one of Rust's first responsibilities was to co-ordinate a popular anti-fascist movement.

The result was the 'Drive Out Mosley' campaign which attracted a broad range of support and a pamphlet by Rust which demolished the BUF's programme for cotton. Uniquely for a CPGB publication, the latter was praised by the cotton unions' paper, the *Cotton Factory Times*.[46]

Local party propaganda had previously been criticised for reliance on slogans and lack of understanding of the real problems facing cotton workers. Under Rust, the party began to reverse this tendency. Publications and campaigns dealt with the immediate issues that concerned textile workers. The district was re-organised with sub-districts in the south-east spinning and north-east weaving areas. These changes did not result in a great advance, for most cotton workers remained temperamentally hostile to communism. However, the party did succeed in overcoming its isolation and its sectarian tendencies.[47]

Such progress was not the achievement of one man. It was the result of the changed circumstances of the mid-1930s and the search for anti-fascist unity. Demonstrating his willingness to unquestioningly follow a new line, Rust was thoroughly behind the unity campaign in Manchester. So enthusiastic was he for the new alliances that at one point he joined Gallacher in proposing liquidation of the CPGB and the formation of a new broad-based socialist party.[48]

Integral to this new inclusive mode of politics was the realisation that if the party was to reach a wider audience, it needed to give priority to local and domestic issues as well as international affairs. In this it is possible that Rust was influenced by the success his wife, Tamara, was having in revitalising the party's work with women in Lancashire by focusing on issues such as housing, maternal mortality and malnutrition. Before he returned to London, he warned against complacency and the remnants of sectarianism in the work of district activists, but he was able to leave a much healthier party than the one he had inherited.[49]

BRITON IN SPAIN

According to the eminent scientist and sometime CPGB member J.B.S. Haldane, Rust would have fought in the International Brigade in Spain but for his motor cycle injury.[50] It is impossible to know the truth or otherwise of this but temperamentally Rust was more suited to political work behind the lines. He was in Spain between November 1937 and June 1938. Officially he was a *Daily Worker* correspondent but in fact he was base commissar, the most senior British commissar there. He was sent by the British party to instil discipline. In the summer of

1937, the leadership of the Brigade was recalled to London to explain the alleged lack of discipline within the British forces. Of the original leaders, only Copeman and Tapsell were allowed to return to Spain. Rust was sent with them to oversee the development of a 'strong collective political leadership'. He was entrusted with ensuring that Communist control extended over all the disparate political elements of the brigade.[51]

There is no clear record of his activities in Spain. His own account of the British brigade, *Britons in Spain*, was designed to celebrate the heroism of the volunteers and Rust does not introduce himself into the narrative. The book describes the role of the political commissar as being concerned with morale and ensuring that the soldiers understood the wider context of the conflict. It was also the commissar's responsibility to deal with political problems. Francis Beckett refers to Rust 'carrying a hand-gun and analysing your politics with cold brutality'. The most recent work by James D. Hopkins concentrates on the role of the CPGB within the brigade and the treatment of 'dissident' volunteers. From this research and from Laurie Lee's references to Rust's card index, it is clear that the latter was responsible for the maintenance of the party's records on individual soldiers. In several cases, these records contained Rust's denunciations of political deviation. In a report written as he was leaving Spain in July 1938, he noted that there was some disillusionment amongst the volunteers but 'such weak elements could be beaten down'. Rust was part of the apparatus by which dissent was crushed amongst the anti-Franco forces in Spain and no doubt he was suited to this role. However, he was also fulfilling the duties given to him by an equally complicit Comintern and CPGB leadership.[52]

The clearest impression of Rust in Spain is given by Charlotte Haldane. As secretary of the Dependents' Aid Committee, she spent much of her time in Spain in the company of Rust. In England she had disliked him but in Spain she found him 'a man of outstanding and obvious ability'. They became close friends despite her awareness that he was cynically exploiting her class and her money.[53] From her account, it is clear that Rust was well aware of the brutal discipline that the Comintern commissars were dispensing. He also enjoyed the trappings of power that his status brought. Her most telling indictment of Rust concerns him fattening himself up at her expense in the black market restaurants of Barcelona while 'the Brigade lads and the Spanish Army were on the shortest rations, while the admirable Catalan people all around me were showing visible signs of starvation'. Rust dismissed her objections and informed her that overcoming such 'sentimental idealism was part of [her] political training'. Whilst this story is credible and as such particularly damning of Rust, it must be treated with caution. The purpose of Haldane's book was to denounce her past and portray party leaders unfavourably. She is careful not to denigrate the brigades themselves but the Communist officials are uniformly depicted as greedy, cynical and brutal.[54]

The poet Laurie Lee records a more favourable impression. After Rust saved him from a Barcelona jail, he stayed a few days in Rust's flat. Rust is described as 'a quiet, gentle man, tough with bureaucratic bullies, but a kindly uncle to such strays as myself'. However, the value of this unusually favourable account of Rust is as dubious as Haldane's. The legitimacy of Lee's memories have been the subject of claim and counter-claim, with some arguing that he never served in Spain at all.[55]

Rust's assiduous work for the party in Lancashire and Spain seems to have removed some of the stigma over his role in 1929. In 1938, Pollitt informed the Comintern that although Rust previously 'had certain sectarian tendencies', he had overcome them 'in the course of work in the Lancashire District of the Party'. After leaving Spain he rejoined his wife in Lancashire. However, his ambition remained unsatisfied. In November 1938, he travelled to Moscow to meet Comintern representatives. In discussions on the CPGB, Rust campaigned for himself as the 'obvious' choice for the new post of assistant general secretary. It has been suggested that throughout this period Rust and Dutt continued to support leftist politics. This is not very persuasive in Rust's case. It is more realistic to characterise him as a Comintern loyalist regardless of the line. However, the crisis over the CPGB's attitude to the outbreak of war in 1939 presented both with an opportunity to re-establish their pre-eminence.[56]

1939 AND AFTER

In the dispute over the party's attitude to the war, Dutt took the initiative. Initially, Rust supported the 'war on two fronts' as long as the struggle against the British government was waged with the same conviction as the war against Hitler. When Moscow's new line became clear, he joined Dutt and the Comintern's messenger, Springhall, on a self-appointed secretariat advocating the imperialist war analysis. At a bitter CC meeting on 2 October 1939, the triumvirate carried the day against Pollitt and Campbell by reminding members of their primary loyalty to the Comintern. Bad feelings persisted within the party for years. Gallacher said that he had never known anything 'so rotten, so mean, so despicable, so dirty' as the actions of the 'three ruthless revolutionaries'. Pollitt predicted that he would remain in the revolutionary movement when his antagonists were forgotten.[57]

Pollitt was replaced by the Secretariat while Rust was also reinstated as *Daily Worker* editor. Initially the new leadership advanced the revolutionary implications of the imperialist war line, leading Pollitt to comment on the 'fascist propaganda' offensive 'to every sincere antifascist' creeping into Rust's *Daily Worker*. Fearful of the isolation that advocating revolutionary defeatism would bring, they modified the line in practice while maintaining the imperialist war rhetoric. As ever, Rust remained alert to potential deviations and was responsible for the public criticism of Ivor Montagu for the perceived mistakes in his book, *The Traitor Class*.[58]

The *Daily Worker* was to dominate the rest of his life. His first task when the paper was banned in 1941 was, together with Douglas Hyde, to prepare for illegality and underground printing. Then he co-ordinated an effective campaign against the ban. When the *Daily Worker* resumed publication in September 1942, he concentrated on transforming it into a radical, mass circulation daily. Before he died, he had overseen the transfer of the paper's ownership from the party to the broader, but still party dominated, People's Press Printing Society and a massive expansion of printing capacity. He was the able editor of a reasonably successful paper with a skilled and dedicated staff, although dreams of mass circulation were compromised by the returning sectarianism of the Cold War.[59]

He had not given up his political ambitions. He regularly clashed with Pollitt and viewed the paper as his personal fiefdom, the basis for a potential bid for the leadership. He remained as true as ever to the twists and turns of Moscow's policy. As a party official, he enjoyed holidays in Eastern Europe. He became particularly attached to Yugoslavia and was full of admiration for the regime there. After Tito was denounced in 1948, Rust repudiated his earlier praise. Despite the arguments of those close to him, his loyalty to the Kremlin was unshaken.[60]

THE PERSONAL INTRUDES
Rust's personal life was complicated and, through work by Beckett and Macleod, the details have recently come into the public domain. Rust's daughter Rosa was born in 1925, a few months before her father was imprisoned. In 1928, Rust travelled, with his first wife Kathleen, a loyal party member, and their daughter to Moscow to work full time for the

YCI. The marriage ended and Rust began a relationship with a former Komsomol member and teacher at the Modern Languages Institute, Tamara Kravets. Rust and Kravets are thought to have married before he returned to England. Permission for Kravets to join him in England was not granted by the Russians until the end of 1931, ostensibly because her father had not returned from Germany to the USSR in 1927. Once in England, Tamara Rust became active in the CPGB, particularly in the mobilisation of women, and after the war she became National Women's Organiser. However, her father's record meant that she and Rust continued to be viewed with suspicion in Moscow. In 1938, Rust had to justify to Congress his wife's removal from the CC's recommended list. The real reason was that, on Pollitt's recommendation, her name had been withdrawn pending further consultation with the ECCI.[61]

In the meantime, his first wife and daughter remained in Moscow. Kathleen returned to England in 1937 but it was decided that Rosa should remain in the Soviet Union at a boarding school for the children of foreign Communists. When the Germans invaded the USSR, Rosa was evacuated to the Volga. Here she was included in the forced deportation of the Volga Germans to Kazakhstan. After many privations, including hard labour in a copper mine that brought her close to death, she was finally rescued due to her international connections. In 1943, arrangements were made for her to return to Britain where she went to live with her mother. According to Macleod, Rust did not deny his daughter's existence, 'he merely refrained from mentioning it to people who did not need to know'. Publicly acknowledging her past might have meant acknowledging the truth of life under Stalin. After his death, the party continued to marginalise his first wife and daughter. One-line memorial messages to Rust placed by a 'Rosa' and a 'Kathleen' were buried in the small print in the *Daily Worker*. Gallacher, angered by the party's refusal to let her mother attend the funeral, offered a public gesture of condolence to Rust's otherwise unacknowledged 'young daughter'. Rust's family were lucky to survive their brushes with Stalin's Russia. Their experiences ensured that Rust was intimately aware of the true nature of that society. However, he elected to keep that knowledge to himself.[62]

CONCLUSION

When Rust died, he was a formidable CPGB leader who had achieved much in a short life. He had shown considerable talent as an editor and organiser and his rise through the party had been rapid. However, his career remained unfulfilled. Although some believe that he could have been the next party leader, it seems unlikely. His past promotions had owed much to the influence of the International rather than support within the CPGB. His service to the Comintern had created many personal enemies. As Moscow's direct intervention in the affairs of the British party diminished, their enmity would surely have prevented further advancement. It is hard to escape the consequences of the observation that he would never be popular 'among those who knew him best'.[63]

Rust was the prime example of a generation of revolutionary activists. They joined the party in their youth under the influence of Lenin and the Bolshevik revolution. Lacking experience, they knew little of political struggle outside the insular world of the party. Isolated from real life in Britain and inspired by what they saw as the triumphs of the USSR, they embraced the sectarian politics espoused by the Comintern. In this atmosphere, they learnt that ruthlessness and lack of sentiment were cherished revolutionary values. Many like Rust also received their political education in the International Lenin School or the YCI, while in the party they owed their preferment to the patron-age of the Comintern. This youthful enthusiasm for Moscow would lead to eventual complicity in the crimes of that regime.

However there were also individual choices to be made. Rust chose to remain loyal to Moscow despite his knowledge of what was happening under Stalin. Various explanations are advanced as to why British Communist leaders sacrificed their independence and refused to acknowledge what they knew to be true. Some suggest it was necessary to suppress all doubts, given the indispensability of the USSR in the fight against fascism. Others, it is argued, calculated that the ultimate benefits of the Communist cause would outweigh the crimes committed in its name. However, alternative choices were available. In the 1920s, Walter Tapsell seemed to be from the same mould as Rust and together they led the attack on the party leadership. Ten years later, Tapsell saw enough in Spain to change his mind. According to Copeman, Tapsell was asked to investigate the May 1937 uprising in Barcelona. His report placed the blame with the Spanish Communist Party rather than with the United Workers' Marxist Party (POUM) branded as Trotskyists by the CPGB. Copeman further alleges that Tapsell was subsequently killed in myste-rious circumstances, though Hopkins believes these claims to be erroneous. Charlotte Haldane remembered Tapsell as a man of indepen-dent mind not afraid to have political disagreements, even with the Russians. Unlike Tapsell, Rust's choice was to be ruthless in his actions and unswerving in his loyalty. Haldane thought that he envied her for being able 'to defy the Soviet bureaucrats' but, even after he had learnt of his own daughter's experiences, he remained silent.[64]

Hyde believed that for Rust personal and political ambition were inextricably linked. Unlike others, Rust was not sacrificing greater influence elsewhere by remaining in the party. For dedicated apparatchiks like him, the party was the only path to the privilege that leadership would bring after the revolution. Rust enjoyed the trappings of power, the food, the holidays, the theatre tickets, to which his influence gave him access. MacEwen realised in retrospect that the luxury holiday he spent with Rust on the Yugoslavian coast as guests of the Yugoslav party newspaper was 'the first stage of the corruption of an elite'. Always the bureaucrat and administrator rather than the ideologue, Rust saw the party as not only the means to bring about the emancipation of his class but also to further his own career. His unswerving loyalty to the movement and his complicity in its crimes was a product of these personal and political ambitions.[65]

I am grateful to John McIlroy, Kevin Morgan and Gidon Cohen for all their help and suggestions in the writing of this chapter.

NOTES

1. C. Cockburn, *I Claud*, Middlesex 1967, p220; National Museum of Labour History (NMLH) CP/BIOG, Rust file, miscellaneous obituaries; L. Lee, *A Moment of War*, 1991, p121.
2. University of Warwick, Modern Records Centre, MSS 292/770/4; M. McCarthy, *Generation In Revolt* (1953), pp133-4; *Daily Worker (DW)*, 5 February 1949.
3. MSS.292/770/4; D. Hyde, *I Believed*, 1950, p148; *The Times*, 4 February 1949; CP/BIOG; Cockburn, op.cit., p221; M. MacEwen, *The Greening of a Red*, 1991, pp108-10; *DW*, 10 February 1949.
4. *DW*, 4, 5, 9, 10 February 1949; S. Russell in J. Attfield and S. Williams (eds), *1939: The Communist Party and the War*, 1984, pp118-19; K. Morgan, *Harry Pollitt*, Manchester 1993, pp148-9.
5. C. Haldane, *Truth Will Out*, 1949, pp132-133, 176; Hyde, *op. cit.*, pp106-7, 147-9; H. McShane, *No Mean Fighter*, 1978, p237; F. Copeman, *Reason in Revolt*, 1948, pp166-7.
6. Rust never wrote an autobiography or revealed much of his past. Accounts of his early life did not appear in the party press. In consequence, it is only possible to piece together a partial version of his background. I am grateful to Kevin Morgan for providing me with a copy of his forthcoming entry on Rust in the *Dictionary of National Biography*.
7. Haldane, *op. cit.*, p133; Russian State Archive of Socio-Political History (RGASPI) 495/100/491, telegram from Rust to his father, 20 October 1928;

F. Beckett, *Enemy Within: the rise and fall of the British Communist Party*, 1995, p118; Lee, *op. cit.*, p175.

8. C. Booth, *Life and Labour in London. 1st Series: Poverty. II Streets and Population*, 1902, p30 and Appendix, p50; H. Pelling, *Social Geography of British Elections*, 1967, pp52-3.

9. Haldane, *op. cit.*, p133.

10. *Ibid.*; A. Macleod, *The Death of Uncle Joe*, Woodbridge 1997, p17; Hyde, *op. cit.*, p148.

11. *DW*, 4 February 1949; J. & B. Braddock, *The Braddocks*, 1963, pp55-8.

12. *Sunday Worker (SW)*, 5 October 1925; RGASPI 493/1/632, Questionnaire for delegates of the VI Congress of the Communist International.

13. *SW*, 5 October 1925; *Communist*, 6 May 1922; *DW*, 7 February 1949.

14. O. Carlson, 'Six months of progress in Great Britain', *International of Youth*, 4, 1, 1924; J. Klugmann, *History of the Communist Party of Great Britain, vol 1*, 1968, p224.

15. J. Callaghan, *Rajani Palme Dutt: a study in British Stalinism*, 1993, p120; *DW*, 9 February 1949.

16. Discussion with John McIlroy and information from RGASPI 495/100/597, CC, 23 March 1929.

17. *Weekly Worker*, 12 December 1924; *Workers' Life (WL)*, 14 October 1927.

18. W. Rust, *What the Young Communist League Stands For*, 1925 and *A Call to Youth, Opening Speech to YCL Congress 1926*; J. Klugmann, *History of the Communist Party of Great Britain, vol 2*, 1969, pp353-4; *WL*, 14 October 1927.

19. *The Times*, 24 October, 26 November 1925.

20. *SW*, 25 October 1925; *DW*, 5 February 1949.

21. J.T. Murphy, *New Horizons*, 1941, pp242-8; McCarthy, *op. cit.*, pp134-5.

22. Klugmann, *op. cit.*, 1969, p326.

23. N. Branson, *History of the Communist Party of Great Britain, 1927-1941*, 1985, p23; *WL*, 12 October 1928, 11 January 1929; W. Rust 'The coming congress of the CPGB', *Communist International*, 6, 4, 1929.

24. L.J. Macfarlane, *The British Communist Party*, 1966, pp218-9.

25. *Inprecorr*, 25 September 1929.

26. Branson, *op. cit.*, p46; A. Thorpe, 'The Communist International and the British Communist Party', in T. Rees and A. Thorpe (eds), *International Communism and the Communist International 1919-43*, Manchester 1998, p74; B. Pearce and M. Woodhouse, *A History of Communism in Britain*, 1995, pp194-5.

27. N. Fishman, *The British Communist Party and the Trade Unions, 1933-45*, Aldershot 1995, p33; Callaghan, *op. cit.*, pp120, 128.

28. Branson, *op. cit.*, pp35-6.

29. J. Mahon, *Harry Pollitt: a biography*, 1976, p159, NMLH CI26, ECCI Presidium, 13, 27 February 1929; NMLH CP/CENT/CI/1/1, 'Closed Letter' and 'E.C. Statement'.

30. 'The 10th Plenum of the ECCI and the British Party', *Communist International*, October 1929, p873; Pearce and Woodhouse, *op. cit.*, pp194-5.

31. Macfarlane, *op. cit.*, pp231-3; Branson, *op. cit.*, pp44-50; CI 28, ECCI Political Secretariat, 1, 11 July 1929; *Inprecorr*, 21 August, 11, 17, 25 September 1929; *Communist International, ibid.*

32. *Inprecorr*, 29 November 1929; W. Thompson, *The Good Old Cause: British communism 1920-1991*, 1992, p45; Morgan, *op. cit.*, 1993, pp70-1.
33. CI28, ECCI Political Secretariat, 11 July 1929; 495/100/597, CC, 23 March 1929; 495/100/599, CC, 26 October 1929; 495/100/604, PB, 20 October 1929; CP/IND/MISC/2/3 Idris Cox, Draft Autobiography, pp30, 34-9.
34. *Inprecorr*, 25 September 1929; Morgan, *op. cit.*, 1993, pp68-9.
35. W. Rust, *The Story of the Daily Worker*, 1949, pp9-10; K. Morgan, 'The Communist Party and the *Daily Worker* 1930-56', in G. Andrews, N. Fishman and K. Morgan (eds), *Opening the Books*, 1995, p144.
36. Morgan, *ibid.*; Callaghan, *op. cit.*, p134; R. Groves, *The Balham Group: how British Trotskyism began*, 1974; Rust, *ibid.*, p17.
37. MacEwen, *op. cit.*, p110; Cockburn, *op. cit.*, p220; *Inprecorr*, 6 July 1931. See *DW*, 4 February 1949, for tributes from other Fleet Street editors.
38. *DW*, 10 April 1930, 17 April 1931; *Inprecorr*, 15 January, 6 July 1931; W. Rust, 'The workers' counter-offensive', *Labour Monthly*, March 1931; Fishman, *op. cit.*, pp36-40.
39. CP/CENT/CI/1/4, 'Resolution of the Presidium of the ECCI', 29 December 1931; MSS/292/770/8, 'Resolutions of 12th Plenum of ECCI', 17 October 1932; Thorpe, *op. cit.*, p77; Morgan, *op. cit.*, 1993, pp78-9; *DW*, pre-congress discussion August-November 1932: contributions by Pollitt (20 August, 26 September), Dutt (19 September), Gallacher (21 September), Rust (29 September), Campbell (8 November) and Page Arnot (11 November).
40. CP/IND/POLL/3/5, Rust to Pollitt, 11, 13 September 1932.
41. *DW*, 22 November 1932; Fishman, *op. cit.*, pp56-7; Groves, *op. cit.*
42. W. Rust, 'The Communist Party Congress', *Labour Monthly*, December 1932, p739; *Inprecorr*, 24 November 1932.
43. *Inprecorr*, 17 September 1929; 495/100/597, CC, 23 March 1929.
44. CP/CENT/CI/1/4, 'Resolution of the Presidium of the ECCI'; CI14, PB, 19 February, 1 June 1933, 5, 8 January 1934; CPGB CC, 'An open letter to Lancashire Communists', *Communist Review*, February 1934, pp12-14; 495/100/943, 495/100/951 and 495/100/993, correspondence between Pollitt and McIlhone, 10, 26 June, 12 July, 6 December 1934, 3 March 1935; Cox, *op. cit.*, pp48-50.
45. *DW*, 2 January 1939; CP/HIST/2/7, K. Morgan interview with E. Frow, 10 September 1987. In his novel, *Gild the Brass Farthing*, 1963, Brian Almond provides a somewhat unlikely portrait of Rust as an inspirational speaker, able to talk to Lancashire cotton workers in their own language, see pp78-81.
46. CI6, CC, 1 February 1935; *DW*, 25 May, 8 June, 17 August 1935; W. Rust, 'Mosley and Lancashire', *Labour Monthly*, May 1935; *Cotton Factory Times*, 12 July 1935.
47. CI5, CC, 10 August 1934; W. Rust, 'Cotton and the Left', *Labour Monthly*, November 1935; W. Rust, *Communism and Cotton*, 1936; *DW*, 1 June 1937; CI16, PB, 12 November 1937.
48. CI15, PB, 15 November 1934; *DW*, 30 January 1935, 25 February, 12 March 1937; W. Rust, 'Unity in Lancashire', *Labour Monthly*, March 1936; CI7, CC, 10 October 1936.

49. CI8, CC, 6 August 1937; CI9, 9 October 1938; CI16, PB, 11 February, 12 November 1937; *DW,* 9 April, 3 June 1937; CP/CENT/CONG/4/9, Tamara Rust's speech to CPGB Fifteenth Congress.
50. *DW,* 4, 10 February 1949.
51. B. Alexander, *British Volunteers For Liberty*, 1982, pp158, 200; Copeman, *op. cit.*, pp139-40; Imperial War Museum IWM 794/13, Copeman interview; W. Rust, *Britons in Spain*, 1939, pp87, 98; CI16, PB, 14, 29 October 1937.
52. Rust, ibid., pp31-2; Beckett, *op. cit.*, p53; CI8, CC, 30 October 1937; J.K. Hopkins, *Into The Heart Of The Fire: the British in the Spanish Civil War*,California 1998, pp158-60, 277-8, 284-5; Lee, *op. cit.*, pp174-5; T. Buchanan, *Britain and the Spanish Civil War*, Oxford 1997, p140.
53. Haldane, *op. cit.*, p132.
54. *Ibid.*, pp126-7, 131-9.
55. Lee, *op. cit.*, pp172-5; *Guardian*, 31 December 1997. Former Brigade commander, Bill Alexander, claimed that Lee had been sent back from Spain by Rust after failing his medical. The poet's family refuted this.
56. Information from Monty Johnstone; *DW,* 2 January 1939; Beckett, *op. cit.*, p64; Fishman, *op. cit.*, pp253-4.
57. Attfield and Williams, *op. cit.*; CI10,CC, 24 September, 2 October 1939.
58. Morgan, *op. cit.*, 1993, p112; Fishman, *op. cit.*, pp256-9; K. Morgan, *Against Fascism and War*, Manchester 1989, pp183-4.
59. Hyde, *op. cit.*, pp88-111; Rust, *op. cit.*, 1949; Morgan, *op. cit.*, 1995, pp150-2.
60. Morgan, *op. cit.*, 1993, pp149-50; Hyde, *op. cit.*, pp221-2, MacEwen, *op. cit.*, p152; H. Pelling, *The British Communist Party* (1975), pp148-9; Macleod, op.cit., p15.
61. Beckett, *op. cit.*, pp126-7; F. Beckett, 'Obituary: Rosa Thornton', *Guardian*, 18 April 2000, Macleod; *op. cit.*, pp3-17; 495/74/38, Report of meeting of ECCI Cadres Department with Rust, 11 November 1938; information from Monty Johnstone.
62. Beckett, *op. cit.*, 1995; Beckett, *op. cit.*, 2000; Macleod, *ibid.*; *DW*, 9, 10 February 1949.
63. Thompson, *op. cit.*, p85; MSS.292/770/4, note on Rust; Hyde, *op. cit.*, p148.
64. Beckett, *op. cit.*, 1995, pp73-6; Copeman, *op. cit.*, pp119-20, 136-7; Copeman interview; Haldane, *op. cit.*, pp137, 260; Hopkins, *op. cit.*, p287.
65. Hyde, *op. cit.*, pp148-9; MacEwen, *op. cit.*, p152.

Shoulder to Shoulder: Rose Smith, who stood for 'Different But Equal and United'

GISELA CHAN MAN FONG

On 6th August 1985, a *Morning Star* obituary paid tribute to Rose Smith as a 'foundation member of the CPGB', 'an outstanding activist in Lancashire in the 1930s' and an 'outstanding reporter of industrial struggles and living conditions' for the *Daily Worker*. After having been ostracised for more than a decade by comrades in Britain for her support of the Chinese position during the Sino-Soviet rift, Smith was reclaimed. She had died on 23rd July 1985 at the age of 94 in Beijing, where she had worked in the Chinese media since 1962. After a long and often hazardous life fighting for social justice and gender equality, her ashes were buried, in the presence of family, friends and high-ranking leaders of the Chinese Communist Party and government, in the Revolutionary Martyrs' Cemetery in Beijing.

Rose Smith probably never thought that she deserved such state honours. She rarely spoke, even to friends, about her life as a Communist militant until she adopted China as her 'socialist home' in the 1970s. Like many Communists of her generation, she denied the uniqueness of her individual self by submerging it into a collective unified entity: the working class, the Communist movement and women. In 1978, in an interview with Roland Berger, Smith formulated this position in relation to biography and history: 'I reflected the mood to some extent and the movements taking place, but my puzzle is how I can get myself out without being personal, but having in all the personal thing ... The personal must be integrated and be an intimate part of the general picture ... So I'd rather have it in the third person'.[1]

Similar difficulties have been experienced by historians of the CPGB when integrating women comrades as 'makers' of its history and popular memory into their writings. Early party histories such as those by

Klugmann and MacFarlane paid little attention to women. With more recent work by Noreen Branson and Sue Bruley, the position is changing.[2] This essay intends to help in filling the gap by adding the voice of one woman activist who played a significant role in the party to the historical record. Who, then, was this woman comrade? What kind of CPGB cadre was she? What was her role during the 'mass' strikes in interwar Britain?

EARLY INFLUENCES

For all of us, in one way or another, our life and our work is an extension of our personality, shaped by nature and nurture. With Rose Smith her actions and writings grew out of her engagement with the material and social world in a continual dialogue. Both the social segregation and the Dickensian conditions under which her family and neighbours existed and laboured conditioned her attitude towards work, social justice, and class and gender relations.

Rose Smith was born on 10 May 1891 in Putney, London. She was the second of seven children, the eldest daughter of an artisan family who later settled in Whittington Moor, a working-class suburb of Chesterfield, Derbyshire. Samuel Ellis, her father, was a potter by trade and an active member of the potters' union. He was employed as a thrower in the Robinson pottery works, except when tramping during economic downturns. Sarah Ellis, née Gardiner, was the illiterate daughter of a Bristol family of ship's carpenters and stone masons. She was a self-sacrificing and thrifty wife and mother. In her children she inculcated the artisan's moral values of 'work' and 'production' and socialised them into their specific roles as workers. Being the eldest daughter, Rose Smith naturally became the right hand of her mother, assisting with all the laborious household chores as well as looking after her younger brothers and sisters.

Encouraged by her mother to take advantage of the emerging state education system and the new career opportunities for working-class girls developing in Edwardian England, Smith secured her secondary education with the award of a two-year Minor County Scholarship at Clay Cross Science School.[3] As a 'graded school', it offered a more female-orientated and less academic curriculum for girls whose occupational destinations were either clerical jobs or elementary school teaching. In 1903, Smith passed the Preliminary Certificate, and the Pupil Teachers' Examination in 1907, but she did not enter university because the payment of fees was completely beyond the income of the Ellis family.[4] For the next decade, Smith taught as an infant teacher in

Chesterfield and Windsor, and, as expected of an unmarried working-class woman, she contributed her wages to the Ellis family economy.

By that time, Britain's economic and social development had reached a decisive juncture. Challenged by the Osborne Judgement in 1909, which outlawed the trade unions' financial contributions to the Labour Party, sections of the trade-union movement engaged in widespread industrial action stimulated by growing interest in syndicalist ideas. In 1911, Rose Smith witnessed the setting ablaze of the Chesterfield railway station by a crowd of strikers, and repeated bayonet charges by the army. On the welfare front, the enactment of the National Insurance Act of 1911 triggered heated debates among socialist and labour activists about the best way to achieve material improvements for the working class, through state reforms or through independent working-class actions. Meanwhile the number of female trade unionists grew and the movement for women's suffrage expanded and diversified its activities.

Searching eagerly for a better understanding of these class and gender issues, Smith joined the Chesterfield branch of the Social Democratic Federation (SDF) in 1910.[5] Its various activities soon fostered in her a sense of belonging to a socialist community with history and traditions. By means of its literature, she pondered over the role of human agency and the general principles underlying the process of history. She also attended a tutorial class on political science, organised by the Workers' Education Association (WEA), held at the Chesterfield Settlement, and attended two summer schools at Balliol College, Oxford in 1913 and 1914.[6] She mixed easily with her male classmates who were mostly from artisan backgrounds and espoused various leftwing causes. She got on particularly well with those Central Labour College sympathisers who were eloquently critical of the lectures given by the Oxford dons. Listening to their challenging repartee, Smith thought that 'there was something more than words' behind their argument.[7] By the summer of 1914, she was ready to question the 'political neutrality' of the WEA's broadly liberal, pluralistic teaching. She thought that some of the Oxford University lecturers 'may have been very sincere people like Cole, Cameron, A.L. Smith, they may have been quite good thinking people but they were not revolutionaries . . . And I realised by then that it had to be a complete overthrow'.[8] From then on, the concept of class struggle and the materialist conception of history were her spiritual guides.

After the founding of the British Socialist Party (BSP) in 1911, she associated with those of its members in Chesterfield who were active in trade unions and sympathetic to the emerging new idea of industrial unionism as propounded by the syndicalist movement. She felt that such a strategy could also be applied to working women, raise their consciousness as workers and safeguard their economic independence. Her first attempt at improving conditions of work for women was as a voluntary trade union organiser when a Friendly Society for female workers producing cardboard and surgical dressings was set up at the Robinson Company in 1912.[9]

The First World War began as she was attending her second WEA summer school at Balliol College. The next few months were for her 'a very confusing time' because the majority of socialists supported the capitalist-instigated war and her own Marxist classmates 'were obviously whiffling and whaffling about how they stood in relation to the war'. In Chesterfield, she found the small BSP group were also split on the war, and those few 'who opposed it strenuously, they had a hard time'. Smith felt particularly betrayed by middle-class women and the suffragist movement. She remembered that some women were so pro-war that they 'were completely swept off their feet'. In the big cities, 'there were all these society dames and middle-class women going about giving white feathers to anyone they saw not in uniform'. The suffragettes 'switched off their campaign'.[10] In 1916 she married Alfred Smith, a house decorator and sign painter from Sheffield. They had got to know each other at meetings organised by the BSP. When he was sent off to the trenches, she went into munitions production. But she was so shocked by what she saw in these factories that she organised the women into trade union membership so as to obtain better working and safety conditions.[11]

THE POLITICAL ACTIVIST

It is not easy to assess the political work of a socialist woman activist because, as Marie Marmo Mullaney has argued in her study of the first generation of socialist revolutionary women, women had not joined the socialist and communist movement out of a desire for attaining personal power and for making a successful 'career' within political organisations.[12] They sought regular contact with the 'masses', particularly working-class women, for two reasons. First, they wanted to understand poor people's oppression and the personal sufferings caused by material and spiritual deprivation; second, they wanted to learn from the inner strength, cooperative spirit, and human resourcefulness that working women displayed, how best to revolutionise class and gender relations.

The path taken by Rose Smith, the CPGB organiser of women and propagandist of inter-war Britain, appears to confirm these findings. She saw her life as a search for the essence of socialism, as a voyage to discover how to put socialist ideas into practice. She called it 'a struggle with the best yet to come', implying a revolutionary change in the management of political life and the economy, as well as a way of living and conducting equal and caring relationships within the family, among friends, colleagues and CP comrades.[13] To these ends, as she confessed later in life, 'I found my working-class family's pride of craftsmanship urging me to make as good a job as I could.'[14]

In 1919 the Smiths moved to the mining town of Mansfield, Nottinghamshire, where their twin boys, Percy and Ted, were born a year later. Local and national stoppages in the coal industry enlivened the town's politics and provided opportunities for Rose, a housewife with a social conscience, to enter the political arena. She joined the Mansfield branch of the Women's Cooperative Guild (WCG) and became a student at the Mansfield and District Labour College, established in 1921. By 1925 she had become its secretary.[15] On the political front, the Smiths, together with members of the Socialist Labour Party, founded the Mansfield local of the CPGB in 1922. Regular meetings were held in the Smith home; Rose served as the local's first treasurer but was admitted to full membership only in 1923. According to her recollection, this delay was due to her being a woman, housewife and having small children, and was understandable in the context of 'the coalfield [where] women were mainly confined to their homes'.[16]

By 1927 she had decided to commit herself even more to the CPGB. She welcomed its reorganisation at this time in the hope that this would lead to a more effective political leadership and became a party organiser in Lancashire from 1929 to 1934. The CPGB was known by reputation rather than by worker's experience of its approach and remained weak in this area of Britain, where political allegiances were still shifting from the Conservative Party to the Labour Party. So her assigned 'pioneering work' of setting up a new party cell in the spinning town of Oldham proved quite a challenge for Smith, a total stranger to the textile areas. Within a year she had succeeded. She then transferred to the weaving town of Burnley and coordinated, in her capacity as elected chairwoman, the work of twelve groups of Workers' International Relief in the county. It was the reports about her good 'mass' work in Lancashire and the adoption of the new leftist Comintern line of Class Against Class which favoured her rise to the post of National Women's Organiser (1929-33) and to positions on both the Central Committee (1930-38) and Political Bureau (PB) (1931-38).[17]

The essence of her work as spokeswoman for working-class women was, however, moulded by her association with the Minority Movement (MM) which began in late 1923.[18] Barred from her teaching profession and regular trade union membership as a married woman and mother, Smith entered the milieu of local class struggle and political activism through the Mansfield branch of the Miners' Minority Movement (MMM) (1923-27) and the Textile Minority Movement (TMM) in Lancashire (1930-34).[19] She believed that the capitalist system consisted only of two classes: she generally referred to 'the people' opposed to 'the bosses' or 'labour' opposed to 'capital'. Both classes were for her socially changing but constant economic entities which were interlocked in a fundamental socio-economic conflict. Initially, influenced by syndicalist perceptions, she hoped that 'the people' could achieve political power through strikes and trade union struggle. To achieve socialism, she fervently believed in the necessity of team work, in which working-class women and men were united, co-operated, worked and raised their consciousness together as equal but different partners in the class struggle. Later, as a cadre she applied the same beliefs to her party work. She stood for an equal distribution of power among men and women in the party. She also believed that all members should be treated equally, irrespective of the position they held in the party. With regard to changes in policies, she advocated achieving consensus for political changes and party strategies by giving careful thought and discussion to their content and implementation. At party meetings, her frank, 'constructive criticisms' were generally well received because her political understanding was known to be rooted in her direct experiences of class conflict.

'THE PERSONAL IS THE POLITICAL'

Her upbringing in a working-class home with its strict division of labour made Smith conscious not only of class oppression but also of the unequal status of women in working-class families. The elimination of these two types of oppression became a life-long objective. After having studied Engels' *The Origins of the Family* and Olive Schreiner's *Woman and Labour*, she challenged the established feminine ideal underlying her mother's marriage. Instead of serving selflessly the interests and needs of her husband and children, Smith sought an equal and intellectually stimulating companionship in her marriage. As she confessed, 'I wasn't concerned with getting married at all because marriage wasn't my goal in life. I like men but I like their company so as to talk and explain things'.[20] She sought to enjoy the same freedom, opportunities outside the home and the self-fulfilment in political work that her father had claimed for himself in his life.

Smith was also a believer in birth control. In order to safeguard the health of working-class mothers and children, she supported campaigns demanding a better dissemination of birth control information to working-class women in government-funded clinics. This, however, was neither permitted by the governments in power nor supported by the male-dominated political parties. As recent research by Sue Bruley and Sheila Rowbotham has shown, Communist women did not fare much better, as the CPGB was equally intransigent in its opposition to developing any policy in favour of birth control.[21] In 1926, under the 'three-year rule', the National Executive Committee (NEC) of the Labour Party forbade discussion of any resolution on birth control, which had already been put forward at three successive conferences and on which a ruling had been made. This infuriated the women of the radical leftwing Workers' Birth Control Group (WBCG). They launched a nationwide campaign. It soon enlisted support from many working-class organisations, including the powerful Miners' Federation of Great Britain (MFGB), in order to place the issue of family planning back on the agenda at all annual Labour Party conferences.

By that time, Smith had already gained wide experience of the social conditions in the Nottinghamshire coalfields. At this critical moment in 1926, with miners locked out, she decided to place the question of reproductive choice within a realistic working-class setting and ensure that on no account did it become a divisive issue in the working class generally and in miners' families specifically. To enhance the credibility of such a campaign, she secured the help of A.J. Cook, the Secretary of the MFGB, who was respected and trusted by miners and their wives. His views about birth control were published in the *Sunday Worker* and led to an exchange of letters between Rose Smith and Dora Russell, one of the WBCG's secretaries.

In this exchange A.J. Cook stressed that the dissemination of scientific birth control to workers' wives would 'free our comrades and give them more leisure and even greater energy to work shoulder to shoulder with us men in the class struggle'. Smith linked the issue of birth control with the economic basis of women's oppression. Contrary to middle-class birth-controllers' assumptions, she stressed that miners' wives were neither ignorant of, nor opposed to, family planning and that 'the present system is directly responsible for the fact that one sees everywhere prematurely aged and delicate women, victims of too frequent child bearing, coupled with insufficient food and rest'.[22] She demanded that the spread of birth control information had to be accompanied by better wages which would make safer contraceptives more affordable to miners' wives. Dora Russell, however, presented herself as the WBCG's feminist spokeswoman and insisted that miners' wives had to be vigilant concerning their rights as women, for the coming into power of workers would not automatically benefit women and improve their rights. She advised that 'the moment the workers came to power we should have the organisation to keep the men up to the promise'.[23]

A few months later, at the 1926 Labour Party Conference the WBCG's leaders moved a resolution to get the NEC's three-year ban on birth control discussions lifted. In her speech appealing to the MFGB's delegates at the conference, Dora Russell purposely cited A.J. Cook's words which had been taken from his interview arranged by Rose Smith for the *Sunday Worker*.[24] When the vote was taken, the women had won the right to further discussion by 1,656,000 votes to 1,620,000. It was, and would remain, a narrow and precarious victory, because it had been achieved in the main by the miners' votes. Indirectly, Smith had done her bit to help the Labour women and the MFGB at a crucial moment in their struggles. In the summer of 1926, the miners' union found itself isolated and rejected by most sections of the labour movement. Smith had then smoothed the way for Labour women and Dora Russell, an upper-middle-class feminist, to come into contact with the miners' union. They became temporary allies, each with their respective position.

Smith also considered housework as one of the three entrenched conditions in capitalist society that fostered 'a woman's enslavement', the lack of equal rights and economic equality being the other two. All her life she fought in different settings to get these conditions changed for women. At a personal level, tensions were mounting in the Smith household in the early 1930s. The main causes were financial difficulties and the unequal sharing of housework. While Rose complained that her husband did not help sufficiently with domestic chores, he, in his turn, might have accused her of absenting herself from home and children too frequently, for the sake of the well-being of the CPGB. Alfred, cast in the mould of the socialist and craftsman-artist William Morris, disliked much of the workerism that the CPGB propagated at that time. He preferred to be his own boss rather than work in a factory. Rose decided to leave Alfred, but the couple never divorced. After their separation, Alfred became an art collector and dealer. Rose raised her two boys with the help of family members and political friends. One of her sons became a lecturer in nursing and the other continued the family's artisan tradition as a fully qualified carpenter and union activist.

Smith consistently advocated greater collective responsibility for housework. In August 1933, she stood as the CPGB candidate in a by-election in St Peter's Ward, Burnley. During her house-to-house canvassing, she devoted much time to the social issue of 'free meals' for school children. In an efficiency drive for savings, the Conservative-dominated Town Council had allocated less money for the provisions of these meals. Poor families were told to make up for it themselves and an extra shilling per week per child was deducted from their relief allowances. For Smith, 'free meals' were, however, more than a class issue whereby the town's resources were to be shared out more fairly. As a socialist woman, she characterised it as an important issue in the fight for female emancipation. As she explained to her male comrades on the Central Committee

> There is this question of feeding school children. Some [women] say they would rather their children came home. I think if we explain this properly we can get women to drive for this. One of the drives we want to make is to break down the enslavement of women inside the home. We have to destroy this among the working class.[25]

Thus, in her election campaign she presented the issue of 'free school meals' as bringing about the socialisation of housework rather than as a method of social control over the working-class household.

'THE POLITICAL IS THE PERSONAL'
Inter-war industrial conflicts in the old staple industries of coal and cotton confronted Rose Smith with the question of how wives and daughters of workers as well as female operatives were to be organised as 'different but equal partners' in these 'direct actions'.[26] It was in the Mansfield coalfield during the stormy period of 1925-26 that she had the first chance to test her ideas of how to do this. Called upon in 1925 by the men of the local Miners' Minority Movement branch to assist them with preparations for a General Strike in the community, she opened her home as a 'distribution, propaganda and recoupment centre for the miners in Mansfield'.[27] She liased with local women's groups

and took up public speaking in the town and the surrounding mining villages. She was then in her thirties, of medium height, slim with brown bobbed hair shaping her long oval face. She was an attractive woman but she had 'no air of frivolity about her'.[28] In the locality, she was soon well known for her passionate and well-reasoned 'rallying of the troops' around issues in the community whose solution demanded a new and wider solidarity.

Conscious of the strict sexual segregation and division of labour in Mansfield and of the absence of a clear lead from the CPGB in the run-up to the General Strike, she argued forcefully in a letter addressed to the party leaders in summer 1925 that they must prepare for a forth-coming conflict between the miners and the state, and they must not conceive its organisation just as 'a man's job'. She pointed out that 'wherever there is a definite issue before the men, there is a definite issue before the women – both attack it from a different angle, and I would like to see a definite method of attack before each section, so that all locals experiencing the same problems may function according to one plan of campaign'.[29] A few weeks later, in front of Mansfield's women leaders of the WCG, Independent Labour Party and Labour Party, she expounded this political position for the eventuality of a miners' strike. She argued that, irrespective of their political allegiance, women should coordinate all their activities to one end – the overthrow of the system that created the exploitation of the workers and their families:

> We sent our boys to fight the Capitalist War for 'Freedom' in 1914-1918 and today we will arrange ourselves beside them in the workers' only real fight – 'The Fight For Bread', for a decent standard of living and the overthrow of this vile system, and the ownership of the mines and facto-ries by the workers to be run in the interest of the workers.[30]

Hers was a political position that tried to incorporate women as equals into the syndicalist perception of a workers' state. A.J. Cook seems to have toyed with similar ideas when, at a women's meeting in Mansfield in March 1926, 'he prophesied that the time was rapidly approaching when every miner's wife would be in a special section of the miners' union'.[31] It was this aspect that, during the summer of 1926, the MM tried to institutionalise by making, in Tom Mann's words, 'trade unionism as the real concern of every family, not exclusively or chiefly for men'.[32] Working-class women of all categories and ages were encouraged to become members of trade unions, co-operative guilds, and trade councils, and thereby to mould the policy of these institutions. Wives and daughters of trade unionists were accepted as associate members of the MM. In this way, a sense of unity was to be fostered, based upon class rather than sectional and sexist mobilisation, a unity which aimed at projecting and bringing about a new social order.[33]

The defeat of the miners in December 1926 put an end to this envisaged restructuring of the trade union movement. Within the MFGB a new struggle for unity began; the Nottinghamshire Miners' Association was challenged by George Spencer's new Company Union. Nevertheless, in Mansfield, the great industrial confrontation of 1926 also left a positive mark on the housewives' perception of their public role in society and labour movement. While the CPGB local recorded fifty new women members, other women sought their political identity in new organisations or unions of miners' wives that were attached to the MFGB and affiliated to the Labour Party. It seems that the ideas of the MM leaders for women to stand shoulder to shoulder with their men in matters of community struggle had survived the defeat of the miners.[34]

The Smiths were victimised by the coalowners and they had to leave Mansfield. However, remembering her father's words, 'We've never bred a quitter. You stick it out, believe in it, you stick it out', Rose Smith remained utterly committed to the MM and CPGB.[35] Her gender-neutral training as a Communist functionary exposed her to 'tough situations'.[36] She had to go against the established norms of proper behaviour for a 'respectable' working-class woman and became the object of police harassment, arrest and imprisonment.[37] She had to put up with moments of intense fear when confronted by hostile working-class crowds at some of the strike meetings. Due to the CPGB not being able to pay her cadre allowance on time, she suffered financial insecurity and hunger. On the other hand, this risky life had its compensations. She learned more about her nature. She loved action and challenges in life and came to regard her party work as a positive way to teach her a sense of self-effacement, sacrifice, adaptability and self-reliance. And she never lost her sense of humour while being 'in the thick of things'. This led to her being remembered by the former miner and Labour peer, Lord Taylor of Mansfield, as someone who 'fought valiantly in the miners' cause' in 1926. Annie Powell, the long-standing Communist councillor in the Rhondda, recalled her as 'a tower of strength' and 'having those qualities of deep human understanding which made her very close to the workers everywhere'.[38]

In 1930, Rose Smith arrived in Burnley, Lancashire, to assist with the building of a revolutionary trade union movement among textile operatives. Due to shrinking overseas markets for the cloth produced in its weaving sheds, Burnley was in the grip of economic stagnation and mass unemployment. To halt this decline, the employers proposed a new production system based on increased working hours and raising the number of looms per operative from four to six or even eight. This new system and the Labour Government's Anomalies Act of 1931 sparked off militant protests between 1930 and 1934 in the weaving sector of the cotton industry.

The majority of the weavers were women: they worked under similar conditions to men and were paid the same wage rates. Most belonged to the Amalgamated Weavers' Association (AWA) but they were generally not actively involved in the policy-making processes of the union. This had not greatly disadvantaged female workers' interests when the British cotton industry was enjoying a monopoly position in world markets and peaceful industrial relations boosted the family wage. However, gender problems between male union leaders and female rank-and-file operatives cropped up after the end of the postwar boom. The CPGB tried to exploit these tensions within the AWA to extend its own growth and influence among the working class.

Having just returned from Moscow, where she had attended the Fifth World Congress and the First Women's Conference of the Red International of Labour Unions (RILU), Smith was naturally inclined to undertake 'hard spade-work' amongst factory women, who showed 'growing dissatisfaction' with their male union leaders, by 'making the women's committees strongholds for the support of Revolutionary Trade Union organisations'.[39] She propagated the Textile Minority Movements's (TMM) 'call to action' in meetings and public speeches. She is thought to have written the TMM's agitational pamphlet entitled *Fight the Eight Looms*. It aimed at arousing the weavers' rank-and-file against their 'colluding' AWA officials. Smith emphasised that the 'more loom system' was an all out attack on women workers: it increased their workload, reduced their wages, made older women unemployed, to be replaced by men, and encouraged the transfer of unmarried women weavers into unskilled and low-paid domestic service. So Smith demanded that all operatives strongly oppose the 'more loom system' and arbitration procedures and continue to fight for the retention of the old piece price list; for a 25 per cent increase in wages; a minimum wage of £2 per week for all cotton workers; and for the immediate abolition of all fines and compensation for bad materials.

113

Being a very astute and practical organiser, Smith overcame her status of an outsider to the locality and the cotton industry by acquiring knowledge which helped to create a bridge between the workers and herself. She collaborated closely with local political activists, talked with all kinds of people in the textile towns and worked systematically through local and trades papers, and company and trade union reports in the local reference library.[40] Above all, Smith liased between regional activists and the CPGB's executive in London who were not fully aware of the 'tempo of the fight' in the factories. In view of the limited resources available to the party, she requested a realistic, less dogmatic strike strategy. She pointed out that the CPGB's future directives must consider in earnest how to discuss the purpose of particular struggles with strikers; how to end a strike or lockout without compromising 'our comrades' as 'isolated' and 'poor fools'; and finally how to consolidate the impact of militant actions through a programme for times of industrial peace so that lasting changes could be achieved.[41]

In mid-January 1932, she attended an enlarged meeting of the Central Committee where the resolution on the liquidation of the MM, described as a 'small organisation, boxed up into itself and thereby isolated from the masses in the factories and trade unions', was discussed.[42] Having been closely associated with the MM and its aims for many years, she joined the members who sprang to its defence. She argued that the MM should not be solely blamed for its isolation. The CPGB should also scrutinise the methods by which 'mass' work had been conducted. To prove her point, she sternly, but with a tinge of impatience, referred to the CPGB's indifference towards work among women:

> This is a vital aspect of Party life. I did not choose to work amongst women, but I realised that this was important. Today we are holding an important meeting, and not one woman is invited to this conference. Local Party committees do not discuss work amongst women. As far as I can see, no woman is going to the National School. [J.T.] Murphy [member of the Central Committee] raises it with me and gets heated about it, and it's time that some other departments understood that this work is important.[43]

Her complaint about the party's lack of support for her work as National Women's Organiser was not new. In her first report on 'Work Among Women', submitted to the PB in July 1930, she had countered the idea prevailing among her male comrades that 'unless a woman is employed in industry, she cannot take her place in the class struggle'. She was against this kind of pure industrial workerism and emphasised that all women could play a useful part in the class struggle. She had also complained that she found her work among women difficult due to her isolation in the party organisation. Subsequently Central Committee members, Willie Gallacher, Wally Tapsell and Idris Cox provided some support, admitting that 'the Women's department had been badly neglected' and 'the Party has no special women's policy'.[44] And in late September 1930, the Central Women's Committee had been reorganised and linked to the Industrial Committee of the party with J.T. Murphy as the responsible PB member. It had been hoped that, at least at the head office in London, the work among women would not come to a standstill while Smith did her 'mass work' in the provinces. Nevertheless, to her great disappointment, the allocation of party tasks continued along gender lines in all branches. She warned that the prac-tice of allowing only women to do social work within the party helped to strengthen the tendency for women to constitute 'a floating membership'.[45] She demanded that female cadres should be trained carefully and rigorously in order to give them self-confidence. She pointed her finger accusingly at the male CPGB district organisers of whom not one had 'thought that there is a woman with sufficient intel-ligence who can be sent to be trained. The comrades do the work, but they are not intelligent enough to be sent to the National School'.[46] Among the male cadres, she lobbied tirelessly so that such women's issues as 'school meals', 'housing and rents', 'the increase in the cost of living' and 'religion' would become integral parts of all party campaigns.[47] However, what she did not realise was that it was essen-tially the male-conceived Bolshevik organisation of the party, its increasingly centralised command structure and the qualities that it privileged which boosted male power and disadvantaged the female minority in the CPGB.

In the summer of 1932, Smith had to admit 'that the MM, like the Party and the unemployed movement, has not tackled the problems of the women of the working class'. As evidence, she pointed out the mistakes committed during a textile workers' strike at Earby. First, the TMM had not sufficiently considered the relationship between striking unionised operatives and women who had been made redundant and received no unemployment pay but still needed to feed their families. Second, the TMM had not really explained to the women why it was better to strike rather than to continue to work for decreased wages. Third, the TMM had not clarified whether or not a TMM-organised

female striker had the same right as an AWA-unionised female operative to return to her loom once the strike had ended. And finally, the
TMM had not developed 'some sense of responsibility and leadership
in regard to work amongst women in the district' and had not proven
itself a better organisation for women than the AWA.[48] As shown
above, this female consciousness had been raised in Mansfield but not
in Lancashire. She attributed this failure to the party's incapability of
convincing the Lancashire weavers 'to deal with the question of cotton
politically' rather than 'to follow the policy of Naesmith where they
believe that they are going to get increased wages'.[49]

By early 1933, the MM had virtually disappeared and, at the
Comintern's behest, the Central Women's Department was merged
with the CPGB's PB. It was said that, in line with the Comintern's
latest extravagant thinking, this was to strengthen working women's
position on the home front in the eventuality of a coming war.
Although Smith thought that 'perhaps it is not wholly true of events in
Great Britain', she supported this new policy.[50] She had privately come
to regard her work among women as thankless and too restrictive for
women cadres. She hoped to be able to direct her attention to other
'mass' work.

THE MESSENGER OF UNITY

In 1934, Smith was transferred to the *Daily Worker* as a 'special correspondent'. This occurred more by accident than design. She had not
thought of becoming a journalist but she did not object to her new
'trade'. In her eyes, it was just another means of communication with
working-class men and women on behalf of the party. As a result of the
emergence of fascism in Europe, the CPGB was now preparing the
ground for united front work and a new collaborative relationship with
other labour organisations in Britain. It naturally followed that the
revolutionary slant of the *Daily Worker* needed to be reined in without
compromising basic Communist principles. So the initial purpose of
Smith's transfer was to act as a 'language polisher'.[51]

As a novice in the editorial office in Cayton Street, London, she
worked long hours, sometimes seven days a week. To keep herself
awake, she began to chain smoke. Yet, the diversity of each day's tasks
became her best reward. She was taught the basics of reporting by
Allen Hutt, the chief sub-editor of the *Daily Worker,* and she soon
wrote her own articles in a terse if rather pedestrian style, supported by
statistics and with punchy headlines. She still believed most working-
class readers lacked sophistication: the innate contradictions of the

capitalist world had to be explained to them in simple English. With working-class women in particular, Smith believed that 'facts had to be spelt out in order to force them gradually within reach of the proletarian reading public'.[52]

Much of her reporting work involved travelling about the country, always looking for new sources of grassroots information. She became the first working-class female reporter specialising in the world of industrial affairs. She wrote about strikes and covered conferences of trade unions and other political organisations in the new co-operative spirit of party work.[53] For her, the world of labour was always gendered. Her factual and informative accounts focused on unionised workers and such issues as wages, working conditions and the recognition of trade unions as the legitimate representatives of the workers, secured by agreed collective bargaining procedures. She also wrote about unorganised women workers. In 1936, only one female worker in five was a union member. As the employers took advantage of weak organisation among women and lack of coordination between men and women at the workplace, Smith lobbied for unionisation of women workers. This was in conformity with the CPGB's new tactics vis-a-vis the unions, as adopted at its Thirteenth Party Congress in February 1935.

Another topic which was of interest to her, particularly in the light of her experience working in a food factory, was the question of workers' control over the labour process.[54] In late 1937, the British economic upturn had encountered problems and management circles discussed a new grading structure of skill and various systems of payment by results so as to maintain the competitiveness of British manufacturing. As worker resistance to the Bedaux plan, a new wage incentive system favoured by employers, was fierce, Smith investigated how it had been applied in British factories since 1926. It was claimed that a substantial increase in output had been achieved at much lower labour costs. Production had been speeded up so that 60 men did the work formerly done by 100. To Smith, however, this gain had been achieved at the expense of the workforce, and speed up, time study and payment by results needed to be contained. The TUC had commissioned an inquiry into the Bedaux plan. It concluded that the unions should oppose all management systems which reduced 'the worker to the status of machines' but thought that 'Bedaux is capable of being applied, in a manner, and with modifications, that may make it less harmful than many other systems'.[55] Four years later, the TUC reacted lethargically to a possible new employers' offensive of introducing even more subtle and harmful timing systems at the workplace. To create some awareness and public pressure from below, Smith investigated conditions in Birmingham's engineering workshops and she published her findings in the CPGB press.

She observed that in a large number of instances where strikes had forced modification of the Bedaux system, the impact on workers, particularly female workers, remained harmful. The 'Point System' used in engineering workshops was a prime example. She stated that women engineers had to cope with 'considerable speeding-up of production' and 'the dodge first employed of swelling the pay packet has now led to wholesale sacking of girls, and considerable reduction in wages'.[56] By taking up the defence of female workers in a male-dominated trade, Smith wanted to press the TUC to reassess its position, show greater vigilance and encourage unity between women and men at the workplace when facing the employers. She believed in restricting the deskilling and degradation of labour in British factories by ensuring that the workers themselves, men and women rather than the managers, modified the labour process and division of labour according to skill and gender.

It was this consistent and sustained opposition of Rose Smith to class and gender oppressions that should become an integral part of the CPGB's historiography. She believed fully and fiercely that capitalism structures inequality for women as well as men in working-class families, factories, labour organisations and political parties. Although she never doubted the ideological premises of the CPGB, she saw a need to improve the party's performance. Her experiences, gained as a militant and a cadre in different localities, made her demand a politics based upon careful assessment of material conditions and power constellations, the development of realistic and non-antagonistic gender practices, and the adoption of campaign issues which reflected the experiences and interests of both working-class women and men. Whenever she felt it necessary, Smith frankly raised women's issues and she fought for them with bravery and tenacity. She did this not out of political expediency but because she firmly believed in them as a feminist socialist.

NOTES

1. The National Museum of Labour History (NMLH), interview with Rose Smith by Roland Berger, 1978, Tape 1; see C. Peneff, 'Autobiographies de militants ouvriers', *Revue Française de Science Politique*, 29, 1, 1979, p65.
2. J. Klugmann, *History of the Communist Party of Great Britain*, 1969; L.J.

MacFarlane, *The British Communist Party*, 1966; N. Branson, *History of the Communist Party of Great Britain, 1927-1941*, 1985, pp96, 192-6; N. Branson, *History of the Communist Party of Great Britain, 1941-1951*, 1997, pp38-49; S. Bruley, *Leninism, Stalinism, and the Women's Movement in Britain, 1920-1939*, New York 1986. See also the references to Communist women in P. Graves, *Labour Women: women in British working-class politics*, Cambridge 1994.

3. The founder and paternalist sponsor of this school was George Stephenson, the railway engineer. F. Hunt, 'Social class and the grading of schools: realities in girls' secondary education, 1880-1940', in J. Purvis (ed), *The Education of Girls and Women. Proceedings of the 1984 Annual Conference of the History of Education Society of Great Britain*, 1985, pp27-46.

4. Smith interview, Tape 6; Derbyshire Record Office D 19C/1/17/1, 1903 Minute Book of the Education Committee; *Derbyshire Times*, 3 July 1909.

5. The Chesterfield SDF branch was founded in early 1905 and from 1906 onwards was a loud voice in local politics. Prominent SDF speakers, such as Harry Quelch, Dan Irving and Rose Jarvis, included Chesterfield in their national circuit, see *Justice*, 17 March, 18 August 1906.

6. The Chesterfield branch came into being in 1909. See *Highway*, 2, 16, 1910, p63; ibid., 5, 58, 1913, p199. On Rose Smith's activities in the branch, see *Highway* 6, 63, 17 December 1913, p58.

7. Smith interview, Tape 7.

8. *Ibid.*

9. *Workers' Life*, 26 April 1929; *The Mansfield, Sutton and Kirkby Chronicle*, 19 April 1929. On the 'Friendly Society', see *Robinson Historical Ledger*, Ref B.78/2; for a photo of the foundation meeting on 26 June 1912, see Chesterfield and District Local History Society (ed) , *Robinson & Sons Ltd Chesterfield, 1839-1989*, Chesterfield 1989, p20.

10. Smith interview, Tape 7.

11. C. Esterson, 'Unforgettable Rose of Beijing', *Daily Worker*, 19 August 1985.

12. M. Marmo Mullaney, *Revolutionary Women: gender and socialist revolutionary role*, New York 1983, examines the lives of Eleanor Marx, Alexandra Kollontai, Rosa Luxemburg, Angelica Balabanoff, and Dolores lbarruri.

13. E. Bidien, 'So much love for so many', *Beijing Review*, 12 August 1985, p23.

14. R. Smith, 'How I became a journalist', Speech to postgraduates of the Institute of Journalism, Beijing, 28 October 1978, p2.

15. Smith interview, Tapes 4, 5, 8 and 9; *Plebs*, 15, 2, p93; *Plebs* 17, pp53, 415, 453; Lord Taylor of Mansfield, *Uphill All the Way*, 1972, Ch. 9.

16. Smith interview, Tape 9.

17. Working Class Movement Library, Salford (WCML), Minutes of Burnley WIR, November 1932; *Searchlight*, September 1932; NMLH Cl 1, Central Committee (CC), 19-20 July 1930; Cl 12, Political Bureau (PB), 6 August, 17 September 1931.

18. J. Hinton and R. Hyman, *Trades Unions and Revolution*, 1975, pp23, 32, 46-9; R. Martin, *Communism and the British Trade Unions, 1924-33: a study of the National Minority Movement*, Oxford 1969.

19. A.M. Oram, 'Serving two masters? The introduction of a marriage bar in teaching in the 1920s', in London Feminist History Group (ed), *The Sexual Dynamics of History*, 1983, pp134-48.
20. Smith interview, Tape 4.
21. Bruley, *op.cit.*, pp77-81; S. Rowbotham, *A New World for Women: Stella Brown – socialist feminist*, 1977.
22. *Sunday Worker,* 20 June 1926. A.J. Cook's arguments resemble those made by the Wobblies' (IWW) publications in the early twentieth century and by Margaret Sanger in her *Family Limitation*. See A. Schofield, 'Rebel girls and union maids: the woman question and the journals of the AFL and IWW, 1905-1920', *Feminist Studies*, 9, 2 , 1983, pp84-100.
23. *Sunday Worker,* 27 June 1926.
24. *Labour Party Report,1926*, p201.
25. Cl 3, CC, 4 June 1932.
26. On Smith's 'direct actions' see G. Chan Man Fong, 'The times and life of Rose Smith in Britain and China, 1891-1985: an interplay between community, class and gender', Ph.D. thesis, Concordia University, Montreal 1998, pp79-136.
27. A.R. Griffin, *The Miners of Nottinghamshire, 1914-1944: a history of the Nottinghamshire miners' union*, 1962, pp55-62.
28. Interview with I. Hackett, Mansfield, 13 November 1993. During the General Strike, Ida Hackett, then a teenager, had often accompanied her father to hear Rose Smith deliver her rousing speeches.
29. *Workers' Weekly,* 14 August 1925.
30. *Ibid.*, 9 October 1925.
31. *Ibid.*, 26 March 1926.
32. *Sunday Worker,* 13 June, 25 July 1926; *Report of the Third National Conference of the NMM* (1926); 'Women wend their way to Battersea', *Woman Worker*, 5, 1926.
33. R.J. Holton, 'Revolutionary syndicalism and the British labour movement', in W.J. Mommsen and H.G. Husung (eds), *The Development of Trade Unionism in Great Britain and Germany, 1880-1914*, 1985, pp269-70. For a similar stance on wives' involvement in unions and industrial strife by the Wobblies, see M. Tax, *The Rising of the Women*, New York 1980, pp125-63.
34. J. Gier, 'Miners' wives: gender, culture and society in the South Wales coalfields, 1919-39', PhD thesis, Northwestern University, Evanston, Illinois 1993, pp286-99. On the Mansfield section, see *Sunday Worker,* 10 April, 27 June 1927.
35. Smith interview, Tape 9.
36. On Smith's activities as a political cadre, see Chan Man Fong, *op.cit.*, pp137-207.
37. On Rose Smith's arrests, fines and imprisonment, see: (a) Mansfield: *Mansfield and North Notts. Advertiser*, 5 June, 2 July 1926; *Mansfield and Kirkby Chronicle*, 5 June 1926; (b) Oldham: *Oldham Evening Chronicle and Standard*, 23 December 1929, 18 January 1930; (c) Burnley: A. Bullen, 'Watching and besetting: the Burnley police and the "more looms" dispute, 1931-32', *North-West Labour History Society Bulletin*, 5, pp1-10. On her arrest, see *Worker*, 17 October 1931; on her trial, see *Express and Advertiser,*

14 October 1931 and *Burnley News,* 14 October 1931; on her release from prison, see *Worker,* 26 December 1931; (d) Preston: *Daily Worker,* 2 March 1931.

38. Extracts of letters read by Fred Westacott at the farewell dinner to Rose Smith, Chesterfield, 4 March 1960.
39. *Worker,* 10 October 1930.
40. Smith, *op.cit.,* p8. On local comrades, see S. Bruley, 'Gender, class and party: the Communist Party and the crisis in the cotton industry in England between the two world wars', *Women's History Review,* 2, 1, 1993, pp94-6; WCML, B. Dickenson, *James Rushton and his Times, 1880-1956* (n.d.); Margaret McCarthy, *Generation in Revolt,* 1953, Ch. 8.
41. CI 2, CC, 19-20 September 1931.
42. CI 3, CC, 17 January 1932.
43. *Ibid.*
44. CI 11, PB, 10 July 1930.
45. CI 14, PB, 16 February 1933.
46. CI 3, CC, 4 June 1932.
47. On her successful treatment of these social welfare issues, see Chan Man Fong, *op.cit.,* pp217-39.
48. CI 3, CC, 4 June 1932.
49. CI 15, PB, 18 November 1934. Andrew Naesmith (1888-1961), Oldham Weavers' Association; Assistant Secretary, AWA, 1925-28; Secretary, AWA, 1928-53.
50. CI 14, PB, 16 February 19331; on the demise of the Women's Department, see Bruley, 1986, *op.cit.,* pp226-32; on the MM in decline, see Hinton and Hyman, *op. cit.,* pp46-9; Martin, *op. cit.,* pp122-78.
51. Smith, *op.cit.,* p11.
52. R. Kovnator, 'The press as means of organising the proletarian women', in CPGB, *Work Among Women,* 1924, p37. For Smith's, 'Report on Women's Work', see CI 3, CC, 4 June 1932.
53. For Smith's articles on the mining strikes in Yorkshire and Nottinghamshire, see *Daily Worker,* 19, 20, 21, 25, 26, 29 January, 4, 5 February, 2 March 1937.
54. R. Smith, 'A day in a chocolate factory', *Working Woman,* January 1928.
55. Modern Record Centre, University of Warwick MSS 292/112/2, Trades Union Congress, *Bedaux: The TUC Examines the Bedaux System of Payment by Results,* 1933.
56. 'There is profit in speed-up', *Daily Worker,* 30 November 1937.

Horner and Hornerism

NINA FISHMAN

Arthur Horner was one of the most prominent Communists in British public life between 1936, when he was elected President of the South Wales Miners' Federation (SWMF), and 1959, when he retired as General Secretary of the National Union of Mineworkers (NUM). At this time the coal industry occupied a central place in the British economy. There were over 700,000 members of the NUM when Horner was elected general secretary in 1946. He played a critical role in the birth of the nationalised coal industry and subsequently in ensuring that the union contributed to its success. Despite the onset of Cold War politics and advancing alcoholism, Horner remained highly respected in the labour movement, and the broad pattern of his life is not significantly different from that of the cohort of union leaders across the political spectrum who made their way in the interwar period.[1]

Horner was the leading Communist Party (CPGB) miner during the 1926 General Strike and ten months' lock-out. He also occupied an important position inside the party. However, he became increasingly alienated during 1929. The reason was the party's policy towards trade unions, adopted as a result of pressure from the Communist International (Comintern) and its sister organisation the Red International of Labour Unions (RILU). The Comintern's new line, 'Class Against Class', first signalled at its Ninth Plenum in February 1928, was being interpreted in an increasingly left sectarian manner, and Horner was not alone amongst union militants in reacting against it.

In January 1931, Horner took his established leading role in determining the policy of communists in South Wales towards the SWMF strike against the coalowners' bid to lengthen the working day and reduce wages. He used his influence to ensure that the Communist Party did not challenge the SWMF decision to call the strike off after a

122

fortnight. The extreme left section of the CPGB leadership, led by Bill Rust and Wally Tapsell, accused him of sabotage. They claimed that he had never accepted the Class Against Class line as it applied to trade unions. The CPGB Central Committee required him to account for his behaviour. Horner refused, arguing that the problems were practical, and that the whole of the South Wales party shared responsibility for the strike's collapse. Faced with his unrepentant response, Horner's defenders on the Central Committee, including Harry Pollitt and Horner's friend Wally Hannington, had little choice but to condemn him.

Rust labelled Horner's transgression against Comintern policy as Hornerism. Local parties were encouraged to affirm the leadership's decision, as projected in Rust's exposures of Hornerism in the *Daily Worker*. In May 1931, Horner went to Moscow to plead his case to the Comintern. He accepted their verdict that he had erred, but that the South Wales party had also made mistakes. He arrived back in Britain, apparently a model penitent. He appeared before the CC and articles in the *Daily Worker* repeated his full admission of mistakes.

After a look at Horner's early life, this chapter focuses on the conflict between Horner and the CPGB leadership in 1931. One interpretation is that Horner returned from Moscow chastened, and that the extreme left prevailed, though 'it had taken two full years finally to reconcile the most important of the South Wales Communists to the full implications of "Class Against Class"'.[2] Upon investigation, the picture which emerges is that Horner was not completely isolated in his views. They were shared by others in the leadership who had been attempting to propel the party back towards a more pragmatic approach since mid-1930. It was Horner's impulsive, passionate character, combined with his leading role in the South Wales strike, which rendered him vulnerable to attack from the ultra-left section who made him the scapegoat for the failure of their own prescriptions.

EARLY LIFE
Horner was born in Merthyr Tydfil on 5 April 1894. He was the eldest surviving son in a family of seventeen children, six of whom lived past infancy. His father, James, had come to South Wales as a young boy from Northumberland. His mother, Emily, moved to Merthyr from mid-Wales with her family. James Horner started as a porter and rose to become the foreman at Merthyr railway goods station. He was an officeholder in the Rechabites, a temperance friendly society. He accumulated sufficient capital to buy land in Clare Street on which he built

two houses. The Horner family occupied one of them, and Emily ran the first Merthyr Co-operative Society shop from the front room, with James doing the books in the evenings.[3]

Horner began work aged eight, as a lather boy in a barber's shop, where he probably listened to Labour politics being discussed for the first time. His father was a union member, but indifferent to socialism. Since the 1867 Reform Act, 'Merthyr politics had been characterised by a degree of popular participation of a peculiarly intense kind'.[4] The Merthyr branch of the Independent Labour Party (ILP) was founded in 1895, and Keir Hardie won a singular victory for Labour in 1900.[5]

Hardie nursed the constituency attentively, holding it until his death in 1915. Horner recalled listening to Hardie speak at 'his open-air meetings at the Fountain ... in the poorest part of the town ... I used to watch him with real hero worship'.[6] Horner left school when he was twelve, and held a succession of jobs in the town. He developed a strong vocation for preaching in the Churches of Christ, probably being drawn in by two brothers, Urbane and John Nicholls, for whom he worked delivering green groceries. The sect's traditions of using reason and logic to prove its Christianity and its refusal to employ full-time ministers enabled Horner to develop talents he would later use as a union leader.[7] Horner was so promising that the Churches of Christ financed him to go to study with their prominent evangelist, the Brother Lancelot Oliver.[8] He recalled having learned how to develop arguments and speak fluently. Returning to Merthyr after six months, he continued to combine religiosity with his two other keen interests. He was boxing to a high amateur level at the local gymnasium, and maintained his active ILP membership, writing for Hardie's paper, the *Merthyr Pioneer*.[9]

Had Horner remained in Merthyr, he might never have become a coalminer or a Communist. But he answered a call from the deacons of Ynyshir, some ten miles south-west in the prosperous Rhondda coalfield, to assist in the new Church they had founded there. He travelled to preach to them, and eventually moved there, probably in 1915. Since the Churches of Christ made no provision for salaried ministers, he found work on the surface at the Standard Colliery.[10]

It was at this point that Horner met Noah Ablett, who lived in Ynyshir and travelled some five miles up the Rhondda Fach to his duties as checkweighman at the Mardy colliery. Ablett was arguably the most creative thinker in the impressive group of miner-intellectuals who had provided the militant leadership in the Cambrian Combine strike in 1910, and as a result had formed the Miners' Unofficial

Reform Committee. Ablett was the principal author of their manifesto, *The Miners' Next Step,* published in 1912.[11] Ablett warmed to Horner, and began to influence him away from Christianity towards materialism and Marxism.[12] Horner continued to preach, and shed his belief slowly. He had to find a replacement not merely for spiritual faith, but also the densely reasoned theology which the autodidacts of the Churches of Christ assembled so doggedly. It was only after many Sunday afternoon discussions with Ablett and comrades in the Aberystwyth Restaurant, Tonypandy, that Horner was able to slough off Christianity.[13]

It was Horner's deepening antagonism to the First World War which precipitated his break with the Churches of Christ. He had always based his sermons on everyday examples, being keen to illustrate the gospel's relevance. He began to preach openly against the war in 1916. Instead of using Christian pacifist arguments, he spoke from the pulpit against a war being waged for capitalist ends. The deacons, particularly those with sons who had volunteered, were outraged.[14] Horner's opposition to the war was soon tested. Though the War Office had been compelled to conscript miners, South Wales miners were largely exempted from the first draft in order to pre-empt possible opposition. However, when 50,000 more miners were called up in January 1918, young South Walians became liable to conscription.[15] Horner went on the run, along with many others who were ILP socialists and/or Christian pacifists, or simply reluctant to meet an early death. His escape to Ireland was not untypical, though most refugees did not enlist in the Citizens' Army, as Horner did. They were given forged documents and then were able to go to London to find war work under their assumed Irish identity.[16]

Horner returned to see his wife and new-born daughter in the summer of 1918. He was arrested, convicted for avoiding the draft, and imprisoned in Wormwood Scrubs. After the Armistice, draft resisters were released, but immediately handed over to the army who prosecuted them for absenteeism. Most of Horner's fellow offenders were speedily released under a Home Office scheme. Horner, however, was scheduled to spend two years in Carmarthen gaol, because of his notoriety as an agitator.[17] Horner and Ablett concocted a brilliant means of escape, and he served just over half a year of his sentence. The post of checkweighman at Mardy became vacant in April 1919. Ablett championed Horner's cause and he was elected with a decisive majority. Horner went on hunger strike, calculating that his determination to starve was greater than the authorities' will to keep him locked up in the face of strong pressure from the SWMF leaders to release their newly elected lay official. His gamble was successful, and after six days, the authorities released him.[18]

He took up his checkweighman's position on 1 May 1919. He moved his family to Mardy and took over as chairman of the South Wales Miners' Unofficial Reform Committee. Horner and his wife became foundation members of the CPGB in August 1920, by virtue of their membership of the Rhondda Socialist Society. But Horner took little interest in the party. He was pre-occupied not only with the daily economic struggle at the colliery, perhaps the most militant in South Wales, but also with the intensifying triangular conflict between the Miners' Federation of Great Britain (MFGB), the coalowners and the Coalition Government.

RISING REVOLUTIONARY STAR

The 1920s were marked by bitter conflict between miners and coalowners. Horner soon made his mark as an energetic and effective class warrior. In the 1921 lock-out, the Mardy Lodge decided to withdraw the safety men, an illegal action for which forty miners were charged at Swansea Assizes. Horner and the Mardy Lodge Chairman, his fellow Communist Dai Lloyd Davies, were the chief defendants.[19] After his release from gaol, Horner's activities continued to centre around the SWMF. It was the older Communist, Nat Watkins, who represented the South Wales miners at early London conferences of revolutionary trade unionists, and attended the first RILU Congress in Moscow in May 1921.[20]

Horner's serious involvement in communism dates from his first trip to Russia in June 1923. Watkins was now secretary of the British Bureau of RILU, and eager to further this promising young agitator. Horner recalled, 'I was sitting in the tub, naked, after coming home from the pit, when Nat Watkins burst in to ask me if I could go to Russia the following week for a conference of the RILU in Moscow. Wal Hannington and I had been elected as delegates.' He went after being given three months' leave of absence as checkweighman, and was able to visit the Donbass coalmines.[21]

The RILU conference coincided with a Commission on Britain held at the Third Enlarged Plenum of the Executive Committee of the Comintern (ECCI), and Horner attended the meetings, along with most of the CPGB Executive. It was anticipated that the Commission would recommend Bolshevising the CPGB, in line with decisions taken at the Comintern's Third Congress. The Commission decided that the CPGB should bring 'comrades prominent in mass industrial work' onto the CC. Three RILU delegates were co-opted, Johnnie Campbell, a former leading light on the wartime Clyde Workers' Committee, Horner and Wal Hannington, a toolmaker from Kentish Town, London. They were also promoted to the CPGB's 'inner cabinet', the Political Bureau (PB).[22] Horner shared a lack of sectarian pre-conceptions with Hannington and Campbell. Along with Harry Pollitt, who had been elected to the CC in October 1922, they were keen to fan the flames of proletarian militancy inside the unions.

Despite his elevation to the party leadership, Horner's activities continued to be centred around the miners' economic struggle. This was not unusual. The men and women who had been inspired to become Communists were overwhelmingly young, and the men were mainly union members. From their experiences during the 1914-18 war, they were confident of winning the rank-and-file to support socialist revolution, and consequently viewed their task as resuscitating the wartime unofficial movements. These had continued, with Communist encouragement, in a desultory and truncated manner through the early 1920s. The Bolshevised CPGB now focused on revamping them. The Miners' Minority Movement was launched in South Wales in August 1923. In January 1924, a meeting of Minority Movements from five coalfields founded the national Miners' Minority Movement (MMM) and announced a 'militant programme' to revive the MFGB. Watkins became National Organiser.[23]

Horner was part of the nucleus of Communists who founded the National Minority Movement (MM) in August 1924. The veteran Tom Mann presided while Pollitt moved and Horner seconded the resolution which concluded the founding conference.[24] Many left-wing socialists joined Communists as committed participants. Prominent militants like Jack Tanner and Arthur Cook, both of whom had briefly joined the CPGB, viewed the MM as a positive development, and were important in promoting it in engineering and mining.

Horner's imagination was caught by the new movement, and he impulsively lavished time and enthusiasm on it, travelling to all the coalfields and successfully evangelising for its programme. The South Wales MMM became a powerful lobby inside the SWMF, with Horner arguing the case for the modernisation of unions to better fight the capitalist class.[25] During the imprisonment of leading Communists in October 1925, Horner replaced Pollitt as head of the CPGB Industrial Department. But he relinquished the post upon being appointed to the Executive Council of the SWMF representing the Rhondda, a position of considerable importance for the widely anticipated national strike in May 1926.[26]

THE AFTERMATH OF 1926

Horner was the CPGB spokesman inside the MFGB during the lock-out of the miners from May to December 1926. He deployed impassioned, rapier-sharp oratory to devastating effect in the conferences held at critical points in the conflict. The points he scored pushed delegates to the left in support of uncompromising motions of no surrender. He incurred the bitter wrath of leaders from other coalfields, including Joseph Jones of Yorkshire and MFGB President Herbert Smith. In the aftermath of the MFGB's surrender to the coalowners in November, Horner became even more radical. In common with many Communists, he expected the CPGB to give a more revolutionary lead, since the TUC refused to lead the working class forward; and with Pollitt in the forefront, the CPGB leadership executed a leftward turn in 1927.

This did not receive automatic approval from the Comintern, whose functionaries were preoccupied by the intensifying political conflict inside the Soviet Party, though they were also focused on the inner-party conflict in the German Communist Party. The CPGB leadership had to take simultaneous account of their indigenous terrain and the lie of the land in Moscow. Actions and pronouncements appropriate to one might be unacceptable in the other. Until 1928, the CPSU required the Comintern to support a prudent, centrist position still stressing the importance of working with reformists.[27]

The situation inside Russia changed dramatically in early 1928 and remained highly fluid. Stalin drove the CPSU unstintingly to enforce collectivisation and eliminate the kulaks. In January 1930, Stalin executed a sudden, expeditious retreat and only proceeded on the rural front with great caution.[28] Though he displayed little interest in the Comintern, the ECCI had been shadowing the CPSU's position for some time, and the Sixth Comintern Congress in the summer of 1928 formalised the left turn. The new line, Class Against Class, stressed the need to intensify the struggle against the bourgeoisie, but also against the social democrats who were deemed to have irrevocably joined the forces of reaction.

As usual, Comintern pronouncements permitted a range of interpretations as to how the move to the left was to be implemented in practice. Moreover, Class Against Class retained the injunction from the previous line that, when appropriate, Communists should forge 'united fronts from below' with sincere but misguided social democratic workers. It did not issue an absolute injunction that all workers should leave 'reformist' unions, but rather counselled transforming them into instruments of struggle. However, both the Comintern and the RILU emphasised the dangers of right-wing legalism and ignored the danger of left-wing infantilism until January 1930, when Stalin's 'Dizzy with Success' speech inaugurated a period of consolidation. The ECCI responded immediately by initiating its own move back towards the centre. The RILU did not follow until August, probably reflecting the extreme left political dispositions of its secretary Lozovsky.[29]

The space inside Class Against Class enabled advocates of a more centrist approach to maintain some purchase inside Comintern affiliates throughout 1928-29, providing they deployed intellectual dexterity to clothe their case in the language of the new line and could cite events on their own terrain in justification. This occurred in Britain where the CPGB had turned leftwards earlier than the CPSU in the expectation of an indigenous revolutionary upsurge. However, the aftermath of the General Strike and the miners' lock-out did not produce a move left by the working class, to the disappointment and often demoralisation of union militants, ILP activists and Communists. In the circumstances, those activists who had retained a will to fight participated in a consolidation inside the unions. Led by Pollitt, the MM promoted 'Back to the Union' campaigns in every industry, and enjoyed considerable success.

The ECCI's move back towards the centre eased the position of both centrists and pragmatists, who recognised that the situation was not revolutionary. Nevertheless, there were still formidable advocates who insisted that the extreme left interpretation was the only correct reading of the line. In European parties, the left enthusiasts were typically leaders of their party's youth section.[30] Britain was no exception, with YCL officials Bill Rust and Wally Tapsell leading the offensive against pragmatists, whom they accused of harbouring right-wing legalist tendencies. I have described Rust and his allies as Young Turks.[31]

Rust and Tapsell had enjoyed a meteoric rise inside the CPGB leadership since the Sixth Comintern Congress. Their zealous commitment to extreme left interpretation of the new line and their skilful negotiation of the ECCI's internal political vicissitudes enabled them to lead a successful assault, with Comintern support, on the more pragmatic British party leadership. Their bid for power culminated in December 1929 at the CPGB's Eleventh Congress in Leeds. However, their hold on power proved remarkably short, because their revolutionary zeal failed to produce any revolutionary fruit. Whilst they led an enthusiastic crusade against social fascism and espoused the foundation of revolutionary unions, the CPGB's already poor position grew palpably worse.

The RILU had responded to events inside the CPSU by moving further left than the Comintern. The new policy of Independent Leadership, enunciated at the Fourth RILU Congress in October 1928, contained let-out nuances comparable to the qualifications in the Comintern's Class and Against Class. But under the guidance of RILU leader Alexander Lozovsky, affiliates, including the MM, were told to lead workers out of 'social fascist' unions forthwith. When this turn was resisted by the MM leadership, which included leading non-Communists, the Young Turks seized their advantage and effected a virtual take-over of the MM.

Citing the CPGB's loss of members and isolation, pragmatic members of the leadership convinced the Comintern to withdraw support from the Young Turks. Pollitt had moved from the MM secretaryship to the three person CPGB Secretariat in July 1929. By 1930, he was exercised by the erosion in the MM's support. He increasingly distanced himself from Rust and his allies whom he regarded as having a wholly misguided approach.[32] By the autumn of 1930, the Young Turks had lost the initiative. In step with the Russians and the ECCI, the CPGB leadership began to adopt a more consistently centrist position.

HORNER AND THE YOUNG TURKS

In common with other union militants in the party leadership, Horner remained orientated towards the existing unions throughout the Third Period. He rejected interpretations of Class Against Class which prescribed splitting established unions. He did not, however, act like a right-wing trade union legalist and he never shirked from attacking union bureaucrats. As chairman of the South Wales Miners' Unofficial Reform Committee and evangelist for the MMM, he argued for a radical change in the MFGB and SWMF structures to make them more effective fighting vehicles.

Horner was used to speaking his mind. He made little attempt to hide his contempt for Rust and his allies despite their increasingly powerful position. Thus, at the CC meeting on 21 September 1929, he referred to delegates' accusations at the Scottish Conference that Pollitt was a right-winger as a libel, and described 'much of the criticism

taking place ... [as] the most unscrupulous kind that ever has been prac-
tised in the history of the Party'.[33] At the CPGB Eleventh Congress,
Horner was amongst the right-wing transgressors dropped from the
CC list by the Commission deputed to prepare it, chaired by Rust.
There was a move to nominate Horner from the floor, but he declared,
'I would rather do anything than stop there'. He was not elected, losing
by 25 to 56 votes.[34]

After the Congress, Horner was sent to Moscow where he spent
most of 1930 working for the RILU. Johnnie Campbell had used his
influence at the Comintern to effect Horner's removal, calculating if he
remained in Britain an open breach with the new party leadership was
inevitable.[35] Horner, his wife and youngest daughter lived in Moscow,
but he travelled frequently to Berlin where the Miners' International
Committee (MIC) was located. He had ample opportunities to observe
the manoeuvrings in the RILU, Comintern and inside the CPSU.
Horner was in Moscow for the Sixth Session of the RILU Central
Council from 16-24 December 1929, and is likely to have remained
into the new year, and would have witnessed the almost instantaneous
impact of 'Dizzy with Success' in moderating the behaviour of the
Komsomol (Young Communist) crusaders. He evidently concluded
that he could make his peace with the new line, and acquired facility in
writing and speaking in the language of Independent Leadership. His
distaste for the Russian winter may have provided an additional incentive for his reconciliation with the CPGB. Rehabilitated, he returned to
Britain in August 1930.[36]

Horner had lost his checkweighman's position when the Mardy
colliery was closed in 1927. But he had become too integrated into the
Moscow machine to resume life as an unemployed Communist activist.
His activity inside the MIC continued unabated. At the end of
November 1930, the RILU instructed him to go to Berlin 'to discuss
the mining situation in Germany, Belgium, France and Britain'.[37]
Horner returned to London with directions to organise by 14
December a national conference 'under revolutionary auspices' and
also 'to secure the election of delegates to attend an Essen Conference
of International Miners in order to co-ordinate the various national
miners' struggles ... and this was given as my principal job'.[38]

Horner made a serious attempt to fulfil his instructions. He was
determined to implement Independent Leadership within the latitude
he had observed in Moscow and Berlin. But his attempts to organise
class struggle were continually frustrated by the shortcomings of the
Young Turks in the party and MM *apparat*. On 4 December, his first

day back in Britain, Horner went to the MM headquarters. He could obtain no help either for organising the national mining conference or assisting a strike of 90,000 Scottish miners then taking place. He found only one person in the office, John Mahon, who said 'it is nothing to do with me ... you must ask someone else'. The same occurred on the following two days and Horner went to the party office, where he found J.T. Murphy who helped.[39]

The MM conference took place in Sheffield. Delegates pledged themselves to organise resistance over the issue of payment for the 7 ½ hour day, a change in miners' working hours included in the Labour Government's Coal Mines Act in August 1930. The change was due to be implemented on 1 January 1931, and it was widely anticipated that the coalowners would enforce wage reductions.[40] His British task accomplished, Horner proceeded to Essen in the Ruhr for the MIC conference, before returning to South Wales for Christmas.

The militant declarations made in Sheffield produced no results, except in South Wales, where the SWMF embarked on an official strike on New Year's Day 1931. As the leading Communist in the union, Horner agreed the party line with the South Wales leadership, including Idris Cox, the district secretary, PB member and enthusiastic supporter of Independent Leadership: 'There was no difference between us. We never had an argument right through the strike ... Never any friction between Cox, Stead, Williams and myself.'[41] The strike lasted a fortnight, during which Horner was shocked at the lack of assistance from the Party Centre and angered by the steady stream of criticism which they did send, mostly directed at him.[42] These recriminations were evidently a pre-emptive move by the Party leadership to safeguard themselves against criticism for providing insufficient help and failing to mobilise other coalfields. Meanwhile, the SWMF leadership were doing their best to quickly end the stoppage.

> At this point the total membership of the SWMF was 75,480 but the workforce was in excess of 140,000 ... The SWMF EC were anxious for a settlement and the [Labour] Government pressed the owners to make concessions over what Noah Ablett called 'trivial issues'. The strike itself was fairly solid ... [43]

The strike was called off by a delegate conference on 16 January. Horner told a meeting of the CPGB District Committee that neither the party nor the MMM had the resources to challenge this decision. The force of his argument swayed the meeting. Most miners present expressed agreement with him, and proceeded back to their collieries to rebuild morale and militancy. The PB proved unwilling to accept the common-sense view that the situation had prevented party members from leading South Wales miners to defy the Executive and continue the strike unofficially. Cox changed his mind, and now told the PB that: 'the situation throughout the whole Party in South Wales is very serious ... because the mass of the membership have not yet been brought to a clear understanding of what is involved in the new line ... many leading comrades in South Wales are not convinced of the new line' and the district needed 'systematic attention'. Rust blamed Horner: '... it is quite clear ... that Horner has returned [from Moscow] ... all the time oppressed with these old influences ... and feeling that the leadership of the Party is no good and cannot be supported'.[44]

Rust and his allies manoeuvred to keep the discussion away from the facts. They pressed the charge that Horner had committed an ideological error deviating from the line of Independent Leadership. Horner was outraged that his revolutionary credentials were being questioned. He was thirty-six years old and had been, as he reminded the CC, 'for more than 20 years actively connected, taking an active part in the revolutionary struggle in this country'.[45] He hit back in an ill-considered statement written in hot blood, prompting Pollitt to observe that Horner's 'tongue is many times his worst enemy'.[46] In an attempt to defuse the conflict, the Party Secretariat, which included Pollitt and Campbell, declined to circulate it either to the PB or the CC. Horner quoted extensively from it when he eventually appeared before the CC in late May:

> If there was one thing the miners in South Wales were looking for it was some sort of promise of assistance from outside ... and everybody understood that unless support could be got for the South Wales miners – the men believed this – their markets would be filled by the production of other districts ... I instanced the treatment in the *Daily Worker* of the Lancashire Executive resolution demanding an MFGB conference in order to discuss support for South Wales. What did the *Daily Worker* say? 'Don't take any notice of it. It means nothing' ... Now I condemned them [PB] too for lack of practical support. I know money is short. I know it is hard but I know it was worth at least £10 to carry on ... During [the] whole of that 18 days ...Williams and Stead never received a single farthing from headquarters of this movement. Williams was never in possession of his train fare to go to a strike committee, even ten

miles away, continually borrowing, begging, doing what he could ... These comrades were kept on typing machines and duplicate [*sic*] turning out circulars from morning to night and doing it very inefficiently ... taking twice the time that any girl at £2 a week would take ... During the whole of that strike, except for these casual chats between Stead, Williams and myself, there was not a single Party meeting held in South Wales in the centre, never a single DPC [District Party Committee] called on the question. Three locals in minefield throughout the whole struggle held one meeting ... The Party was liquidated in practice. It became merged in the strike committee movement.[47]

The Secretariat had pressing reasons for enforcing an armistice between Horner and his critics. Inside the CC and PB an irresistible compulsion to declare against Horner was operating, of which the Secretariat was well aware, but they recognised his value as a militant and agitator, and they wanted him to be both able and willing to take a leading role in organising coalfield conflict. Wage reductions were still looming, and the Secretariat hoped to stimulate a national miners' strike. On 23 January, Pollitt said, 'We want him [Horner] to work with the new cadres, to give them the benefit of his experience.'[48]

A lull in hostilities followed in February during which the pragmatic section of the leadership resumed their centrewards tack. On 11 February Pollitt wrote in the *Daily Worker* that 'because of incorrect interpretations placed on the trade union questions, there had been in our Party and the Minority Movement a marked reluctance to carry forward the new line inside the trade unions'. He cited the SWMF conference decision on 16 January as evidence of the party's weakness, offering an implicit criticism of the South Wales comrades for not taking union activity sufficiently seriously. Only one lodge had voted against the Executive, whereas there had previously been large numbers supporting the MM. He said that union officials were characterising the CPGB as a party of 'nons' who were encouraging others to leave unions. Pollitt concluded that 'we [must] advise workers to join the unions under our leadership ... our Party should again go forward with this line inside the reformist trade unions ... organising Party fractions, securing election as delegates to all conferences and taking advantage of every opportunity of winning official positions...'

Rust, as *Daily Worker* editor, denied the substance of Pollitt's thrust in the next issue. He insisted that the party had nearly achieved its goal of winning the masses:

Independent leadership is not a phrase, but a reality ... We are closer to the masses than before the [SWMF] strike ... Let us get down to mass work and discussion with a vengeance. The last meeting of the South Wales DPC showed that the biggest danger is the lagging behind the masses. From top to bottom of the district we need more energy and fire, more burning conviction of the greatness of our responsibility of the big things we can do and of the stirring times we live in (emphasis in original).[49]

RECANTATION AND RECONCILIATION

Rust and his allies now renewed their attack on Horner as the source of the party's poor performance in South Wales. They used their dominant position inside the MM to remove him from the leadership. He was accused of paying lip-service to Independent Leadership whilst concerting 'sabotage in practice'. The MM Executive had decided 'to conduct an intense enlightenment campaign throughout the ranks ... in explanation of the role of the trade union bureaucracy and in popularisation of the Minority Movement policy and its application in the immediate struggles of the miners against coal capitalism and its Labour and trade union allies'.[50] However, the MM signally failed to build on the sporadic outbreaks of miners' strikes which occurred in March and again in June-July in South Wales, Yorkshire and Scotland. The South Wales DPC tried to spark a strike independently of the SWMF without success.[51] The party mining activist Mel Thomas told the Maesteg local that Cox was mainly responsible for Communists' failure to march to their pit and bring the men out. He called on the DPC to admit its own errors.[52] Another veteran recalled:

> [T]he Communists weren't strong enough see and Horner then, I remember the time, said, 'The Minority Movement found itself effectively bankrupt at the period to bring the men out' ... We really weren't strong enough see ... [W]e didn't come out ... in [March] 1931 because I was the [lodge] delegate and I wasn't so eager to bring them out, because I knew we might have a meeting in Cardiff and perhaps 3 or 4 lodges would try to bring the men out, but they wouldn't be successful I thought.[53]

The erstwhile promoters of Independent Leadership had been unable to push either party activists or the rank-and-file beyond sporadic action within union institutions. But they redoubled their attack on Horner. Throughout March, the *Daily Worker* condemned

Horner's errors. The Young Turks mounted a campaign inside the Party against him. On 6 March, the *Worker* reported that the Middlesbrough aggregate had condemned Hornerism. On 10 March, the Birmingham aggregate's reference to Horner's 'deeply ingrained opposition to the line of the Leeds Congress' (which had enthusiastically endorsed the line of the Comintern) was recorded, along with Horner's refusal to accept the PB resolution which blamed all party members in South Wales (including himself) for failing to produce a coalfield strike. His 'long declaration' in reply to the PB had 'fallen into the language of renegades and social fascists'.[54]

Will Paynter remembered the campaign for 'the stereotype decisions that were being taken at Party branches all over the country. They were supporting the official Central Committee decision ... without any knowledge of what the real issues were. And at the time there was a lot of this sort of mechanical support, this sort of mechanical underwriting.'[55] Under pressure, Horner finally began an expeditious retreat. He wrote to the CC on 19 March 1931 stating that he had 'practically decided that the path of my revolutionary duty lies in the direction of submission to the Party and intend to prepare a statement to this effect'.[56] Meanwhile, Rust kept up unremitting political pressure, and Cox swung the South Wales party against Horner. In early April, the DPC passed an anti-Horner resolution, by a 19-1 vote. Cox admitted that he had made mistakes at Maesteg, but he had made them *'in trying to carry out the line* and [this] was totally different from *actual opposition* to the line as in the case of Cde Horner'(emphasis in original).[57] Paynter's defence of Horner at the time is relevant. In a letter published in the *Daily Worker*, he wrote that Horner's disagreement with Cox 'is now being construed as lack of faith in the workers to fight on, submission to [SWMF] conference decisions, trade union legalism etc. But it was merely a recognition of the dominant influence of the SWMF and the adoption of a tactic by which it could be combated [taking the fight against the settlement to the SWMF lodges].' [58]

Had the Young Turks' ambitious expectations of revolutionary victories been realised, they would have had no difficulty in forcing the pragmatists onto the defensive. The extreme left were still advancing against their inner party opponents in the German Communist Party. But the real position was encapsulated in a *Daily Worker* letter from J. Carter of Pontypridd, who had earnestly tried to make Independent Leadership work: 'The greatest danger is not Hornerism, but those comrades who accept fully the new line of the Party, but who are inactive as regards going to the pits because they feel the difficulties of operating the new line are so tremendous ... Comrades cannot overcome their own prejudices ...'[59] In these adverse circumstances, the Young Turks' strategy was exemplary. They utilised Horner's earlier recalcitrance to convict him not only for his own supposed mistakes, but also their own shortcomings. They blamed the failure of either a South Wales coalfield strike or a national miners' strike to materialise on Hornerism, not their interpretation of Independent Leadership. Such opportunism at his expense brought Horner's blood to the boil. On 15 April he withdrew his earlier offer to recant: 'I cannot be a party to such deceit and refuse to submit a statement which would assist in perpetuating these weaknesses [of the South Wales party]'.[60]

The opponents of the Young Turks concluded that they could not save Horner if he would not repent, and prepared to sacrifice him. On 16 April Pollitt told the PB that he 'thought Horner should attend CC [Central Committee] and CC should decide on question of expulsion'.[61] When Horner made his 'final stand', a thoroughly uncompromising statement to the Central Committee at the end of May, he was clearly in the mood to be martyred: 'I regard this matter as a vitally serious matter to me – it is life and death for me ... in the sense that to be outside of the revolutionary working class movement is something that I have never thought about when thinking of living in the future.'[62]

Had Horner been expelled, it is a matter for counter-factual speculation as to which direction he might have taken. Oswald Mosley's New Party was advocating solutions to the slump and unemployment which were remarkably similar to those put forward by others on the left. The autobiographies of Walter Citrine and Horner both recorded the coincidental meeting of Citrine, Horner and Mosley around Arthur Cook's bedside in Manor House Hospital, Golders Green, in May 1931.[63] John Strachey, a strong Mosley supporter, knew Cook and Horner well. He was possibly deputed to see them about the New Party.[64] In June, Strachey reported that Cook had responded favourably and press reports appeared 'that Arthur Horner ... was also on the point of joining the New Party.' [65]

Horner was extricated from his martyr's crown at the last minute. Moves originating in the Comintern, perhaps from Page Arnot, sent the secretary of the MIC, Grusha Slutsky, to Mardy in great haste. 'When he arrived at our house ... I at first would not come from the pit to see him. I was so angry.'[66] The Politburo and Central Committee minutes recorded that a letter from the ECCI addressed to the Secretariat was duly forwarded to Horner. On 11 June, Pollitt reported that Horner had written 'regretting inability to make unconditional submission and expressing willingness to go to Moscow to discuss points raised in their letter' and that he would leave on 24 June. [67]

Horner's reconciliation with the movement was protracted. His case proceeded at a leisurely pace throughout summer and early autumn. He had time to go swimming at the Dynamo Club between hearings.[68] The description of the Comintern Commission in the CPGB minutes reverberates with echoes of the heresy trials conducted by the Roman Catholic Church in the fifteenth and sixteenth centuries. Horner's case, like those of Jan Hus and Martin Luther, turned on semantics and finally the willingness of the accused to submit to the authority of the mother church. Horner's ultimate recantation was full, but not without mitigation. The Commission found him guilty of tactical errors, but flatly dismissed the charge that he had strayed into the murky waters of ideological deviation. He won his point that other comrades in South Wales had also committed tactical errors.

Horner returned to Britain in September 1931. Paynter recalled that: 'He came back with a story, I remember meeting him privately ... He said, he described to us the way that the discussion had proceeded with the sort of collection of facts, analyses of the facts and all this sort of thing.'[69] Having made the first obeisance in Moscow, he now brought himself to make a ritual recantation in Britain. It was remarkably similar to the one which Pollitt had urged him to make in the previous January. The *Daily Worker* reported the event under the headline 'Comrade Horner Submits to the Party'.[70] Further articles reiterating and emphasising his *mea culpa* were published in November.[71]

AFTERMATH

In December 1931, the Comintern convened another British Commission, whose report was adopted by the ECCI in January 1932. Its findings vindicated the pragmatists. From the New Year, the British Secretariat began a strong campaign leading up to the CPGB's Twelfth Party Congress. They began to invoke Lenin's writings on 'British sectarianism' in the *Daily Worker*. For example:

> There are four million organised workers in this country ... Unless we can, by our work and personal example, win the leadership of these workers, it's idle to talk of revolutionary struggles ... The trade unions have been described [by Lenin] as 'schools for Communism' and we have to regularly attend and work within these schools and win the workers for our principles.[72]

The immediate impact on Horner was to redouble his revolutionary ardour. Ensconced in Mardy, he threw himself into the battles of unemployed miners and their families. He was soon apprehended for his leading role in a confrontation with bailiffs executing an eviction order. During the trial at Glamorgan Assizes, he was labelled 'the dictator at Mardy'. It was implied that he was a Russian agent, and that Mardy returned to normality during his absences in Moscow.[73]

Horner was sentenced to fifteen months' hard labour. But his incarceration in Cardiff gaol was transformed by the Governor's decision to make him the prison librarian. He now had the leisure to read. During this period of intense reflection, he developed a clear-sighted perspective of how he should lead the South Wales miners, which he lost no time in putting into practice.[74] His intellectual development was not accompanied by a healing of the scars of his battle with the Young Turks. In a letter written to his wife in the week before his release, Horner wrote:

> The news on Saturday [probably from Paynter] was not very good, particularly that about Wally [Hannington]. The political vendetta is apparently being deepened and extended regardless of the meritorious actions of the individuals attacked. You say Harry Pollitt is coming down to see me upon my release. I shall be very glad to have a heart to heart talk about a number of questions, and this visit should provide the opportunity.[75]

With the exception of Horner himself, there is no mention of the incident in any of the published autobiographies or official biographies of the main participants. It is understandable that Horner should continue to regard the pursuit of his 'errors' by Rust as a vendetta. The balance of evidence had never justified Rust's verdict that Horner had sold out to the 'reformist' union leaders. Horner was to retain a lasting scepticism about the party bureaucracy and a distrust of its potential hold over members.

Thanks to Alan Campbell, John McIlroy and Kevin Morgan for their help.

NOTES
1. See N. Fishman, *Arthur Horner, a political biography* (Lawrence and Wishart, forthcoming).

2. H. Pelling, *The British Communist Party: a historical profile*, 1975, p61; see also W. Thompson, *The Good Old Cause: British communism 1920-1991*, 1992, p46.

3. A. Horner, *Incorrigible Rebel*, 1960, p11.

4. K. O. Morgan, 'The Merthyr of Keir Hardie' in G. Williams (ed), *Merthyr Politics: the making of a working-class tradition*, Cardiff 1966, p59.

5. *Ibid.*, pp65, 68-70.

6. Horner, *op. cit.*, p15.

7. *Ibid.*, pp12-14. Horner consistently described the Churches of Christ as Baptist, probably because they were comparatively unknown, whilst having a strict injunction for adult baptism. Horner insisted that his fiancée be baptised before their marriage (*Ibid.*, p23). See A. F. Adams, *A Brief Survey of the History of the Churches of Christ in South Wales, 1870-1939*, Brecon 1939; M.W. Casey and P. Ackers, 'The Enigma of the young Arthur Horner: from Churches of Christ preacher to Communist militant (1894-1920)', *Labour History Review*, 66, 1, 2001, pp3-23..

8. *Churches of Christ Yearbook, 1913,* p118, states that Horner stayed six months.

9. Horner, *op. cit.*, p15.

10. Casey and Ackers, *op. cit.*; Fishman, *op. cit.*

11. D. Egan, 'Noah Ablett, 1883-1935', *Llafur*, 4, 3, 1986, pp19-30; R. Lewis, *Leaders and Teachers: adult education and the challenge of labour in South Wales 1906-1940*, Cardiff 1993, pp91-3.

12. Fishman, *op. cit.*

13. Horner, *op. cit.*, p21. Horner retained his Christian habits and rhetoric longer than he recalled in his autobiography.

14. South Wales Coalfield Archive, Swansea (SWCA) MNA/PP/46/48, Interview with Arthur Horner by John Griffiths for BBC Radio, n.d., *ca.* 1960.

15. B. Supple, *The History of the British Coal Industry, Volume 4 1913-1946: the political economy of decline*, Oxford 1987, pp93-4.

16. H. Francis and D. Smith, *The Fed: a history of the South Wales miners in the twentieth century*, 1980, pp22-3; South Wales Miners' Library, Swansea (SWML), interview with D.J. Davies, by David Egan, 3 November 1972; interview with Mr and Mrs D.J. Davies by Hywel Francis, 14 October 1974; Horner, *op. cit.*, pp24-5.

17. Horner, *op. cit.*, p31; Mr and Mrs D.J. Davies interview.

18. Horner, *op. cit.*, pp34-7.

19. *Ibid.*, pp55-6.

20. R. Martin, *Communism and the British Trade Unions 1924-1933*, Oxford 1969, p21.

21. Horner, *op. cit.*, pp64-5.

22. J. Klugmann, *History of the Communist Party of Great Britain, Volume 1, 1919-1924*, 1968, p212; L.J. Macfarlane, *The British Communist Party: its origin and development until 1929*, 1966, p83.

23. Klugmann, *op. cit.*, p279; N. Fishman, 'Heroes and anti-heroes: communists in the coalfields', in A. Campbell, N. Fishman and D. Howell (eds), *Miners, Unions and Politics 1910-1947*, Aldershot 1996, pp96-7; Macfarlane, *op. cit.*, p129-30.

24. Klugmann, *op. cit.*, pp282-3.
25. Fishman *op. cit.*, MacFarlane *op. cit.*, pp158-9.
26. Horner, *op. cit.*, p71.
27. MacFarlane, *op. cit.*, chs 8 and 9; G. Gorodetsky, *The Precarious Truce: Anglo-Soviet relations, 1924-27*, Cambridge 1977, ch. 6. (Thanks to Steve Smith for this reference.)
28. See C. Ward, *Stalin's Russia*, 1995, pp40-47.
29. E.H. Carr, *Twilight of the Comintern, 1930-1935*, 1982, ch. 1.
30. M. Worley, 'The Communist International, The Communist Party of Great Britain, and the "Third Period", 1928-1932', *European History Quarterly*, 30, 2, 2000 p189.
31. N. Fishman, *The British Communist Party and the Trade Unions 1933-1945*, Aldershot 1995, p33.
32. *Ibid.*, chs 2 and 3.
33. Quoted in N. Branson, *History of the Communist Party of Great Britain, 1927-1941* (1985), p48.
34. *Ibid.*, p50.
35. Campbell reminded the Central Committee in 1931 that Horner 'never saw the fundamental justice of the change of leadership in this Party [in December 1929]. He saw some people whom he considered good people being slighted and other people whom he considered not quite so good put in their place.' National Museum of Labour History, Manchester, CI2, Central Committee (CC), 15 March 1931. For Horner's provocative behaviour, see MacFarlane, *op. cit.*, pp247, 250.
36. Campbell interceded for Horner in August 1930 at the Comintern's British Commission, citing his 'value as a mass worker', and he subsequently returned to Britain (CI2, CC, 15 March 1931); Fishman, *op. cit.* forthcoming.
37. CI2, CC, 31 May 1931.
38. *Ibid.*
39. *Ibid.* Mahon was a leading Young Turk who had risen to prominence in the MM.
40. Supple, *op. cit.*, pp335-6; Francis and Smith, *op. cit.*, p175.
41. CI2, CC, 31 May 1931; Martin, *op. cit.*, p91.
42. CI12, Politburo (PB), 15, 22-23, 29 January 1931.
43. Francis and Smith, *op. cit.*, p176.
44. CI12, PB, 23 January 1931.
45. CI2, CC, 31 May 1931.
46. CI12, PB, 23 January 1931.
47. CI2, CC, 31 May 1931.
48. CI12, PB, 29 January 1931. See also A. Thorpe, *The British Communist Party and Moscow 1920-43*, Manchester 2000, pp175-6.
49. *Daily Worker (DW)*, 12 February 1931.
50. *DW*, 28 February 1931.
51. Francis and Smith, *op. cit.*, p179.
52. *DW*, 19 March 1931.
53. SWML, interview with Frank Williams, Mardy, by Francis and Smith, 15 May 1973.
54. *DW*, 3-7, 9-12, 14, 16, 24 March 1931.

55. SWML, interview with Will Paynter by H. Francis, 6 March 1973.
56. *DW*, 27 April 1931.
57. *DW*, 9, 10 April 1931.
58. *DW*, 30 April 1931.
59. *DW*, 21 April 1931. For the German Communist Party, see Worley, *op. cit.*, pp188-197.
60. *DW*, 27 April 1931.
61. CI12, PB, 16 April 1931.
62. CI2, CC, 31 May 1931.
63. Horner, *op. cit.*, pp107-8; W. Citrine, *Men and Work: an autobiography*, 1964, p210. Both misremember the incident's date. Horner recorded it as 1930 and Citrine wrote that it occurred shortly before Cook's death on 2 November 1931.
64. Cook signed the Mosley Manifesto, issued in December 1930. Cook's biographer states that he had come to know Mosley well in 1926. Since Horner and Cook were frequent partners at meetings, Horner probably also knew Mosley. P. Davies, *A.J. Cook*, Manchester 1987, pp175-6.
65. R. Skidelsky, *Oswald Mosley*, 1975, p255.
66. Horner, *op. cit.*, p111. Robin Page Arnot told Jim Fyrth that 'he had negotiated the compromise – he was the go-between. The CI was all set to expel Horner when he arrived, and it was really due to RPA that this did not happen ...' Arnot told Hywel Francis that 'he was shocked when the message came [to Moscow] from Pollitt that the intention was to expel Horner'. Transcript of discussion on Hornerism in Communist History Group, 28 March 1987.
67. CI12, PB, 4,11 June 1931.
68. Horner, *op. cit.*, p111. He remembered that five 'internationally known members were appointed to hear the appeal. Kuusinen was chairman ...'. Arnot was present 'as Communist International representative....[and] put the case against me in a very kindly and objective way ... Robin and I were the best of friends then ...'
69. Paynter interview.
70. *DW*, 8 October 1931.
71. *DW*, 6 and 17 November 1931.
72. *DW*, 19 January 1932.
73. Francis and Smith, *op. cit.*, pp180-2.
74. Fishman, *op. cit.*, 1996, pp103-5.
75. SWCA MNA/PP/46/1-5, letter, 2 December 1932.

Miner Heroes:
Three Communist Trade
Union Leaders

ALAN CAMPBELL AND JOHN McILROY

In 1927, James MacDougall, the assistant of the great Scottish socialist John Maclean and animator of the reform committee movement in the Scots coalfields during the First World War, reflected upon the victories of Communist candidates in the Scottish miners' union elections that year:

> Conferences of the Minority Movement met with a surprising amount of success. There were to be seen the men, still comparatively young, who had been thrown up by the agitation of the Miners' Reform Committee. Several of them were now checkweighmen and officials, and no doubt their original enthusiasm had been chastened by experience, but they could not resist the call. Side by side with them sat the new generation that had arisen since 1917 – very young, very confident, Communist to the core. The impression got from these conferences of 'Red' trade unionists is that they are very much machine made – everything done on the Moscow model – and yet the energy and vitality of the miners' union is definitely there too.[1]

Willie Allan, David Proudfoot and Abe Moffat were, successively, general secretaries of the United Mineworkers of Scotland (UMS), the more important of the two 'red' unions formed by the Communist Party of Great Britain in 1929 following the drawn out crisis provoked by these electoral successes. The history of this short-lived union has recently been analysed.[2] Our intention here is to examine the lives of its three leaders, who ranked among the most important Communist trade union leaders of the inter-war period – two were Central Committee (CC) members – but who are largely neglected in existing historiography. All were born in the Scottish coalfields between 1892 and 1900 and were members of the generation of miners radicalised by the First World War and its aftermath: all joined the party during its first five years. Yet although their backgrounds were similar and their political careers, for a time, closely interlinked, their paths to communism were different and their personalities and approaches to politics – despite their best endeavours to 'Bolshevise' themselves – remained highly distinctive. A study of their lives to 1936 provides a prism through which we can evaluate one of the party's few opportunities to exercise leadership of a trade union and explore the tensions this engendered between the imperatives of Comintern policy and the compelling pressures of everyday trade unionism alluded to by MacDougall.

THREE ROADS TO COMMUNISM

'He was some man, ye know ... To me he was a bloody god', recalled Johnny Boyle, a Communist activist in the 1920s, of his mentor, David Proudfoot.[3] Proudfoot was born in 1892 in the Fife mining village of Methil. Its population grew rapidly in the following two decades as the coal industry and the local docks were developed by the paternalistic Wemyss Coal Company to export coal to Europe. Proudfoot's father was employed for many years as a docker. After leaving school, David, the eldest son in a family of five children, commenced an engineering apprenticeship, but was soon drawn to the higher wages offered in the pits.[4]

Proudfoot enlisted in 1914, served as a machine gunner in France and Salonika and became an NCO before being discharged in 1918 suffering from dysentery and malaria. Upon his return to Methil, he began work in the Wemyss Coal Company's Wellesley Colliery, a modern, mechanised mine employing almost two thousand men. Bouts of malaria prevented him continuing underground work and he was elected checkweigher at the Wellesley the following year, a position he retained until the mining lockout of 1926.[5]

Proudfoot's appointment as checkweighman at the largest pit in East Fife at the age of 26 suggests recognition of his talents by fellow colliers. A tall man with dark, receding hair which made him look older than his years, he was, according to his fellow Fife Communist, John McArthur, 'not a showy speaker. He was slow, steady, more of a stodgy speaker, but generally he had well-prepared material, well-thought-out arguments'. Johnny Boyle concurred: 'he wisnae much of an orator, but he was a bloody good organiser'.[6]

A Miners' Reform Committee had been established in Fife by 1918 and coordinated support for militant policies within the county union, the Fife, Kinross and Clackmannanshire Miners' Association (FKCMA). Proudfoot was soon involved and by the 1921 national lockout had emerged as a prominent activist. The dispute was characterised in Fife by extreme militancy, with mass pickets stopping pumping operations in order to flood pits. Proudfoot was one of the leaders of several thousand East Fife miners who made a midnight rendezvous with a two-thousand-strong contingent from West Fife at Thornton railway junction. Railwaymen were prevented at gunpoint from working and wagons and shops looted before police and armed marines dispersed the crowd.[7]

Proudfoot's early views were marked by rejection of religion – his mother was a member of the Church of Scotland – support for the suffragettes and espousal of temperance. His father had been a member of the Social Democratic Federation (SDF), later the British Socialist Party (BSP), which possessed a significant presence in Fife before 1914. Immediately after the war, Proudfoot, too, was associated with the SDF which was re-established from the pro-war rump of the BSP and affiliated to the Labour Party. He quickly abandoned that organisation and drew closer to the revolutionaries who had coalesced in the Fife Communist League which merged into the CPGB at the Leeds Convention in January 1921.[8] It is not clear precisely when Proudfoot joined the CPGB but his participation in the British delegation to the Congress of the Red International of Labour Unions (RILU) in Moscow in June 1921 suggests he was by then a member.[9]

Subsequently, he threw himself into union and party activity despite long hours as a checkweighman and recurring malaria. In his regular correspondence with Allen Hutt, his London comrade and confidant, Proudfoot adumbrated his numerous responsibilities in 1925:

> 1. Group leader and representative on District Party Committee; 2. Group trainer (oh, hell); 3. Chief literature distributor ... 4. Delegate for Union Branch to local Trades and Labour Council; 5. Delegate for Trades and Labour Council to Divisional Executive [of Labour Party]; 6. Collector of subscriptions for Communist Book Club; 7. Doormat for local industrial disputes; 8. Checkweighman in spare time.[10]

'He was', said McArthur, 'a wonderful organiser. He did not spare himself. He worked like a Trojan'. Yet such efforts had to be on Proudfoot's terms: 'He would work with a team provided he proposed the action ... then he would work himself to the bone and not spare any others in the doing of it'.[11] The results were often meagre. A new CPGB group had been formed in East Fife in September 1923 with Proudfoot as secretary, but by the end of the year, its strength was only eight; in 1924, he pronounced it 'as dead as the dodo'. Such failures were disheartening not only for Proudfoot but also for his young comrades of whom he could be critical. Hugh Sloan recalled, 'Davie was always a kinda pessimistic, sort of sardonic kind of a character', while Johnny Boyle remembered, 'Oh Christ, he could be sarcastic and bitter'.[12] His political career was to develop a pattern of ceaseless activity punctuated by depression born of illness and frustration at lack of results.

An enduring feature of Proudfoot's political outlook was the need to organise at the point of production. In line with the party's Bolshevisation in the 1920s, he enthusiastically supported the formation of CPGB Factory Groups 'to popularise the idea of Industrial Unions with Pit and Factory Committees as the unit of organisation'.[13] In 1925, Proudfoot was the driving force behind the publication of the Wellesley Colliery pit paper, the *Spark*, the longest running Communist workplace bulletin in Britain, which appeared regularly until 1932 with a circulation of over 600 copies. Methil was perhaps the best organised mining village in Britain in 1926. Ernie Wooley, a CPGB full-timer sent to Fife during the dispute, hyperbolically asserted that 'Methil is to Fife what Petrograd was to Russia during the revolution'.[14] Proudfoot was the convenor of the Methil central strike committee, which organised transport, propaganda and entertainment as well as an 800-strong workers' defence corps, and his prominence as the leading local Communist was further enhanced by his arrest for making a seditious speech.[15]

Proudfoot's correspondence with Hutt kept him more informed of political developments within the CPGB than were other Fife activists, who equated trade unionism with revolutionary struggle. Moreover, he managed to make occasional trips to London which helped overcome his sense of isolation in Methil and dispel 'the impression sometimes forced on one in this kind of place – that the Party only exists in one's own imagination'.[16]

* * *

'Very capable, a good speaker, arrogant, officious, conceited – all the attributes of a leader! Ruthless, too, I would think, making sure the proper people got into the proper positions at the right time ... auto-

cratic but capable', was one recollection of Abe Moffat by a Fife
Communist who knew him in later life. Those closer to him saw 'a very
strong character' masking a shy personality.[17] Moffat was born in 1894
at Lumphinnans in central Fife, into a large mining family with eleven
children living in a two-roomed house. There was a family tradition of
activism, for his grandfather had migrated to Fife after being victimised
for his union activities in the Lothians. Lumphinnans was a small but
rapidly expanding village almost entirely composed of mining families,
lying between the mining towns of Cowdenbeath and Lochgelly. Its
two pits were operated by the Fife Coal Company, the largest in the
coalfield, with a reputation for a harsh industrial relations regime.[18]

Abe started work underground in 1910 at the age of 14 in
Lumphinnans No. 1 pit. As a young man he was a keen athlete and,
briefly, a gambler. Upon the outbreak of war, 'carried away with the
imperialist propaganda', he volunteered for the army, serving in
France. The experience prompted self-questioning on the slaughter and
his radicalism was reinforced by the unrest in the Fife coalfield upon
his demobilisation. In particular, the events of the 1921 lockout, with
violent clashes between police and miners, exerted a powerful influence.[19] A short spell of unemployment through victimisation, when he
was forced to play his much-loved violin for pennies on the beach at
Auchtertool – he was described as 'a fairly good fiddler' – may have
been another factor.[20] He discussed politics with Laurence Storione, a
French anarcho-communist who had settled in Lumphinnans as a
miner and opened a communist bookshop there. At Storione's urging,
Abe and his elder brother Jim joined the CPGB in January 1922: 'I
began to realise that a political struggle is important as well as an industrial struggle. That was the reason why I joined the Communist Party,
because I believed that it was the Party which was leading the workers
in the right way. I was impressed by the Communists in 1921'.[21]
However, according to one Fife veteran who knew the 'Little Moscow'
of Lumphinnans well, 'Abe joined the party in 1922 ... But he didnae
do very much political activity at that time for the party. But it was in
later years that he came forward in the union ... But in between that
time he never came forward'.[22]

His first wife died young and Abe married Helen McQueen, a
pithead worker, in 1924, the year he was elected to represent
Lumphinnans on Ballingry Parish Council. During 1926 he was among
councillors surcharged for granting relief to locked-out miners and was
arrested and fined for leading a riotous mob against blacklegs. Two of
Moffat's younger brothers – David and Alex – were imprisoned during

the dispute and subsequently his entire family was victimised by the Fife Coal Company.[23]

While these activities brought Abe local prominence, his brother Alex, seven years his junior and also a CPGB member, appeared more likely to rise in the party. While Abe was a member of the union branch committee, Alex held the more important post of branch delegate to the FKCMA Executive Board and became the union's vice-president prior to formation of the UMS. It was a measure of Alex's standing that in 1927, at an aggregate to elect the CPGB slate for Fife's nominations to the Executive of the federal National Union of Scottish Mineworkers (NUSMW), he topped the poll with 90 votes. Proudfoot was a close second with 85 while Abe trailed sixth with 64.[24] Alex was elected to Fife County Council in 1928 while Abe lost his local government post consequent on the abolition of parish councils the following year. Both Abe and Alex were elected checkweighmen at Lumphinnans No. 11 Pit early in 1929 but the Fife Coal Company secured an injunction removing them, claiming they had incited a strike and the case attracted national attention. Alex also stood in that year's general election as CP candidate in Rutherglen, Lanarkshire.[25]

The two brothers were sometimes confused and Willie Allan found it necessary to inform a CC discussion of potential candidates that 'there are two Comrades Moffat – Alex and Abraham. Although Abraham is a much finer and more solid type, there are good reasons why I am supporting Alex now ... Most of the references to Comrade Moffat have indicated that members are referring to Alex Moffat'.[26]

But it was Abe not Alex who was elected to the CC in December 1929. The reason lay in the brothers' contrasting personalities. While both were well built, tough-looking men – one former party organiser recalled their cropped hair cuts made them look 'like boxers' – Abe was more controlled, disciplined and single minded. Their father was a lay preacher in the Plymouth Brethren and Abe inherited his Calvinistic character while Alex was more extrovert, a 'fiery' personality liable to 'flare up', with a fondness for the good life, including whisky. Alex's involvement in a street brawl in Cowdenbeath caused scandal in a party which prided itself on high standards of personal conduct. According to McArthur, non-Communists 'could get away with bad behaviour, excessive drunkenness, kicking up rows ... or womanising', but 'members of the Communist Party should keep in mind that the Party's prestige was all-important ... '[27] Similarly, the leading Scottish Communist Harry McShane initially rejected Alex as his assistant on the 1936 Hunger March 'because Alex had been involved in two or three fights wi' the police when drinking. But I got a promise he wouldn't take any drink ... He was a tremendous help ... He had a great sense of humour'.[28] A party activist compared the brothers: 'The build of the man [Abe], the jib of the man. He was upstanding, always well dressed and careful in his behaviour, social behaviour, and had this air of authority which was quite commanding ... Alex was completely different ... He was a very warm-hearted character ... Abe was a cross he had to bear'.[29]

Alex was sent to the International Lenin School in Moscow in 1930 but the CPGB quickly requested his return. In a missive redolent of the chaos in King Street at the time, Harry Pollitt informed the Comintern that Moffat could not afford to miss a statutory meeting of the Fife County Council. In what must have smacked of the parish pump to the plenipotentiaries of world revolution, he proffered the perennial explanation that the CPGB had confused Alex with Abe. Abe could be domineering towards his brother while Alex displayed greater volatility and independence than the party demanded. For example, when the CPGB instructed the UMS to call a strike throughout the Scottish coalfields in 1931, it was a dismal failure, supported mainly by miners at Lumphinnans No. 11 pit. Alex pragmatically advised the men to return to work, defying the instructions of the party's Scottish secretariat and was censured for his 'impermissible and demoralising' conduct. It was Abe who had the necessary qualities – and ambition – to become a leading Communist. That he later secured Comintern approval is suggested by his being entrusted to act as a courier delivering Swiss francs from Moscow upon his return from the 1935 Seventh Comintern Congress.[30]

* * *

'Willie was a brilliant young lad, a very capable, powerful speaker. He was also a wonderful mimic. He could mimic all the Lanarkshire and Scottish miners' union officials and often he had us in stitches at his performance. He made a terrific impact on the Lanarkshire coalfield', recalled John McArthur.[31] Willie Allan was born in 1900 in Blantyre, Lanarkshire, to Lithuanian parents. In 1891, less than 10 per cent of Blantyre's miners had been born in the parish, while almost 20 per cent were Irish-born; many others were of Irish descent. In the following decades, the mines also attracted Lithuanians or 'Poles'. By 1911, almost 4,000 'Russians and Poles' had settled in Lanarkshire. Blantyre's heterogeneous population established a reputation for resistance to the ruthless exploitation by the large mining companies: for example, during a strike in 1887, police and cavalry were deployed to quell several days of rioting and looting by its miners.[32]

The Lithuanian community succeeded in constructing an impressive range of social institutions to preserve its cultural independence, including Catholic priests who conducted mass in their native tongue, ethnic food stores and three newspapers. Initially employed as strikebreakers, Lithuanians increasingly became loyal supporters of the burgeoning Lanarkshire Miners' Union (LMU). A branch of the Lithuanian Social Democratic Party had been founded in Lanarkshire in 1903, and later renamed the Lithuanian Socialist Federation of Great Britain. Intelligence sources expressed recurring concern at 'the presence of a strong alien element among the miners of Lanarkshire in particular, and to whom these agitators and their Bolshevik associations appeal ... '[33]

This was the world in which Allan began work at a pithead aged 12, becoming a miner two years later in 1914. During the war, Blantyre was the insurgent storm centre of the Lanarkshire Miners' Reform Committee, established in 1917 with the support of Maclean and MacDougall, who then worked at a pithead in the district.[34] The committee initiated strikes against rising food prices and conscription and Blantyre miners were among its most prominent supporters during militant unofficial strikes in January 1919.

Allan was inevitably influenced by this atmosphere. His parents were staunch Catholics and his early rejection of religion led to family disputes: Allan joked that every time his mother made a donation to the Church, he took a shift off work to compensate. Aged only 19, he was elected a Workmen's Inspector under the provisions of the Mines Act at Loanend Colliery. Further recognition came the following year when he was selected by the LMU to be one of their three full-time students at Maclean's Scottish Labour College (SLC). James MacDougall remembered him as 'curly haired ... a strongly-built young fellow, talented and vigorous, an excellent speaker ... '[35] By April 1921, at the beginning of the lockout, 'Comrade Allan of the Scottish Labour College' was chairing a meeting of the Blantyre branch of the Socialist Labour Party (SLP). When Allan became an SLP member is unclear, but he may have been influenced by Maclean's decision to join the party earlier that year. Subsequently, he contributed to the SLP's *Socialist*. Intriguingly, he was critical of the 'harum-scarum tactics of the Communists' during the lockout, which he attributed to their being 'rendered despondent and desperate by the steady going under of Russia' and so 'considered it their duty to strive by every means at their disposal to precipitate any upheaval in this country, no matter how premature or local it may have turned out ... '[36]

Nevertheless, Allan was an active supporter of the Miners' Section of the CPGB-led National Workers' Committee Movement (NWCM), formed in March 1921 from the remnants of the shop stewards' and miners' reform movements, and soon became its Lanarkshire Secretary. When the NWCM put forward a slate for the LMU annual elections, Allan secured fourth place in the vote for the finance committee.[37] Participation in the Lanarkshire county union led to Allan finding himself in a minority within the SLP which in 1922 readopted the policy of dual unionism. Allan insisted that 'to try and build up a legal, safe, Industrial Union outside of and hostile to the existing unions is to attempt the impossible'. He was critical of attempts to establish a Workers' International Industrial Union (WIIU) in Britain, declaring: 'the NWC policy is practicable. The WIIU is impossible'. Although he participated in the SLP's conference in 1923, this was his last recorded involvement. By the end of that year, he was a member of the CPGB's Glasgow District Committee.[38]

Victimised after the 1921 lockout, Allan was agitating amongst the unemployed in Blantyre later that year, as well as conducting a class in economics and industrial history at the Lanarkshire village of Stonehouse. He went to Yorkshire as an underground stoneman but was soon back in Blantyre where he threw himself into political activity. There he was the tutor of an SLC class in history and economics between 1923-4 and the following year taught economics at the Lanarkshire mining villages of Bellshill and Burnbank.[39] By then he was contributing regular reports to the *Worker* and was active in the Miners' Minority Movement (MMM), established in January 1924 from the mining section of the NWCM. That year he was elected as a Lanarkshire representative to the NUSMW executive. This success led him to become president of the MMM Scottish section in early 1925 and secretary the following year. In the summer of 1925, he also served as district organiser of the National Unemployed Workers' Committee Movement in Lanarkshire, agitating throughout the county, 'expending a tremendous amount of energy' and setting up fourteen local unemployment committees. Still only 24, he stood for the post of LMU secretary and secured a remarkable 42 per cent of the vote in a straight fight with the long-established incumbent.[40]

At some point in the 1920s, Allan married Jennie Lowrie, the daughter of a steel smelter, whom he had met at the Cambuslang Socialist Sunday School. Shortly before the 1926 lockout, he was elected checkweighman at Tannochside Colliery. He played a prominent part in the dispute in Lanarkshire and was arrested in October for 'conspiracy and riot', although the case was found not proven. He also penned numerous articles lambasting the union leadership. Writing in the *Worker* under the headline 'The Cowardly Leaders of Lanarkshire', he complained of the 'innumerable instances of capitulation and spineless policy' of the county leaders since 1921. At the CPGB Congress in October, his growing status was symbolised by his election to the CC.[41] His rise to membership of the party elite was therefore dramatically swift.

UNION REFORM AND NEW UNIONISM
A central theme of Allan's political views in the 1920s was the need to work within the official union structures. When NWCM candidates stood for LMU office in 1921, Allan argued against his SLP comrades:

> Quite apart from what any of the 'pure' Socialists may say, we think that the presence of a number of comrades working within the union in an official capacity (even if it is a 'county' union) should give us more material assistance and opportunity for educating the mass of workers than ever we have had before.[42]

Although not then a party member, Allan was entirely at one with CPGB strategy. The formation of a breakaway Mineworkers' Reform Union (MRU) in Fife in December 1922 following a series of manoeuvrings by the right-wing leadership of the FKCMA under William Adamson provoked dismay among the CPGB leadership. The party opposed the establishment of the MRU in which many of its Fife cadre took leading positions, including Proudfoot who was vice-president, and in 1924, the CC sent a 'special organiser' to Fife 'to demand that the comrades work for unity'.[43]

This provoked some heart-searching. Proudfoot, who 'played a great part in building up' the organisation, resigned from its Executive in July 1924, urging a ballot on unification. Proudfoot admitted his views were 'decidedly unpopular' among CPGB members and many remained active in the union's leadership. Proudfoot represented only 'a small section' of Fife Communists and the majority, including the Moffats, remained in the MRU until its fusion with the FKCMA early in 1927.[44]

The dispute also caused tension with MMM militants elsewhere which prefigured later divisions within the UMS. Allan chaired a meeting of the MMM Scottish executive which heard complaints from MRU representatives of lack of support from that body. In reply, Allan insisted that 'the existence of the Reform Union in Fife [was] a positive hindrance to Left-wing progress inside the Scottish Miners' Union' to which the MRU was unable to affiliate because the NUSMW recognised only the right-wing-led FKCMA. He forcefully affirmed that the MRU was 'frittering away good energy in trying to build up a Reform Union ... In Lanarkshire they would welcome a speedy liquidation of ... the Reform Union'.[45]

At the same meeting Proudfoot expressed his support for the policy of the MM and 'the Lanarkshire comrades', sentiments which could not have enhanced his popularity in Fife. As the dispute festered on, Proudfoot maintained his insistence that the 'only solution ... is One Union in Fife' but despaired that the District Party Committee was 'too damned timid' because of the MRU's popular support. By March 1926, he contemplated leaving the party and taking the MRU Methil branch into Adamson's union: 'the Party can then be exonerated and not get any mud that would be thrown ... '[46] Nothing came of this stratagem as developments were overtaken by the lockout.

Despite victimisation after the dispute, Proudfoot married on Christmas Eve, 1926, a move he admitted seemed 'damned foolish with no prospects of work'. His wife, Jemima, a second cousin and the daughter of a miner, was a divorcée with children.[47] The pressures of married life as an unemployed step-father added to the demands of his political activities: 'Here I am with little or no prospects of work, will have to furnish a house when I get work (Christ knows when) clothes, boots, etc, to provide for four; to mention only the "domestic circumstances".'[48] By the summer of 1927, he complained:

> The thought of it [the *Spark*] never mind the sight of it, nearly makes me sick ... it is absolutely hellish at present; rushing to West and Central Fife for Public and Campaign Ctee meetings, rushing back and knocking at a typewriter and duplicator, while some of the others take the kids to the sands and give the wife an airing.[49]

However, the Communists' role in the lockout paved the way for successes by CPGB candidates in Fife and Lanarkshire that year. Proudfoot was elected an FKCMA agent while Allan secured the secretaryship of the LMU. More importantly, the combined votes in these county unions were sufficient to guarantee the election of members of the MM slate to the NUSMW Executive, including Allan as general secretary. The anti-democratic manoeuvres of the incumbent Scottish officials, in collusion with the leadership of the Miners' Federation of Great Britain (MFGB), require no detail here, but for over 18 months they repeatedly postponed the NUSMW annual conference to prevent the Communist officials-elect from taking office and ultimately recognised a breakaway union in Fife formed by the right-wing Adamson.[50] Of greater interest is the attitudes of our protagonists and their response to increasing pressure from the Comintern, which was now developing the ultra-leftist, sectarian and ultimately disastrous new line of Class Against Class, to form a new 'red' miners' union.

Proudfoot was presciently anxious that factional divisions within the FKCMA should not produce a new split:

> Better in my opinion to have one union with a right wing leadership in the Central Office and one union operating AT THE PITS which at least gives some basis of unity amongst the men than two unions operating, one with a party leadership and the other of Non-Pol nature with the result of having the men AT THE PITS split in two definate [sic] unions and the antagonisms of the past four years reopened.[51]

In Lanarkshire, Allan had only a minority of MM supporters on the LMU executive and the right wing harried him at every opportunity. While rank and file support remained strong, membership plummeted as a result of closures, victimisation and the virulent factional struggle within the shell of the LMU. He was also in a small minority on the NUSMW Executive where his defeated opponents remained in post and called the police to expel him from meetings. They refused to endorse his election by the LMU to the MFGB annual conference in 1928 and when he sought to address the gathering he was physically ejected.[52]

When Proudfoot visited Blantyre in December 1928 he found that: 'The prevalent feeling in Lanarkshire is that there is no Union to save, that we should immediately set about the formation of a new Union'. In contrast, he advocated a superior assessment of the party's interests: 'Organise the Lanarkshire mineworkers around struggle at the Pits (unionists and nons) continually appeal to them to come into the union *to fight* the R.W. who refuse to struggle at the pit and who also refuse to accept rank and file decisions on struggle ...'[53] A few days later, he expanded his position further in a realistic appraisal of rank and file miners' attitudes:

> I hope my statement re the Party line on the Lanarkshire situation did not convey the impression that I was opposed to the formation of New Unions *when the time is ripe* ... It is a very easy thing to declare and prove that the Workers are getting fed up with the R.W. leadership, but they are *not so fed up* that they have come solidly over to us or we should have them along with us inside the Unions fighting the R.W. (emphasis in original).[54]

Proudfoot's views reflected those of the majority of the CPGB leadership which was under increasing criticism from Moscow for not immediately forming a new union from the Communist-led 'Save the Union' campaign, established to reverse membership decline.[55] That same month, Harry Pollitt informed the Comintern that only in Fife was there a sufficiently experienced cadre to manage the affairs of the union, while in Lanarkshire the party lacked control:

> We oppose any suggestion that there should be a date fixed to form a new union in Scotland. Such a step would be *suicidal, ridiculous and premature* ... the line of the Central Committee is therefore to develop this Save the Union campaign ... then upon the basis of the response to this campaign, making the decision, *if necessary*, of forming one union for the Scottish miners (our emphasis).[56]

The CPGB Congress in January 1929, which accepted that Communists faced a new Third Period of revolutions and war, devoted considerable attention to the Scottish coalfields. Abe Moffat warned it would be 'dangerous' to establish a new union until the Save the Union Committees 'had gained much more strength'. But in an implicit criticism of Allan, he contrasted developments in Lanarkshire and Fife, pointing to the need to go 'out to the unorganised miners in the pits (not confining their activities to the Union branches)'. Allan agreed but did not accept that all avenues inside the MFGB were exhausted: to form a new union would be 'a very big mistake'. The resolution was adopted unanimously after Arthur Horner summed up: 'to advocate the immediate formation of a new Scottish Miners' Union, without mass support, would simply mean isolation'.[57]

But the situation was soon transformed. Three weeks later, the NUSMW Executive called a Special Conference which amended the constitution to disaffiliate county unions in arrears. This decision excluded the FKCMA and permitted the entry of Adamson's breakaway union as the Fife affiliate: Lanarkshire was isolated. The patient manoeuvrings of the NUSMW bureaucracy now raised the issue of a new union once more in a situation where a breakaway appeared the only alternative to many Communists and where any other strategy was finally ruled out by the Comintern. Ten days after the NUSMW conference, the Comintern sent a long, highly critical 'closed letter' to the CPGB Executive demanding an end 'to vacillation and wavering in the sphere of trade union work ... The most vigilant attention must be paid to those branches of the unions in which the Communists have already secured the leadership ... particularly in Fife and Lanarkshire ...' While the letter did not explicitly call for the formation of a new union, it did not have to spell out this demand to a leadership who were well aware of the Comintern's current views.[58] A few days later, the Political Bureau (PB) accepted that 'there was now no other step possible than the formation of a new union'. Allan, on behalf of the Save the Union Council, accordingly issued a manifesto calling for the formation of a new Scottish Mineworkers' Union.[59]

CHANGING THE LINE, CHANGING THE CADRES

The UMS was formed in April 1929 with Allan as General Secretary. Proudfoot was appointed an organiser in East Fife, and Abe Moffat, who had played no leading role in the union's creation, took up a similar post in Central Fife early the following year. The union faced enormous difficulties in establishing itself against unremitting, collusive hostility from coalowners and county unions. If, in the context of both Russian foreign policy and conditions in the Scottish coalfields, the decision is understandable, launching a union constitutionally committed to revolution in such an unfavourable balance of forces was – and this could be seen to be so at the time – highly questionable. The CPGB's sectarianism was compounded as Lanarkshire members, stung by condemnation of their earlier 'trade union legalism', mounted a series of ill-prepared strikes to foster what was seen as growing revolutionary consciousness. A report by Allan in 1930 demanded the 'complete elimination of the bad mistake of hurriedly calling for strike action without serious preparation and on issues which are in no way linked up to the grievances existing in the pit'.[60] Proudfoot was also highly critical of the ultra-leftism of some Lanarkshire Communists. Upon being sent to Shotts in September 1930 he described the situation as 'one hell-of-a-mess ... created by the political purists who draft resolutions in the approved 10th plenum etc manner, without understanding what they are drafting or how to apply the decisions some of them are so glib at yapping about'.[61]

Allan's role as leader of a breakaway union whose creation he had cautioned against caused him inner tensions. The 29 year old militant was aware that being 'fairly young and pugnacious ... one may become ultra-leftist'. But although Allan mimicked the rhetoric of the Third Period – 'social fascism is not a deliberate choice but the logical evolution of all social democratic parties' – he was criticised by ultra-left zealots for not having 'taken a critical stand until the last few months when this had become popular'.[62] His position was undermined by the decline of support for militancy amid the industrial devastation of Lanarkshire, and the increasing proportion of UMS members in Fife, a figure which grew from 30 per cent in 1929 to 56 per cent of 'red union' members in 1930.[63] Fife Communists condemned him for pessimism and lack of commitment to the UMS. At the CC in January 1930, Abe Moffat openly attacked Allan's leadership:

> We have a tendency in the Scottish coalfields that the UMS is not the leader of struggle in the pits. Comrade Allan made a statement at a meeting of strikers that the workers must decide and the UMS would help them ... While I say the workers are coming towards us, the leaders of the UMS are saying the UMS is going down ... and the workers have said don't send Allan because of the pessimistic note struck by him.

Allan angrily 'raised the protest that Moffat had not said these things in Scotland' but does not appear to have denied Moffat's allegations.[64] Despite grossly inflated reports of UMS progress 'exceeding our expectation', the union's real predicament – it had less than 3,500 paid up members in 1930 – dissolved what little optimism he might once have harboured for the project.[65] In July 1930, Allan reported that of the union's branches, only eight had single pit committees: 'We have failed to get our roots into the pits'.[66] Such an admission provided fresh ammunition for critics. The previous month the PB had been informed of 'a very serious difference between the leading comrades in Fife, and leading comrades in other parts of the coalfield'. Further evidence of the rift was provided when Moffat and two other UMS organisers submitted a report on the union's Fife gala, highly critical of Allan.[67]

There were also tensions between Proudfoot and helots for the new Comintern line in Central Fife. Once more he contemplated dropping out of party activity and rejected Hutt's suggestion of a holiday: '... the fact remains that I would require to come back to what – to do the same old grind, amongst those that I am more than beginning to despise for their bloody, cowardly, snivelling, crawling and cringing attitude to any and everyone with a little more authority than themselves'.[68] Tensions between UMS activists in East and Central Fife were exacerbated by Abe's domineering personality. In 1930, McArthur complained that he had the most routine work of all the UMS organisers, concluding sarcastically: 'But Christ, I never knew these matters occupied so very little time until Abe told me; and a matter I have had impressed upon me is that Abe spends more time (twice the time in fact) on fighting and attending to cases before the public assistance Coms [Committees] than I do ...'[69]

It was a measure of the desperate plight of the UMS that Allan aligned himself with ultra-leftist moves by Willie Gallacher and Robin Page Arnot, supported by Pollitt, to overcome the union's isolation by making it the driving force in a campaign to build a United Mineworkers of Great Britain during the first half of 1930. But they had misjudged the shifting currents of Comintern policy which condemned the projected adventure as 'a serious mistake and premature'. When Gallacher and Pollitt – not always the consistent opponent of leftism depicted in some recent literature – pursued the issue at the English [sic] Commission of the Comintern in August, they were hammered. The chair, William Weinstone of the CPUSA, ridiculed the weakness of the UMS: 'What was the wisdom that Comrade Pollitt gave us? ... Our union has 1,000 members, the Miners' Federation of Great Britain has over 400,000 ... ' He demanded postponement of its conference 'to effect a change within, to get new cadres', and spelled out a more limited role for the union: it was to act as an exemplary, Communist-led union, not as the vanguard of revolutionary trade unionism in Britain.[70]

These recommendations were acted upon. The CPGB replaced Allan with Proudfoot as general secretary. It had been proposed to Allan 'that he should go to Moscow as MM representative for a period. At first he regarded this as political banishment, but after a careful discussion he accepted the proposals, and admitted that he had not produced the required results'. At the UMS Executive on 10 January 1931, Allan dutifully resigned and moved Proudfoot as his successor. His proposal was unanimously supported.[71]

Proudfoot's appointment was not popular: it was accepted by the other UMS leaders only because it was personally imposed by Pollitt. Taking up office, Proudfoot wrote that it was 'almost impossible to describe the chaos' at the union's Glasgow office; he felt he had been 'left with the baby to hold'.[72] Membership was in dramatic decline, falling from 3,886 in February 1931 to 1,791 a year later, when over

82,000 were employed in the Scots coalfields. After seven months, Proudfoot resigned and withdrew from party activity, declaring himself 'absolutely fed up and disgusted with it all'. The reasons he gave included 'sabotage by leading Party UMS coms' and irregular and inadequate wages which meant that his wife had been forced to approach the Methil branch for money as he had 'gone without dinner four days that week'. He was therefore 'allowing them to make a more popular appointment' which he correctly predicted would be Abe Moffat.[73]

Moffat was left to limit the damage and his term of office was characterised by three developments. First, consolidation of the UMS as a Fife union: by 1934, 80 per cent of members lived there. Second, securing the election of a number of UMS Workmen's Inspectors who campaigned on safety issues. Such appointments established leading activists, including Moffat, as authoritative champions of the miners. It was symptomatic of the refocusing of Communist energies towards more conventional union activity that Moffat informed the CPGB CC in 1933 that: 'In many cases I find our comrades do not know the first thing about workmen's compensation, conditions of employment, etc. To be able to talk on broad political issues, of course, is necessary, but it is an intimate knowledge of these other vital questions which will gain them the confidence of the workers ...'[74] The third policy was the campaign for 'unity' with the reformist unions. Such a strategy was entirely consistent with the drift of Comintern policy towards the popular front, in which the UMS resembled a derelict hulk from a bygone age. Although approaches to the NUSMW received no positive response, the PB took the decision to liquidate the union in December 1935.[75] Pollitt was enthusiastic about the initiative, which he ascribed to Moffat:

> As a result of this the split in the Scottish coalfields has gone. It means we shall soon have an early perspective of one Miners' union for Scotland. It means that comrades like Abe Moffat with influence in Fifeshire will, in my opinion, in the course of six months or so be playing a leading role in the MFGB ... [76]

REFLECTIONS
Miners were different. There is no need to subscribe to the essentialist if politically evasive iconography of their first major historian, the long-term Communist activist Robin Page Arnot, to affirm that our three protagonists were each in their own way indomitable fighters, hard men hewn from hard seams. They grew up in a now vanished

society where hardship, violence, class consciousness and class hatred were part of the air they breathed. With the exception of Allan's months at the SLC, they had little time to read and study. They were essentially schooled in revolutionary politics by their people and their party. Despite their similar ages and backgrounds, their different political histories and personalities provide a corrective to simplified notions of generational unity, the uniformity of party cadres and the processes by which Comintern policies influenced trade unionism. The different paths they took as Communists and their different takes on the party's politics suggest diversity rather than monolithism. This was a CPGB which pursued close control of its cadres, yet did not always attain it. The different responses of our three subjects demonstrates the variability of values and experiences of CPGB activists and their shifting relations with their party.

The destinations our actors moved towards are also suggestive of wider trends in the CPGB. Like so many others, Proudfoot's seam was exhausted by the leftist sectarian excesses of the Third Period. Like so many others, Allan moved from aspiring, all-round political cadre to union official, illustrating the growing bureaucratisation in party and unions. In more striking fashion, Moffat became professional union leader and part-time tribune, operating a distinction between politics and trade unionism which the party would have found intolerable in the early days of the UMS.

Proudfoot was arguably the most strategic and organisationally talented of the three. His cautious approach was born not of timidity but intuitive sensitivity to the shifting moods of the rank and file, honed by years as a checkweighman. His prudent advice to his impetuous Lanarkshire comrades – 'preparation BEFORE and CONSOLIDATION after each move is absolutely essential' – was to be ignored with disastrous consequences. But his own careful preparation for strikes often paid dividends.[77] His sense of when the miners were willing to fight, combined with organisational acumen, permitted him to exercise militant leadership when he judged it timely. Proudfoot's vision was not restricted to militant trade unionism and he was highly critical of the 'syndicalist approach' of many Lanarkshire activists. The pages of the *Spark* stand testimony to his efforts to develop a transformative conception of industrial politics. His commitment to workplace activity was central and he campaigned tirelessly to establish pit committees. In doing so, he cut against the grain of tradition in Fife with its residential, not pit, branches. He railed against the routinism and passivity of the UMS branches and lamented

that the emphasis on internal democracy preceding the union's formation had acted 'to the exclusion of any positive policy we had for
operating at the pits'.[78]

Proudfoot was rightly perceived as antipathetic to Class Against
Class. The CC was informed in 1930 that Proudfoot and McArthur
were 'essentially old liners' who 'do not believe in the radicalisation of
the masses', although it was conceded they had 'the following of the
masses'.[79] This may be one reason why Proudfoot was the least
successful of our trio in achieving national prominence. In addition, his
oscillations between manic activity and depression led to McArthur's
justified condemnation of 'his inability to last the course'.[80] Proudfoot
was not untypical. A Comintern agent in Scotland complained both of
the 'terrible overloading of leading and active comrades with work' as
well as 'a mania among the active comrades to resign from the active
work and even from the Party'.[81]

Allan was a gifted orator and talented agitator. He was tenacious in his
campaign against the 'old gang' in the NUSMW and courageous under
their sustained attacks. Aged only 27, he bested an older generation of
miners' leaders. Allan's constitutional approach to union leadership, and
his faith that rank and file support would eventually translate into
victory, inoculated him against the persistent tendency towards breakaway unionism in the Scottish coalfields. But ultimately he miscalculated
the undemocratic depths to which his opponents would stoop in their
anti-Communist crusade. His former SLP comrades might have more
readily anticipated the mendacity of 'labour fakirs'. Allan was thus
reclaimed for the party line and new unionism. But he was no administrator and the problems of building a revolutionary union in
unpropitious industrial circumstances would have tested the talents of
even the most gifted organiser, as Proudfoot later discovered. McArthur
criticised this flaw in Allan's character: 'a lack of a serious sense of
responsibility, a go-easy, devil-may-care, sometimes flippant and jocular
attitude to organisational questions ...' Allan, in his turn, never forgot
what he saw as Moffat's active part in his removal. However, by 1932 he
was back in a more comfortable role bringing directives from the
Comintern on the need to work in the reformist unions.[82]

Moffat was the most politically limited, yet conventionally the
most successful. A branch activist when the UMS was formed, his
installation as general secretary two and half years later is evidence of
his ambition, drive and pugilistic stamina. His increasingly authoritative leadership was characterised by the consolidation of the UMS as
a militant Fife union rather than the seedbed of revolutionary union-

ism in the British coalfields. Such a role appears to have been congenial to him. In a review of the first five years of the UMS, Moffat
painted a glowing picture of 'a militant miners' union', entirely
concerned with wages, safety and 'building the united front of the
Scottish miners' rather than the establishment of the 'Revolutionary
Workers' Government' enshrined in the union's constitution.[83] If the
Third Period disabled Proudfoot and Allan, the move back to reality
and the united front after 1933 provided Moffat with the chance to
consolidate the opportunity Class Against Class had provided for
him. As Comintern policy moved from ultra-leftism towards the
popular front, he was the right man in the right place. Nevertheless,
his search for stability and 'unity' appears to have reflected genuine
beliefs and just before he died he insisted: 'the moment I became
General Secretary in 1930 [sic] I developed the idea of bringing the
miners together and carried on a consistent campaign for that'.[84]
Pollitt's assessment also suggests that Abe's talents were as union
leader rather than Bolshevik cadre: 'When Moffat spoke at the UMS
Congress it was a good statement from a miner, but not a political
statement from the Party'.[85]

These sketches not only provide insights into personalities, they
illuminate Communism in the Scottish coalfields. Powerful characters
such as Moffat and Proudfoot dominating their locality could unintentionally hinder party development. When Gallacher posed the paradox
of the party's failure to build in Fife where 'the situation is more
favourable than anywhere' in 1932, Allan offered a plausible answer:
'But just as we had four or five years ago a position in East Fife with
Proudfoot who was the central man, so also we have a somewhat similar position in Cowdenbeath and Lumphinnans. But we have three or
four active comrades like Moffat, and these are doing so much, that
workers simply regard them as all sufficient ... '[86] Impressive leaders
took the eye but in 1931 there were only a derisory 55 party members
employed in the Scottish mines, and the burden carried by the leading
activists meant that party cells went out of existence during strikes.
Page Arnot observed that whereas in Fife the UMS leaders 'had real
contact with the masses in several villages, this was more as individuals
and not as members of the party'. During strikes, 'the party disinte-
grates, splits up and becomes a series of individual active strikers ... '[87]
Rather than the UMS replenishing the party with new cadres, the party
became submerged in its red union.

As 1933 dawned, the reality was a weak union and a weak party. Placing
the Scottish coalfields under the microscope and taking full account of

variations in CPGB policy validates traditional assessments.[88] In terms of membership and influence, the Third Period was disastrous. Leftism was indigenous but, quite mistakenly in the conditions prevailing, it was licensed and amplified by a party which should have fought against it. The growing weakness of the CPGB was intimately related to a deteriorating economic and industrial situation: the best judgement is that CPGB politics, based on failure to grasp the balance of class forces and over-estimation of workers' consciousness, acted to exacerbate that weakness, not to ameliorate it.

Variations on an ultra-left line do not detract from this judgement: if CPGB leaders at times acted to restrain leftism, they acted at times to extend it. The primary, although not the sole, influence in Class Against Class was not the CPGB adapting to indigenous problems but the Comintern insisting upon a particular, debilitating adaptation which owed more to the requirements of the Russian leadership than the aspirations of the British or Scottish working class. It goes without saying that Comintern policies had to be translated and applied on the national terrain. We have shown the difficulties and the human cost. Our account depicts in personal terms the pathos of Class Against Class. Our protagonists were working class leaders striving to make sense of a changing world, torn between their own revolutionary impulses and what their experience and their members told them was possible in developing strategies for progress. It is difficult to see how the surreal politics of the Third Period helped.

The UMS these three men strove to build was Britain's most significant example of a revolutionary union. If there was, in difficult circumstances, little alternative to a regrouping of left-wing trade unionists, the revolutionary role the CPGB prescribed for the UMS in an era of working-class defeat marginalised it. In practice it never transcended trade unionism, indeed it was only when Moffat re-engaged with conventional collectivism that any stability was attained. Nor, despite brave attempts to develop women's guilds, did the UMS develop in any significant way a pre-figurative social trade unionism. The view that the Third Period provided for the construction of a Communist culture – at least if we are talking of a culture rooted in the working class – receives slender support.[89] There is little evidence that the counter-culture which Macintyre has celebrated in the 'Little Moscows' was given a significant fillip by the UMS or by other developments.[90] By 1933 coalfield communism was weak. Whether in Lumphinnans or more widely (as in Gallacher's election as MP for West Fife in 1935), it was the return to more realistic politics that underpinned what success there was in the 1930s.

EPILOGUE

David Proudfoot was blacklisted and only intermittently employed in labouring jobs. Active in the Methil Cooperative Society, he eventually secured permanent work as an agent for the Cooperative Insurance Society. For the rest of his life, he maintained a strong sympathy for the Soviet Union. But he remained critical of his former comrades. Following the dissolution of the UMS, which he claimed 'was carried out in this area in the most awful fashion', he continued to complain of the 'incompetents and in some cases hoodlums' in the local party.[91] David Proudfoot died in 1958.

Willie Allan's work in the RILU apparatus did not move him, as it did others, in a more sectarian or egotistical direction. He was critical of the view 'that if you come back from Moscow you are a "big cheese" ... '[92] As a full-timer with the Minority Movement, he campaigned against ultra-leftism but the MM was effectively buried by the end of 1932. He gave up full-time party work and in 1934 moved to Northumberland. As check-weighman at Cambois pit, he was elected in 1937 to the executive of the Northumberland Miners' Association. He become treasurer in 1944. A member of the CPGB CC from 1927 to 1935, he served again from 1937-8. But he played no leading part thereafter. He still sported the soft white scarf, outside his jacket, 1920s style. Into his fifties, he still paid attention to his 'paraffin' and to women. He was esteemed as an orator and raconteur. He left the party in 1956 over Khrushchev's revelations about Stalin. Willie Allan died in 1970.

Abe Moffat was elected to the NUSMW executive in 1940. He became President two years later. He served (later as President, Scottish Area NUM) for nineteen years and played an important role in forging unity among the Scottish miners. Time confirmed and hardened the tendencies noted above. He became an enclosed, cautious, dominant leader intent on developing a disciplined trade unionism. He remained intensely loyal to the party and a member of its CC into the 1950s. He refused to follow Alex out of the party in 1956. But in later years he would never have stomached the control the CPGB had sought to extend over its union cadre in the distant days of his youth. He was succeeded as Scottish NUM president by Alex, who had returned to the party, in 1961. Abe Moffat died in 1975.

This essay has been written as part of the Communist Party Biographical Project involving staff of the Universities of Manchester and Liverpool, financed by ESRC Grant No. R000 23 7924.

NOTES

1. J.D. MacDougall, 'The Scottish coalminer', *Nineteenth Century*, December 1927, p779.
2. A. Campbell, *The Scottish Miners, 1874-1939, vol. 2: trade unions and politics*, Aldershot 2000, ch. 7.
3. Interview with Johnny Boyle, 6 August 1986.
4. I. MacDougall, 'David Proudfoot,' in W. Knox (ed), *Scottish Labour Leaders, 1918-1939: a biographical dictionary*, Edinburgh 1984, pp230-1.
5. *Ibid.*, p231.
6. I. MacDougall (ed), *Militant Miners*, Edinburgh 1981, p70; Boyle interview.
7. *Plebs*, October 1917, p209; MacDougall, *op. cit.*, 1981, pp18-19; *Dunfermline Journal*, 16 April 1921.
8. MacDougall, *op. cit.*, 1984, p233; MacDougall, *op. cit.*, 1981, pp46-7, 70, 137-8.
9. MacDougall hazards Proudfoot joined the party 'around the time of its formation in 1920', MacDougall, *op. cit.*, 1984, p233.
10. The letters (PL) are held in Methil Public Library (MPL), Fife. Those written between 1924 and 1926 are published in MacDougall, *op. cit.*, 1981, pp182-323. PL, 27 January 1925.
11. MacDougall, *op. cit.*, 1981, p70.
12. Russian State Archive of Socio-Political History (RGASPI), 495/100/106, Organising Bureau, 18 September 1923; PL, 9 September 1924; interview with Hugh Sloan, 6 August 1986; Boyle interview.
13. PL, 12 October 1924; see also 10 May 1925.
14. PL, 20 July 1925, 23 May 1926.
15. E. Burns, *The General Strike, May 1926: trades councils in action*, 1926, pp143-4; MacDougall, *op. cit.*, 1981, p91; PL, 15, 23 May 1926.
16. MacDougall, *op. cit.*, 1981, p139; PL, 27 January 1925.
17. Interview with Alex Maxwell, 4 May 2000; with Ella Egan (née Moffat), 6 September 2000; with 'Young' Abe Moffat, 2 November 2000.
18. A. Moffat, *My Life With the Miners*, 1965, p9; S. Macintyre, *Little Moscows: communism and working-class militancy in inter-war Britain*, 1980, pp48-9.
19. Moffat, *op. cit.*, pp9-34.
20. Rab Smith in I. MacDougall (comp.), *Voices from the Hunger Marches*, vol.I, Edinburgh 1990, p94; Moffat, *op. cit.*, p15.
21. Moffat, *op. cit.*, pp28-9; P. Long, 'Abe Moffat, the Fife miners and the United Mineworkers of Scotland: transcript by Paul Long of a 1974 interview', *Scottish Labour History Society Journal*, 17, 1982, p7.
22. Smith, *op. cit.*, p93.
23. Long, *op. cit.*, p10; Moffat, *op. cit.*, p45.
24. PL, 14 July 1927.
25. PL, 4 October 1929; *Workers' Life*, 26 April, 10 May, 7 June 1929; 20 September, 4, 18 October 1929; Moffat, *op. cit.*, p49; Macintyre, *op. cit.*, pp68-9; F.W.S. Craig, *British Parliamentary Election Results, 1918-1949*, Glasgow 1969, p636.
26. 495/100/599, Central Committee, 26 October 1929.
27. Interview with Bill Lauchlan, 5 May 2000; Egan, Moffat interviews; Macintyre, *op. cit.*, p184; MacDougall, *op. cit.*, 1981, p143.

28. Harry McShane in MacDougall, *op. cit.*, 1990, p24.
29. Interview with Ian Munro, 3 May 2000.
30. 495/100/754, Pollitt to Comintern Secretariat. 8 October 1930; National Museum of Labour History (NMLH), CI 12, PB, 26 March, 9 April 1931; Public Record Office (PRO) HW 17/19, GCHQ Decrypt of Comintern Radio Messages, 29 August, 3 September 1935.
31. MacDougall, *op. cit.*, 1981, p36.
32. K. Lunn, 'Reactions to Lithuanian and Polish immigrants in the Lanarkshire coalfield, 1880-1914', in K. Lunn (ed), *Hosts, Immigrants and Minorities*, Folkestone 1980; M. Rodgers, 'The Lithuanian community in Lanarkshire, Scotland, c.1885-1914', *Papers presented to the International Oral History Conference, Amsterdam 24-26 October 1980*, 1, Amsterdam, 1980; A. Campbell, *The Scottish Miners, 1874-1939, vol. 1: industry, work and community*, Aldershot, 2000, ch. 6.
33. Rodgers, *op. cit.*, p22; J.D. White, 'Scottish Lithuanians and the Russian Revolution', *Journal of Baltic Studies*, 6, 1, 1975, p5; PRO AIR 1/560, 'General survey for the past month', 6 March 1918.
34. J.D. MacDougall, *op. cit.*, 1927, p767.
35. *Ibid.*, pp762, 778-9.
36. *Socialist*, 13 January, 24 February, 7 April 1921; 26 January 1922.
37. R. Martin, *Communism and the British Trade Unions*, Oxford 1969, pp19-20, 33; *Worker*, 27 August 1921; National Library of Scotland (NLS), Dep. 227/37A, LMU Council, 24 September 1921.
38. *Socialist*, 26 January, 9 February, 16 March, 27 April 1922; May 1923; 495/100/117, 'H' An Das EK, 19 December 1923.
39. *Worker*, 8 October 1921, 22 September 1923, 4 October 1924; *Workers' Weekly*, 26 September 1924.
40. *Worker*, 7 March, 14 November 1925, 27 February 1926; Dep. 227/41, LMU Council, 1 July 1925.
41. Marion Henery in I. MacDougall, *Voices From The Hunger Marches*, vol.I, Edinburgh 1990, pp48-9; *Worker*, 21 August 1926; J. Klugmann, *History of the Communist Party of Great Britain, vol. 2: the General Strike, 1925-1926*, 1969, p362.
42. *Worker*, 27 August 1921.
43. *Communist*, 27 January 1923; 495/100/233, PB, 8, 15 December 1925; 495/100/235, Organising Bureau, 6 January 1925; 495/100/349, PB, 5 April 1925; CI 28, Pollitt to Political Secretariat (PS) of Executive Committee Communist International (ECCI), 10 December 1928.
44. PL, 16 July 1924; MPL B017, Hodge to Proudfoot, 29 December 1924 and B020, Hodge to Proudfoot, 16 February 1925; PL, 25 March, 2 July 1925; MacDougall, *op. cit.*, 1981, pp70, 118; Moffat, *op. cit.*, p36.
45. *Worker*, 17 October 1925.
46. PL, 29 October, 24 December 1925, 12 March 1926.
47. MacDougall, *op. cit.*, 1984, p234; PL, 21 December 1926.
48. PL, 13 April, 4 May 1927.
49. PL, 21 July 1927.
50. Campbell, *op. cit.*, vol. 2, ch. 6.
51. PL, 12 September 1927.
52. *Workers' Life*, 19 July 1928.

53. PL, 25 December 1928.
54. PL, 28 December 1928.
55. 495/100/498, PB, 13 November 1928; 495/100/494, CC, 18/19 November 1928.
56. CI 28, PS ECCI, 10 December 1928.
57. *Inprecorr*, 1 February 1929; NMLH CP/IND/KLUG/04/03, 'Verbatim report of 10th Congress'.
58. L.J. MacFarlane, *The British Communist Party: its origin and development until 1929*, 1966, pp308-19. In 1930, Pollitt stated that 'in resolution after resolution' the CPGB was condemned 'for not forming the UMS before we had formed it, [that] we were missing the tide', CI 32, Anglo-American Secretariat, 11 August 1930.
59. 495/100/604, PB, 6 March 1929; *Workers' Life*, 8 March 1929.
60. Moffat, *op. cit.*, p52; MPL F008, Executive Committee Report.
61. PL, 27 September 1930.
62. 495/100/493, CC, 7-9 January 1928; 495/100/599, CC, 26 October 1929; 495/100/604, PB, 20 October 1929.
63. Campbell, *op. cit.*, vol. 2, ch. 7.
64. CI 1, CC, 11-12 January 1930.
65. 495/100/598, CC, 7-11 August 1929.
66. CI 1, CC, 19-20 July 1930.
67. CI 11, PB, 12 June 1930; MPL F032, Fife Miners' Gala, 12 June 1930.
68. PL, 2 September 1929.
69. MPL I012, McArthur to Proudfoot, 27 October 1930.
70. CI 31, PS ECCI to CC CPGB, 24 May 1930; CI 32, Anglo-American Secretariat, 11, 12 August 1930. It is incorrect that Pollitt opposed the perspective of a British red miners' union as suggested in M. Worley, 'Reflections on recent British Communist Party history', *Historical Materialism*, 4, 1999, p249.
71. CI 11, PB, 23 December 1930; MPL F256, UMS Executive, 10 January 1931.
72. PL, 14 February 1931; CI 12, PB, 9 April 1931.
73. F123, UMS Income, February 1931; F132, UMS Income, February 1932; F262, UMS Executive, 22 August 1931; PL, 13 September 1931.
74. CI 4, CC, 10 September 1933.
75. CI 15, PB, 20 September, 21 December 1935.
76. CI 7, CC, 4 January 1936.
77. PL, 28 July 1928; MPL I010, Strike at Randolph Colliery.
78. PL, 8, 28 February 1930.
79. CI 1, CC, 19-20 July 1930.
80. MacDougall, *op. cit.*, 1981, p70.
81. 495/100/737, Letter no. 16, 14 September 1931.
82. MacDougall, *op. cit.*, 1981, p133; Information from Eric Wade to A. Campbell, August, 2000; 495/100/833, Pollitt to Jimmy Shields, 9 March 1932.
83. A. Moffat, 'Successes in the Scottish miners' struggles', *Labour Monthly*, 16, 1934, pp165-72; F001, UMS Rules.
84. Long, *op. cit.*, p12.
85. CI 13, PB, 29 December 1932.

86. CI 13, PB, 29 December 1932.
87. CI 12, Scottish District Party Organisation Report, 17 February 1931; CI 2, CC, 19/20 September 1931.
88. For revisionist accounts, see A. Thorpe, 'Stalinism and British Politics', *History*, 83, 1998, pp612-15; A. Thorpe, *The British Communist Party and Moscow 1920-43*, Manchester 2000; M. Worley, 'Class Against Class: the Communist Party of Great Britain, 1927-32', PhD thesis, University of Nottingham 1998 and Worley, *op. cit.*, pp247-9. For an in-depth critique of recent revisionism see J. McIlroy and A. Campbell, 'Nina Ponomareva's Hats', *Labour/Le Travail*, Special Issue, February 2002.
89. M. Worley, 'For a proletarian culture', *Socialist History*, 18, 2000, pp70-91.
90. Macintyre, *op. cit.*, pp71, 173.
91. PL, 21 May 1936.
92. CI 32C, Anglo-American Secretariat, 3 December 1931.

The Young Men Are Moving Together: the Case of Randall Swingler

ANDY CROFT

And so we come to Randall. Why was he
  Of all the Viccamickles noblest, dearest?
Poet and Communist (better than me
  At both activities); his mind the rarest
I'd yet encountered; more than others free
  Through grasp of Holy Wisdom at her fairest.
In that somewhat corrupt ancient community
How was it he achieved complete immunity?

It's hard to say. His various perfections
  Included total lack of egoism,
Playing the flute, with delicate inflections,
  Constant support for heresy and schism
Against the establishment and its connections
  (Though sucking archiepiscopal chrism
In with his mother's milk, named after Cantuar,
But more at home in Arcady or Mantua).

                   Thomas Hodgkin, *Don Tomás*

I

On 28 May 1909, a telegram arrived from Lambeth Palace at Glebe House, Church Lane, Aldershot, congratulating the assistant curate of Aldershot Parish Church and his wife on the birth of their fourth child the previous day. Not every child born to a small-town Anglican curate enjoys the personal attention of the Archbishop of Canterbury, but Randall Carline Swingler always occupied a special place in the affections of Archbishop Randall Davidson, the maternal great-uncle and godfather after whom he was named.[1]

The boy was, however, heir to rather more than a name. On his mother's side there was a long and distinguished history of service in the established Church. Her great-great-great-grandfather was the Reverend Thomas Davidson, lecturer at the Tron Church in Edinburgh and Chaplain to Queen Anne. One of Davidson's sons, William, was a successful merchant in Rotterdam, Edinburgh and London, maintained numerous servants dressed in unsilvered white liveries, and was painted by Joshua Reynolds. He left his entire fortune to his nephew, the Reverend Thomas Randall, on the condition that he change his surname to Davidson, a stipulation evidently motivated by a desire to found a dynasty of Scottish landed gentry. The young man changed his name to Thomas Davidson and thus inherited a fortune and the estates of Muirhouse and Hatton. Raeburn painted his portrait. His son Henry Davidson, a prominent and successful figure in the shipping business of Port Leith, married a cousin of Sir Walter Scott; to their eldest son, born in 1848, they gave the lost family name Randall. After serving briefly as a curate in Dartford, Randall Davidson was appointed Resident Chaplain at Lambeth Palace to Archbishop Tait (an old school friend of his father). At Tait's death in 1882 the responsibility for communicating to the Queen the Archbishop's last thoughts on the succession fell to his Chaplain, and the way he discharged his responsibilities in this delicate political matter earned him the Queen's personal respect and trust. His subsequent rise through the Church was spectacular. Victoria made him her advisor on ecclesiastical appointments, then Dean of Windsor, Bishop of Rochester and Bishop of Winchester. In 1903 he was enthroned as the Archbishop of Canterbury.[2]

Randall Davidson had a sister, Mary, who in 1877 married Colonel Charles Elliott CB, late of the Seaforth Highlanders and the Madras Artillery, advisor to the Maharaja of Mysore, tutor to the Maharaja's sons and Keeper of the Maharaja's Jewels. As a Deputy Commissioner in Nagpore, Madras, Elliot had been responsible for the brutal repression of the mutiny in Raipore, ordering the mass-hanging of rebellious sepoys and earning the admiration of a grateful Empire.[3] One of his sons was prison governor in Bombay, the other served in the Royal Navy. They had one daughter, Mabel Henrietta, born in 1878. Her father died when she was only eleven and she grew up a sheltered, lonely child on the edges of the institutions of Queen Victoria's Church, Army and Empire. As a young woman she used to stay for long periods with her uncle at Farnham Castle (the Bishop of Winchester's residence) and was well known in the district for her singing at sacred concerts. It was there that she met and was courted by Henry Swingler, then studying for the priesthood at the Bishop's Hostel. They were married at Farnham Parish Church in 1903 by the Bishop of Kensington after which bride and groom and their two hundred guests retired to a wedding breakfast at Farnham Castle.

Henry Swingler (later vicar of Long Eaton in Nottingham and Cranbrook in the Weald of Kent) was the son of Henry Swingler JP, Derby iron-master, landlord, mine owner and Deputy Lieutenant of Derbyshire. Employing 1,400 hands on a twenty-seven acre site in Derby, the family business of Eastwood and Swingler built and exported steel railway bridges all over the world, notably to South America and Canada. As the business prospered in the last decades of the nineteenth-century, so did Henry Swingler. He was elected to Derby council, served as a county magistrate, as a director of the Derby Commercial Bank and the Derby Savings Bank, as Chairman of the Derby Gas, Light and Coke Company, a governor of Derby School and Derby Royal Infirmary, President of Derby Children's Hospital and of the Derby Society of Engineers. When he died, Henry Swingler left over £350,000.[4]

Church, Army, Empire, iron and steel, railways and coal, land and banking, represented at Westminster and at Court – this was a remark-able inheritance, an extraordinary concentration of wealth, power and influence, even by the standards of the Edwardian upper-middle classes. There was a governess, a cook, a nanny, an under-nanny, a nursery maid, a kitchen maid, a parlour maid, a gardener, a house maid and the 'monthly nurse' who joined the family for two months after each of the Swinglers' seven children were born. It was a convention-ally strict and remote Edwardian household, and for several years the children saw little of their parents, enjoying an independent, self-contained and sometimes wild existence. After family prayers they spent the day in the nursery or the school-room and would not reap-pear until after tea, the girls dressed in Indian muslin dresses and the boys in little sailor suits.

Their father took the older children on long walks, and read to them from Sir Walter Scott on Saturday evenings. Mrs Swingler had a good soprano voice, and encouraged the children to form a little choir, teach-ing them to sing their way through Gilbert and Sullivan (especially the *Mikado*). All the children had dancing lessons. Arthur, Elizabeth and Randall (at the age of five) learned to play the piano, and Dorothy and Stephen the violin. Mrs Swingler taught herself the viola in order to join the children in a family orchestra, whose finest moment was a performance of the Bach Suite in B Minor, Dorothy and little Stephen playing the violin, Mrs Swingler the viola, Humphrey the cello and Randall the flute. At Christmas the vicarage children provided entertainments – songs, sketches, trios, violin and flute solos – for the local workhouse and for the Mothers' Union.

Once, a missionary came to stay on furlough from India. The children were inspired by her stories and decided to become missionaries when they were older. Their parents were pleased that the missionary zeal had caught fire in the family so quickly, for this was a deeply religious household, in which prayer, scripture, hymn-singing, sacred music and – later – theological debate, informed their daily lives. As small children they learned the Psalms and the *Magnificat*. The Reverend Swingler took prayers each morning, removing the telephone from the hook to avoid interruptions as he translated *ex tempore* the gospel from the Greek:

> The house of childhood was a world of rooms
> Each one a separate virtue. The small back garden
> Sunny with naughtiness our stifled Eden
> Over which always the winged lion of Goodness
> Posed heavy paws above us, and his thunderous
> Mane made lurid all the coloured landscape
> Of pleasure, and the sun's forehead malarial.
> How delicately we trod the fire-breathing grass !
> How cautiously contained our web-like flesh
> In terror of being trapped into happiness !
> While the long cold hands of the black father, Sin,
> Palpably pressed upon our cringing shoulders
> Rooting our knees into the blessed stone,
> Rigid, remote, and utterly benign.[5]

Swingler was educated at home until the age of ten, when he was sent to a preparatory school in Sussex. In 1922 he won an Exhibition to Winchester. Among his contemporaries there were several who later distinguished themselves in public life – the poets Charles Madge, William Empson and Robert Conquest; Kenneth Younger, a Minister in Attlee's Government, George Lowther Steer, *The Times* correspondent in Abyssinia and Spain, William Hayter, British Ambassador in Moscow and John Sparrow, Warden of All Souls. John Willett, Brecht's translator, Frank Thompson, future Communist and brother of the more famous Edward and William Whitelaw, Margaret Thatcher's

Deputy Prime Ministet, joined the school shortly afterwards. Swingler's reputation as a scholar, steeplechase-runner, flautist, poet, actor and reforming head of house brought him many friends and admirers at school, including the future Labour Minister Richard Crossman, Patrick Reilly, British Ambassador in Paris and Moscow, and Evelyn Shuckburgh, Assistant Secretary-General of NATO. He spent his summer holidays staying with the future adult educator and Africanist, Thomas Hodgkin and his family at Bamburgh Castle in Northumberland.

II

In 1928 Swingler went to New College, Oxford to read *Literae Humaniores*. He joined the University Climbing Club and went climbing in Corsica. He won a running Blue and in 1930 helped Oxford win the Hare and Hounds match against Cambridge; as *The Times* reported, 'when R.C. Swingler came through the water, seven yards behind an exhausted R.C.J. Goode and overhauled him in the last stretch, Oxford enthusiasm knew no bounds, for in doing so Swingler had given Oxford two points over the bare necessity for victory'.[6] He played in the Oxford Orchestral Society and the Oxford Opera Club Orchestra, and for a while considered a career as professional flautist. New friends at Oxford included the critic Peter Burra, Simon Nowell-Smith, future assistant editor at the *TLS*, the poet Louis MacNeice, Gabriel Carritt and the composer John Sykes. He wrote Christian verse-plays for an Anglican boys' club and contributed poems to the undergraduate magazine *Farrago*. While other young would-be poets looked to European Modernism, Swingler's early poetry was self-consciously Georgian, owing more to Robert Bridges than to T.S. Eliot. Swingler spent his third year in digs with Jo Stephenson, later Lord Justice of Appeal and Francis Brodrick, son of the 9th Viscount and 1st Earl of Middleton, Secretary of State for War during the Boer War and Secretary of State for India in Balfour's Government. It is hard to imagine a world more different from the one which Swingler later inhabited.[7]

After failing Greats, Swingler left Oxford to teach in private schools in London. In 1933 he married the concert pianist Geraldine Peppin, to whom he had dedicated his first book, *Poems* (1932). Two more collections followed the next year, *Reconstruction* and *Difficult Morning*, bringing him the admiration of poets as various as Auden, Day Lewis, Richard Church and George Barker. With a private income derived from Eastwood and Swingler shares in Argentinian railways, the Swinglers moved to the Cotswolds, where in 1935 their daughter Judy was born. For a young man of his class and time and education Swingler's life was so far conspicuous only because of the number and variety of his talents (and because he combined a taste for athletics, poetry and music in an Oxford generation usually divided between 'Hearties' and 'Aesthetes'). Everything this young man touched seemed to turn to gold. Universally loved, many talented, physically courageous, charming, handsome, wealthy and a natural leader – Swingler's privileged early life suggested that he could have chosen almost any career and enjoyed the apparently effortless success which everyone expected of him:

> Randall Swingler leaves a particularly strong impression on my mind. Physically he resembled a quieter, unemphatic Auden. A golden straw-thatch of hair and intensely blue eyes gave him a Scandinavian look ... In this Cotswold setting Randall looked every inch a poet in the romantic English tradition. Great things were expected of him ... To visit them at Milton was to make a firm connection with a very English cultural continuity. Partly it was the landscape ... the warm positive affirmation of Cotswold stone, the bright air stirring with the exuberance of downland, the ability to look over and across so much that was quintessentially English. Partly it was the quality of the rural cottage-home, the high endeavour and the gaiety, the dawning parenthood and the exulting ambitions that we shared. Of all my friends they had most conspicuously a steady tranquillity of spirit. I thought of Randall as a man wholly dedicated to the poetic role for which he seemed so well endowed.[8]

Within a few months, however, Randall Swingler had exchanged this Cotswold idyll and the 'idiocy of rural life' for London and revolutionary politics. For the next twenty years Swingler was the Communist Party's best-known poet, and one of its most prominent cultural spokesmen. He edited the best-selling *Left Review*, one of the key institutions of the Popular Front in Britain, a magazine that wore its Marxism lightly, generally unsectarian, and rarely confusing literary considerations with political ones. At *Left Review* he published and helped edit Nancy Cunard's famous *Authors Take Sides on the Spanish War*, selling five thousand copies in two weeks. He was a regular speaker at party, YCL and *Daily Worker* meetings, taught at the Marx Memorial Library and Workers' School, and spoke at Left Book Club (LBC) meetings, summer schools and week-end schools. In 1937

Swingler gave the first Ralph Fox Memorial lecture. He reviewed books for the *Daily Worker*, where he also worked as an occasional sub-editor. He and Alan Bush edited *The Left Song Book* (1938) for the LBC. That year he launched his own radical paperback publishing company, Fore Publications.[9] He contributed several plays for Unity Theatre, including the Mass Declamation *Spain*, the Munich-play *Crisis* and revues like *Sandbag Follies* and *Get Cracking*. He was active in the Workers Music Association, for whom he and Alan Bush wrote many songs, and in the LBC's Writers and Readers Group, Poets Group, Musicians Group and Theatre Guild. Swingler and Alan Bush wrote *Peace and Prosperity* for the London Choral Union, and a radically re-written production of Handel's *Belshazzar* for the London Co-operative Movement. In 1939 they organised the massive Festival of Music and the People, including an Albert Hall pageant written by Swingler and starring Paul Robeson, and the premier of Britten's *Ballad of Heroes*, for which Swingler and Auden wrote the libretto.

Randall Swingler was a distinguished recruit to the party, a widely-published and respected writer who provided an important link between King Street and literary London. He was involved in negotiations with Allen Lane for the re-launch of *Left Review* by Penguin. He wrote a new version of *Peer Gynt* for Rupert Doone's celebrated Group Theatre (where he was assistant editor of the *Group Theatre Magazine*). His poems were set to music by Benjamin Britten and John Ireland; his 'Music and the People' pageant was set to music by Vaughan Williams, Arnold Cooke, Elizabeth Lutyens, Victor Yates, Edmund Rubbra, Erik Chisholm, Christian Darnton, Frederic Austin, Norman Demuth, Alan Bush, Elizabeth Maconchy and Alan Rawsthorne. He published two novels, *No Escape* (1937) and *To Town* (1939) and contributed reviews, stories and poems to all the most important literary magazines of the period – *New Writing, Life and Letters, Purpose, New English Weekly, Twentieth Century Verse, New Verse*. He and Auden were the only English poets who were included (with Alberti, Aragon, Guillen, Hughes, Lorca, Neruda and Tzara) in *Les Poetes du Monde Defend le Peuple Espagnol* (1937). Swingler also wrote the words of the chorale finale for Alan Bush's first piano concerto, broadcast by the BBC in 1938.[10]

Despite his background (and unmistakably patrician voice) Swingler's loyalty to the party was never doubted. He was close to several senior figures, including Harry Pollitt and J.R. Campbell. Through the party's Ralph Fox (Writers') Group (which often met at the Swinglers' flat) Swingler came into contact with intrigues inside the

French party's cultural apparatus (he attended Le Congrès des Ecrivains in Paris in 1937), and with the League of American Writers. When in 1939 the Comintern apparatus demanded the removal of Ralph Wright as literary editor of the *Daily Worker*, he was replaced by Swingler. In the absence of Walter Holmes, Swingler was a frequent guest-writer of the popular 'Worker's Notebook' in the *Daily Worker*. Although Swingler was fiercely opposed to the Comintern's 'imperialist war' thesis (he had a meeting with Pollitt on 14 September, the day Pollitt received and suppressed the Soviet press telegram characterising the war as 'imperialist') he did not hesitate to prosecute the new line in the 'Men and Books' page in the *Daily Worker*.[11] During the first months of the war he reported on the blitz for the paper, and was on a *Daily Worker* national speaking tour when the paper was banned in 1941. A supporter of the People's Convention, launched by the CPGB to publicise its anti-war stand, he was active on its Committee of Arts and Entertainments. He edited *Poetry and the People*, expanded and re-launched as *Our Time*, first as an anti-war magazine and later (after the invasion of the Soviet Union and the CPGB's turn to supporting the war) as an organ of war-time cultural propaganda. He was called up at the end of 1941.[12]

III

Swingler's political trajectory seems, at a glance, to conform to the caricature of the 1930s upper-class radical satirised by Anthony Powell in the character of Erridge in *Casanova's Chinese Restaurant* (1960), an example of what Orwell called 'the public-school-university-Bloomsbury pattern':

> Here was a church, an army, an orthodoxy, a discipline. Here was a Fatherland and – at any rate since 1935 or thereabouts – a Fuehrer. All the loyalties and superstitions that the intellect had seemingly banished could come rushing back under the thinnest of disguises. Patriotism, religion, empire, military glory – all in one word – Russia. Father, king, leader, hero, saviour – all in one word, Stalin. God – Stalin. The devil – Hitler. Heaven – Moscow. Hell – Berlin. All the gaps were filled up. So, after all, the 'Communism' of the English intellectual is something explicable enough. It is the patriotism of the deracinated.[13]

Considering the importance of this characterisation to anti-Communist historiography, the number of gifted, gilded youths like

Swingler who joined the CPGB in the 1930s is a curiously unexplained, not to say unexplored, phenomenon. Among them were well-known figures such as the Carritt brothers, Philip Toynbee, John Cornford, Wogan Phillips, Noreen Branson, Ivor Montagu, Nancy Cunard and Jessica Mitford. The fact that the godson of the Archbishop of Canterbury (like the Young Man of Great Possessions) gave away most of his inherited wealth to the CPGB and the *Daily Worker* ought to have guaranteed Swingler a special place in Cold War literature. And yet Swingler remains a largely forgotten figure. As a result, an important moment in the party's cultural history is missing from the record – its lively, internal educational and artistic life, its rapid and long-term radicalisation of Fitzrovia, the development of a native Marxist literary criticism and the exploration of ideas of Englishness and popular tradition – rendering the famous 'entry of the intellectuals' a phenomenon explicable only by Cold War cliché.[14]

In the case of Randall Swingler – which is of course at the same time suggestively representative and wholly untypical – the decision to join the party was neither sudden nor short-lived. And it had nothing to do with looking for a new 'faith'. Although it was expressed as the passing of one sensibility – Christian, Wykehamist, and class-bound – his Communism nevertheless owed a good deal to the intellectual formation of that sensibility – Christian Platonism, evangelical witness, the public-school cult of Beauty and Nature, and Wykehamist principles of service. Swingler's Communism was always partly romantic *and* partly puritan. He may have spent his life in flight from his class and kind, but his rejection of the worldly was always combined with a fierce passion for the world.

There are several ways in which Swingler may be said to have negotiated his passage towards Communism in the early 1930s, so that the political events which seem now to give the decade its historical shape – the hunger marches, Abyssinia, Spain, Austria, Manchuria, Czechoslovakia – were felt by him simply as confirmation of firmly held convictions. The first was generational. In April 1930 the literary weekly *Everyman* published a letter from E.M. Barraud 'The Revolt of Youth' (or the lack of it). The letter struck a chord. *Everyman* was overwhelmed by letters supporting Barraud's appeal for 'Youth' to have its say (and thereby proving her wrong in her assessment of the mood of a generation). The correspondence dominated the paper for eleven weeks, and was still running twelve months later. Swingler was one of those who was excited by the idea of the Revolt of Youth, and while a student attended a series of meetings in London called by

Barraud. By June they had founded a new organisation, whose aim was 'to combat the humbug and hypocrisy, the muddle and the inertia and the ugliness that everywhere surrounds us today.' Within a few weeks they had over 600 members.

It was a generational revolt, not an ideological one; they saw themselves pitted against the 'Old Men' who were likely to lead Britain into another war. They took their social criticism from Shaw, Lawrence, Huxley and A.S. Neill, their politics from Lenin and Gandhi, their economics from Marx and Major Douglas, and their psychology from Freud and Havelock Ellis, while in Wells's *The Open Conspiracy* they believed they possessed a text-book for changing the world. The Promethean Society looks now like a false-start in the intellectual history of the period. But for Swingler it was a brief and clarifying moment which alerted him to a moral vocabulary which was neither literary nor scriptural.

Shortly after leaving Oxford Swingler finished a verse-sequence entitled 'Revolutionary Poem', invoking the Holy Spirit and calling for the gift of tongues to express a militant crusade on behalf of the 'people of the sun/ That have been hid so long away':

> But the young men are moving together :
> Have felt the reservoirs crack, have seen
> The shadows lurch down from the hills and the meadow green
> Grown lurid beneath the grave thunder-weather.
>
> The young limbs stir from sleep: as yet
> Outward towards the fingers runs
> The swift blood, always out from the heart: will soon
> The marsh be drained, the channels loud in spate.
>
> Look out you walled in wool of night
> That crouch; these are salvation, these
> Hands turn not back, take all that darkness has
> And with strong tension wrestle it into light.[15]

The sequence runs through the generational iconography of what would soon be called the Audenesque – sunlight against shadow, desire against reason, movement against stasis, spring against winter, youth against middle age, the pressure of the future against the weight of the past. But 'Revolutionary Poem' was finished in December 1931 – five months before the publication of Auden's *The Orators* or Michael

Roberts' *New Signatures* (the anthology which first brought the poetry of Auden, Day Lewis and Spender to a wider audience) and two years before either Spender's *Poems* or Day Lewis's *Magnetic Mountain*.[16] Just what kind of revolution these young men were supposed to be moving towards is not entirely clear (though this was also a characteristic aspect of the Audenesque) but Swingler at least understood it to derive from the Christian tradition.

The second, then, was theological. Until the mid-1930s he was a committed Christian and a practising Anglican. At Oxford he had been active in the St Ebbe's Boys Club and an Oxford representative of the Winchester-College Mission. But the seriousness of his Christian convictions and the passion with which he held them increasingly brought him into conflict with the Church, and with his parents. Family meals in the holidays becoming increasingly animated by theological discussions. Swingler could not conceal his disagreements during the Reverend Swingler's sermons, grimacing and turning round in theatrical protest. When William Temple visited the University in Hilary term 1931 Swingler and his brother Humphrey (now at Worcester College) went to hear Temple preach, excited by the radical, social strain of Temple's teaching. Swingler even briefly became a disciple of Frank Buchman, then at the height of his influence in the universities. For a while, the Buchmanites used to meet in Swingler's digs. It is not difficult to see how the 'muscular Christianity' of the Oxford Group (later known as Moral Rearmament) would have appealed to Swingler, with their evangelical call for a life of sacrifice and service in the world. It seems to have had a natural attraction for a certain kind of Wykehamist:

> He was a spiritual character for whom that kind of exhibitionism, almost, would appeal, although God knows, he wasn't an exhibitionist at all. But I can imagine him being attracted to it. He was self-denying, a very self-denying character, and the fact that he always looked so cold and so hungry and so thin was also an expression of his spiritual attitude. I certainly thought of him like that. He always looked saintly, like one of St Francis' followers. He looked cold and pinched and self-denying. I did get the impression that he ate very little.[17]

Early in 1932 Swingler arranged to have printed a one-act play. *Crucifixus* was a passion play, a verse-drama designed for liturgical rather than dramatic effect. As the play opens on a bare stage, lit from behind, Fear and Waste are preparing the Cross, discussing the folly of the man who will soon die upon it. Fear admires the way he stood up to 'those ferrety priests' but thinks he 'went too far' ('There might have been a revolution'), while Waste believes he was a 'menace to reasonable society'. Having raised the Cross centre-stage, they are replaced by Pedantry ('some quite original ideas./ But of course he was hopelessly muddled') and Policy ('determination like his might have carried him far/ if directed along the proper channels'). There follow three processions – a crowd of shepherds, ploughmen, fishermen, manual labourers, factory hands and clerks, a crowd of usurers, barristers, jailers and soldiers marching blindfold and a third crowd of suicides, thieves and harlots, a drunkard, a plutocrat, a priest and a teacher. The three groups combine to form the play's Chorus, a rising lamentation for the defeat of the world's one hope:

> So at the vacant corners the wind returns
> and we return to our dirty corners and bow
> before our masters, knowing, hoping for nothing.
> Pouncing in the dark we look perpetually
> to have clutched on good luck: but grasping have no joy.
> The long-expected dies, sky falls on harvest,
> the honoured defrauds, turning all to loss.[18]

Crucifixus ends with the death of Christ and not with the Resurrection, using the Easter story to claim a divinity for the resurrection of the common human spirit over adversity, oppression and death. Mary and John then approach the foot of the Cross to claim the vision of Love he has shown them, the valuable dream 'Of the world's harmony and the beautiful/ Communities of men' before the man on the Cross addresses the audience in the moment of his death:

> Renouncing every pretentious tyranny within ourselves
> Advance with the wind from a new station of humility
> To extend governorship over that obscure territory.
> Advance with no bugle clamour nor the imposture of banners
> But with ingrained assurance of the trained
> Muscle's immediate contact with good
> And of the benediction of selfless labour.
>
> This is our valuable dream
> That washes the globe of brain through with brightness
> Of the world's harmony and the beautiful

Communities of men. Of broken thraldoms
Of self in the liberation of service.[19]

John Sykes wrote to say he had heard his friend had written a play. 'Somebody said it was Communist – whatever that may mean, but I think I do know what it means. Dimly I have an idea what *you* mean'.[20] Swingler and Sykes were considerably preoccupied by the idea of 'the Risen Lord' (the title of an essay by D.H. Lawrence which they much admired). From Lawrence they took heart in their arguments against a behaviourist view of humanity, against the twentieth-century cult of the primitive, and against the separation of the 'artist' from the rest of society. They agreed that the central problem was 'Man's Divorce from the Body of God, Nature', and that the Church was largely responsible for this. 'Build us, then, a brighter and better world. Such is the cry. A world rid of Empire and Class and Competition, a world soaring to the skies, a world peopled with men and women working selflessly in harmonious energy, a God-intoxicated world'.

The third was geographical. After prep school in Sussex, Winchester, New College and the vicarages in Long Eaton and Cranbrook, living in London obliged Swingler to reconsider the society in which he occupied such a privileged position. His second collection, *Reconstruction,* was a renunciation of the rural landscape of his early verse in favour of the 'Tentacular town'. Swingler was reconstructing *himself* – as an urban poet, and as an inhabitant of a city which reveals its potential for a different kind of beauty, as in 'Sunset Over Camden Town':

> At whom the sun set over tangled rails,
> spidering gantreys and the tall emaciated
> mansions ghosted into a fading past:
> suddenly those wells of excitement of which he tells
> were true in me, hot springs breaking the heart's crust,
> splashing the sky with the huge emotion of kindness,
> clearance of white decks for a new day, endowment
> to a few arms of unsuspected power.[21]

The poems were an emotional and political response to living in London, the 'snore of metal' and the 'traffic's shingle-roar', 'sprawling industry's benighted limbs' and the 'rank allotment'. But the 'jungle-city' is also 'perplexed England', her 'self-contained defensive/houses' ruined by 'that power which division squanders, that poor love/that rots in hoarding'. When over the next few years Swingler turned repeatedly to the idea that political commitment was unavoidable for his generation, he expressed it, significantly, as a choice between rural and urban living:

> Looking about me I saw a curling country
> Of hills and valleys like a heap of snakes,
> At the edge, beyond their heads, the magnificent mountains
> Like clouds; and at first a comfort like falling water
> And universal delicate sorrow
> Sank out of all my veins.
> I was joined to this hill with roots like a nipple
> To the breast and I thought the plains
> Were flowing with waves of light like eternal lakes
> Where cranes flew up out of the enormous grasses
> Freighted with legends, and the curious grebe
> Darted and elegantly towed their icy reflections
> And sunlight floated warm and rich on the grasses
> Buoying their seeds. And I thought for a time
> I was alone and joined with this delectable
> Land. But I was wrong.
>
> For looking longer that landscape came
> Within a new focus. Not snowy were those mountains
> But rolling trains of smoke; under the hills
> Furnaces glared like lions and the hiss
> Of their running metal was a serpent's laughter.
> Thicker and blacker were those hills forested
> With slums than with cat-like pinewoods, and the rush
> Of people passing in the streets, the crush of their feet
> Denser than any wind in the summer grass.
> No cranes in the air slanted, but planes
> Side-slipped from the hanging clouds
> And ran out, easeful, on to the polished grass
> Like ducks on water, leaving their whale-like hangars
> White-bellied behind them. And I knew
> That I was not alone.[22]

IV

It is not clear exactly when Swingler joined the party, but by early 1934 he was already in touch with the British section of the Writers'

International (WI), launched at the Conway Hall in February of that year. Tom Wintringham, one of the twelve CPGB leaders gaoled in 1925-6, was secretary, the poet Edgell Rickword, formerly editor of *The Calendar of Modern Letters* and *Scrutinies*, was treasurer; John Strachey, Ralph Fox and Michael Davidson constituted the rest of the executive committee. Following the model of the John Reed Clubs in the USA and the *Association des Ecrivains et Artistes Revolutionaires* in France, the organisation saw itself as a focus for 'revolutionary writers' of all classes in Britain, and in October 1934 they launched the magazine *Left Review*. The first issue which carried a little poem by Swingler, reproduced the WI's founding statement:

> There is a crisis of ideas in the capitalist world to-day not less considerable than the crisis in economics. Increasing numbers of people are reading seriously, trying to get some insight as to the causes of events that are shattering the world they know, and some understanding of the reasons for men's actions. And increasingly they are being given, not insight or understanding, but *distraction*. Journalism, literature, the theatre, are developing in technique while narrowing in content; they cannot escape their present triviality until they deal with the events and issues that matter; the death of an old world and the birth of a new.[23]

It is not difficult to see why Randall Swingler should have identified with such welcome clarity and seriousness of purpose after the earnest naivety of the radical literary magazines with which he had hitherto been associated. He immediately joined the discussion in *Left Review* around the statement:

> It is the function of art to resolve problems, not to evade them, and the creed of socialism is a great deal more than a political programme ... the artist is not a special sort of being, inhabiting a rarefied atmosphere beyond the exigencies of common life. Rather it lies in his essence to have more than usual in common with the generality of men. Consequently, while he strives to achieve the maximum of effectiveness in his work, that effectiveness, as with all men, will depend upon the extent to which he himself is a fully alive human being ... He must express the needs of all men, the correlating but inhibited desires of every class. But his work and its effect will be resisted by the individual as strongly as the need itself was suppressed. For the needs are communal, a giving away of the self; the salvation of our present spiritual chaos can only be through the death of self-interest to the resurrection of

community interest and the right relation of men; 'the death of the old
world and the birth of a new.' To undergo communal experience involves
a death of the self, the sacrifice of the seclusion which stifles our happi-
ness in anxiety, and from which so few souls have dared to emerge : to
recognise a communal need is to be liable at once to a claim which will
be desperately hard and perhaps dangerous to answer ... [24]

Swingler was here drawing together all the forces that had shaped
his life up to this point – the Romantic conception of the artist,
Wykehamist notions of public service, Anglican paternalist ideas of
community, the Georgian dream of sharing in the life of the common
people, Marxist ideas of consciousness, ideology and class, and the
New Testament call to be born again. 'We must form ourselves into a
nucleus', he wrote, 'a hard core of understanding in the middle of this
cascade of print and blurb', in order to maintain the integrity of 'the
true function of the artist', and 'the development of life towards freedom'. The apparently discrete vocabularies of generational revolt, of
country and city, and of the Christian story, each represented for
Swingler a desire to belong, to inhabit a larger world than the privileged one into which he had been born.

In the party he had found the intellectual home for which he had
been searching, and where he was to remain until 1956:

> Round and round the prisoner goes
> And his every corner knows,
> Dreams he hides from, on the walls
> Hang like bats. And hidden scrawls
> Chart his rare illuminations
> On the margin of his patience.
>
> Day by day his quivering eye
> Gazes at the passers-by
> And his desperate hand appears
> Signalling between the bars.
> By night, in his own darkness caught,
> He fills the sullen space with thought.
>
> This he knows and this he sees,
> Infinite complexities,
> Useless all while he is locked
> In zero from the world of act,

THE YOUNG MEN ARE MOVING TOGETHER

Useless all when he is dead,
With nothing done and nothing said.

I am that prisoner who strives
To link himself with other lives
But always finds himself alone
Prisoned within walls of stone,
Whose mental world is thin and false
As shadows painted on the walls.

The walls of stone my parents built
By false respect and sense of guilt,
Upon the walls the painted gloss
Is compensation for my loss.
My love of life within the cage
Pent like a panther purrs with rage.

This prison and this iron gate
The safety of my class and state
Constrain the growth of hand and eye,
My dangerous humanity,
And what was love is made by fear
Hatred of all that comes most near.

Yet sometimes I have passed a note
In secret to the world without;
And tapping through the walls have found
Answers returned from underground
Where lives the working multitude
Whom force and fraud have kept subdued.

And now no more my thought repines
In metaphysical designs.
My fingers bleed, my nails are raw
With tunnelling beneath the floor,
That we may meet and move at last
To storm this prison of the past,

And opened to the light of fact
Our thought may become truth in act.
For we could use those walls of stone

> To build a city of our own
> Where truth must work to make us free
> And justice mean our unity.[25]

Swingler soon found himself among old friends in the party – Thomas Hodgkin, Kenneth Knowles, Humphrey Searle, Robert Conquest, Charles Madge (Winchester), Goronwy Rees, Gabriel Carritt, Richard Goodman, Geoffrey Bing (New College), Derek Kahn, Cecil Day Lewis (*Farrago*), Pat Sloan, Geoffrey Trease, E.M. Barraud (the Promethean Society). Both Swingler's brothers and two of his sisters joined the party; so did his wife Geraldine and her twin sister, Mary. Regular visitors to their garden flat on Primrose Hill included party figures like Walter Holmes, Claud Cockburn and Dave Springhall; Communist writers like Montagu Slater, Edgell Rickword, John Sommerfield, Arthur Calder-Marshall, Maurice Carpenter and Honor Arundel; Unity figures like John Allen, Alfie Bass, Ted Willis, Ann Davies and Roger Woddis; musicians like Constant Lambert, Elizabeth Lutyens, James Gibb, Christian Darnton, Alan Rawsthorne, Alan Bush and Arnold Goldsborough; the jazz-band leaders Van Phillips and Ben Frankel; J.B.S. Haldane and his wife Charlotte (dubbed 'hot Lottie' by the Swinglers on account of her revolutionary fervour); Douglas and Paddy Garman moved in with the Swinglers until they could find somewhere to live. Each of these had followed different, though sometimes overlapping, paths towards Communism. But to each it seemed to provide a political home which was adequate to their generation and to the years of social, economic and political crisis in which they came to adulthood. Often sharing an upper-middle-class Anglican background, the same public schools and the same universities, it is not surprising that they should follow a similar political trajectory.

The Swinglers were young, talented, glamorous, funny and famous, an extremely good-looking couple, Geraldine with shoulder-length hair, Swingler the handsome image of Jean Gabin. Their love for each other was obvious to all who knew them, though this did not prevent either of them from embarking on a series of romantic adventures and a great many affairs, some passionate, some casual. Between parties at their flat, meetings of the St Pancras party, nights at Unity Theatre at Collins Music Hall on Islington Green and the pubs and clubs of Soho, the Swinglers were at the social centre of the overlapping worlds of Communism, literature, theatre and music, high-minded Hampstead and boozy Fitzrovia:

The Young Men Are Moving Together

The pub is the place where good comrades are found,
For the day's work is done so we'll call one more round.
Be it cider or guinness or fine tawny port
Or gin by the gill or good ale by the quart.

Here's a plague on the brewer who waters it down,
Till you can't tell the difference 'tween bitter and brown,
And another on the Government that taxes our beer
While profits are mounting by millions a year.

Damnation to the martyr, the saint and the prig,
Whose bladders are too small and whose pride is too big.
And the worst we can wish them is the hell that they fear
A tropical country where you can't buy a beer.

Here's a health to the Red Army whom Hitler detests
And the kick in the panzers we'll give in the west,
Here's a health to the Soviets where the lads own the land
And here's to the day when all workers join hands.

Here's a health to our freedom and may it grow great:
When we take a hand in controlling the state
We'll clear out the fakers and the fat profiteers
And throw all the big-wigs outside on their ears.

Then all may be happy and work with a will,
For we'll own the factory, the farm and the mill,
And when ale's brewed for drinking and not for profit's sake
We'll put plenty of hops in and avoid belly-ache.

So lift up your elbows and lift 'em up high
And tip up your glasses till the heel taps the sky
We'll drink to each other and drink to the day
When working men and women have it all their own way.[26]

I am grateful to Judy Williams for permission to quote from her father's papers, and to Dorothy Swingler, Elizabeth Dart and Mabel Swingler for helping to reconstruct aspects of their brother's early years.

NOTES

1. The birth was of course announced in *The Times*, Saturday 29 May 1909; according to Swingler, the bishops would gather round the baby on visits to Lambeth Palace, saying 'It's my turn to bath the boy tonight', 'no, no, Canterbury, it's York's turn'.

2. See G.K.A. Bell, *Randall Davidson: Archbishop of Canterbury*, Oxford 1952.

3. 'Fortunately there was at Raepore an officer, Lieutenant Charles Elliot, but little known yet, whose stern and lofty determination to support the dignity and authority of Government has not been surpassed by any one during the past eventful year', *Friend of India*, 4 February 1858.

4. Swingler and Eastwood went into liquidation in 1925; the present Rolls Royce foundry now occupies the old Swingler and Eastwood site on Cotton Lane; the account of Henry Swingler's twenty-first birthday celebrations in the *Derby Mercury*, 26 September 1864, reads like a scene from *The Ragged Trousered Philanthropists*.

5. 'Puritan Childhood' in Randall Swingler, *The God in the Cave*, 1950.

6. *The Times*, 15 December 1930; there was a pictorial report of the match in the *Illustrated Sporting and Dramatic News*, 20 December 1930; the *Daily Telegraph*, 5 March 1931, carried a photograph of the Oxford University athletic team against Cambridge, including J.C. Swingler (*sic*).

7. Swingler showed no interest in politics at Oxford; his only contribution to the New College Essay Society was a defence of the public school system.

8. Desmond Hawkins, *When I Was: a memoir of the years between the Wars*, 1989, p151.

9. See A. Croft, 'The boys around the corner: the story of Fore Publications', in A. Croft (ed), *A Weapon in the Struggle: essays on the cultural history of the British Communist Party*, 1998.

10. Because the BBC were uncomfortable with the political implications of Swingler's text, Adrian Boult led the orchestra and choir straight into *God Save the King* in an attempt to undo the effect of the work on its listeners. For an assessment of Swingler's late 1930s verse, see A. Rattenbury, 'Poems by Randall Swingler' and 'Total Attainder and the Helots' in J. Lucas (ed), *The 1930s: a challenge to orthodoxy*, Hassocks 1978.

11. According to Edward Thompson, Swingler was the night editor at the *Daily Worker* on 4 September: 'As the deadline for the press approached, Swingler glancing idly at the incoming ticker-tape noticed with alarm that German tanks had crossed the frontier into Poland ... He ran down, stopped the presses and, on the stone, wrote out a defiant editorial committing the paper (and the movement) to support of the war, concluding, "This is a war which can and must be won." He was met the next morning with grave faces and grave rebukes; how could a *poet* determine the political line of the Party? But the Party, none the less, was committed ...', E.P. Thompson, *Beyond the Frontier*, Woodbridge 1997. This is an unlikely story, not least because the party leadership was at that stage in complete accord with the 4 September editorial, but it is clear that Swingler identified himself with the Pollitt-Campbell-Gallacher line of 4 September, and not with the later Dutt-Rust line of opposition to the war.

12. For Swingler's experiences during the Second World War, see A. Croft,

'The best of corporals: the Italian Campaign in the poetry of Randall Swingler', *London Magazine,* October/November 1998; during the war, Geraldine combined a successful and distinguished career as a concert pianist, playing with her sister Mary on CEMA and ENSA tours, with heavy commitments in the party's women's organisations and in the Musicians Union (where she was notoriously successful in recruiting to the Communist Party).

13. G. Orwell, *Inside the Whale*, 1940, reprinted in *The Collected Essays, Journalism and Letters of George Orwell,* vol 1, Harmondsworth 1970, p565.

14. For the party's literary history see A. Croft, 'Writers, the Communist Party and the Battle of Ideas, 1945-50', *Socialist History,* 5, 1995, and 'Authors take sides: writers and the Communist Party, 1920-56', in G. Andrews, N. Fishman and K. Morgan (eds), *Opening the Books : new perspectives in the history of British communism*, 1995.

15. Part of this poem was later incorporated in 'Sunset Over Camden Town' in *Reconstruction*.

16. For a discussion of Swingler's early poetry, see A. Croft, 'Politics and beauty: the poetry of Randall Swingler', in K. Williams and S. Matthews (eds), *Re-writing the Thirties*, 1997.

17. Interview with Gabriel Carritt, 29 July 1993.

18. R. Swingler, *Crucifixus: a drama*, 1932; part of the play was published in the Promethean Society journal, *Twentieth Century*, October 1932.

19. Swingler continued to employ Christian iconography in his writings, notably in several carols he wrote with John Sykes, in *The Sword of the Spirit*, 1941, *A Winter Journey* (with Alan Bush) 1946, 'The Ballad of Herod Templer', 1952, *A Canticle of Man* (with Alan Rawsthorne) 1953, *The Harvest of Peace* (with Bernard Stevens) 1953, *The Fall of Babylon*, 1957, and *Et Resurrexit* (with Bernard Stevens) 1966; some time during the early 1950s Swingler wrote an unpublished 'Requiem Mass for the Korean War'.

20. John Sykes, undated letter to Swingler, April 1933.

21. 'Sunset over Camden Town', in R. Swingler, *Reconstruction*, Oxford 1933.

22. From 'Entrance to the City', an unpublished 700 line poem written 1934-5.

23. For *Left Review,* see D. Margolies (ed), *Writing the Revolution: cultural criticism from Left Review*, 1998.

24. 'Controversy', *Left Review*, December 1934.

25. R. Swingler, 'The Prisoner', first published in *Life and Letters Today*, Summer 1938.

26. R. Swingler, 'Drinking Song', set to music by Christian Darnton in August 1941, and published in J. Manifold (ed), *The Book of Words*, 1946.

From 'Insufferable Petty Bourgeois' to Trusted Communist: Jack Gaster, the Revolutionary Policy Committee and the Communist Party

GIDON COHEN

So far, history yields only rare glimpses of Jack Gaster. He is typically and minimally encapsulated in a series of labels: 'son of the famous Rabbi', 'a London lawyer' or, more expansively, 'a lawyer who became convinced that the way forward was for the ILP to associate with the Communist International'.[1] Telling us little more about the man, this shorthand usefully denotes Gaster's hitherto unexplored triple interest for historians. Gaster was a Jew who renounced his background to become a Marxist. He was a key player in the inadequately analysed and often misunderstood tragedy of the Independent Labour Party (ILP) in the 1930s. And finally, he was, for more than half a century, a loyal member of the Communist Party of Great Britain (CPGB) in which he performed a low key but indispensable role as a party lawyer. While the man himself looks back with satisfaction on his long years in the CPGB, it is his coming to communism which is of most obvious relevance to historians of the left. From 1931 to 1935, Gaster led the Revolutionary Policy Committee (RPC) which was influential in the ILP's historic disaffiliation from the Labour Party in 1932. Three years later he led the RPC into the CPGB. These episodes, important in the history of the British left, have been insufficiently scrutinised by historians and they form the core of this chapter.

Where Communist historiography sees the RPC's gravitation to the CPGB as a natural, beneficial progression, ILP-centred histories see a harmful CPGB entrist group and Trotskyist analyses are unable to comprehend what they see as the RPC's baffling choices.[2] This chapter seeks to explore Gaster's reasons for becoming a Communist, searching behind these conflicting conventional images. Examining Gaster's background, his movement towards Marxism and his troubled relationship with the CPGB, his RPC emerges as, at times, fiercely independent of both ILP and Communist Party. Yet, despite conflict and abuse directed at Gaster's 'insufferable petty bourgeois mind' from the CPGB leadership, by 1935 the pull of Communism proved irresistible.[3] Internal splits, faction fighting and policy disagreements played a part. However, this reconstruction of Gaster's political development highlights the magnetic attraction internationalism exercised on young people in the 1930s, an attraction often focused by the certitudes of CPGB politics centred on defence of the USSR and uncomplicated by the doubts, divisions, oscillations and absence of comparable theoretical and spiritual anchorage which enlivened but ultimately undermined the ILP. In the decade before World War II, it was compelling images of international communism and the workers' state in Russia which inspired Gaster's political journey traced here

INTO POLITICS

Moses Gaster was born in Bucharest in 1856 into a famous Jewish family which straddled the Ashkenazi and Sephardi communities. After attending university in Bucharest and Leipzig, and Rabbinical Seminary in Breslau, he lectured on Romanian literature and comparative mythology. However, as a Jew with well-known Zionist sympathies, he was expelled from Romania. In 1885, he came to England, soon obtaining an appointment as Ilchester lecturer in Graeco-Slavonic literature at Oxford University. Within two years of arrival, his academic profile ensured he was appointed to the vacant office of Haham (Chief Rabbi) of the Sephardi community in England at the substantial salary of £720 per annum. Moses married Lucy Leah Freidland, the daughter of the principal of Jews College, in 1891. Later, as the family grew, the Sephardi community provided a large house in Maida Vale. He was heavily involved in the Zionist movement, presiding at Herzl's first public meeting in England. In 1907, he was elected president of the English Zionist Federation and later played a significant part in bringing Zionist and Liberal establishments together.[4]

It was into this environment that Jack Gaster, the twelfth of thirteen children, was born on 6 October 1907. However, Jack's early life was distant from both his parents. The five youngest Gaster children lived on the top floor of the house, nurtured by a German nurse. Their father visited them each evening to listen to prayers, their mother came up only three times a week to deal with any problems with nurse and to see the children. Moreover, the children were evacuated to Brighton for the last years of World War I. In such circumstances, even the dominant presence of Judaism in the family of the Haham made a limited impression on young Jack. A life of 'too many prayers' combined with a 'doubting nature' led him by the time of his bar-mitzvah to reject religion. As a son of the Haham, his personal renunciation of religion did not excuse him from his duties. Reluctant and protesting, he was always expected to make up the minyan, the quorum for a service, when required. [5]

Returning from Brighton in 1918, Gaster completed his schooling at a private establishment in Hampstead and went on to the LSE to study Economics and Government, where he was influenced by Hugh Dalton, H.B. Lees Smith, Kingsley Martin and Harold Laski. However, after only a year he left the LSE and began training as a lawyer, taking articles with the solicitor to the United Synagogue. Gaster had 'the usual life of a young bourgeois fellow', taking a keen interest in music, literature and theatre. At school he had developed an interest in politics, which continued at the LSE, under the influence of a close friend, Peter Manheim, a dealer in antique ceramics who was a member of the ILP. Through 1925, as Gaster was beginning work as an articled clerk, it was becoming clear that a conflict between the miners and the state was unavoidable. He spent the months of simmering conflict between 'Red Friday' and the General Strike studying the situation. ILP leaders, including John Wheatley and Jimmy Maxton, predicted the General Strike months before it happened and the party was alive with discussion. Study and argument led the nineteen-year-old Gaster, under Manheim's ILP guidance, into increasing sympathy with the miners. During the General Strike itself, Gaster was horrified at the role of the blacklegs, who included members of his own family:

> All London Transport was on strike, national transport was on strike, 100 per cent solid, and they used to bring out the buses, driven by a blackleg, with a policeman sitting beside him, and barbed wire across the front, a nice friendly atmosphere to show the people were behind the government … It was a most shocking thing. And what influenced me to some extent were all the blacklegs, who were mostly from the universities and suchlike and included one of my brothers.[6]

Gaster shared Wheatley's perceptions of betrayal by the TUC and 'whining and grovelling' Labour leaders. He was drawn to the ILP, the increasingly left-wing party affiliated to the Labour Party, and joined in November 1926. Gaster launched himself into activity in the ILP's Marylebone branch, beginning with street sales of the *New Leader*. Party literature and discussion were, at this time, his only political influences and he was particularly captivated by the leftward shift of the ILP in the late-1920s under the influence of the party chair, the charismatic Scottish MP, Jimmy Maxton. The ILP's official position was for 'Socialism In Our Time' centred on a 'Living Wage' policy. Gaster eagerly seized on the ideas within the 'Living Wage' policy, developed in part by H.N. Brailsford whom he admired enormously. He was particularly attracted to the idea of a family income, based on wages and child benefit, which would be sufficient for all and would provide a solution to unemployment through tackling the problem of 'under-consumption'. Later describing his attitude as almost that of a 'Christian Socialist', he developed education as his special interest and became involved in the Nursery School movement, looking for 'social engineering from the bottom up'. Soon he became a regular speaker for the ILP, first chairing meetings and, within a few years, taking the plat-form alongside prominent figures such as Fenner Brockway, Maxton and the miners' leader A.J. Cook.

By 1929, Gaster was a senior figure in his local Labour Party, and during the general election of that year he was placed in charge of organising open air meetings in the constituency. He again campaigned for Labour in Marylebone in 1931 and stood as a candidate for the London County Council. But Gaster was disillusioned with Ramsay MacDonald even before the 1929 election. The ensuing disputes over unemployment and the means test between Labour and the ILP during 1929-31 increased his antipathy to the Labour leadership. When in 1931 MacDonald left Labour to head the National Government, Gaster described the move as 'the dirtiest ever done'. However, the Labour Party's hysterical reaction to the betrayal, and the personalisa-tion of the crisis, convinced many in the ILP that the larger party would never solve its fundamental problems. Gaster was at the centre of this group who began arguing that the ILP should disaffiliate from the Labour Party.

THE REVOLUTIONARY POLICY COMMITTEE
Gaster joined with others advocating a break with the larger organisa-tion in an informal 'disaffiliation committee'. Inside this unofficial body, Gaster first came into serious contact with Marxist ideas: his new influence was a leading member of Poplar ILP, Dr C.K. Cullen. Cullen arrived in Poplar to work for the local health authority as a tuberculo-

sis doctor in 1923; by 1930, he was spreading Marxist ideas within the ILP. While the disaffiliation committee was campaigning for breaking ties with the Labour Party, Cullen and, increasingly, his willing recruit Jack Gaster, were committed to the wider aim of developing a 'revolutionary policy' for the ILP. A section of the 'disaffiliation committee' under the leadership of Cullen and Gaster established itself as the RPC. Gaster took the role of chair, with his friend Peter Manheim also active, and the RPC began holding meetings across the country.

In its first public statement in January 1932, the RPC attacked both ILP reformism and the Communists' 'tactics and unsound psychology'. Assuming that capitalism would destroy itself, they concluded that there was no chance that Parliament, by itself, could play a major role in the transition to socialism. They suggested peoples' minds would only be shaken from capitalist prejudices during a revolutionary period, when it would be too late for parliamentary activity. Instead, they argued, 'industrial upheaval is more likely to rouse the spirit of the worker than a general election' and the committee proposed a general strike as a much more likely route to socialism. Consequently, emphasis was placed on the need to build up structures of workers' councils.[7]

Gaster was increasingly recognised as one of the RPC's most useful assets. He qualified as a solicitor in January 1931. His considerable verbal flair and keen legal mind soon saw him acknowledged as the RPC's most able and fluent public speaker.[8] The RPC and associated members of the disaffiliation committee quickly came to play an important part in the machinery of the London Divisional Council of the ILP. In early 1932, Cullen launched a narrowly unsuccessful bid to become London representative on the ILP's National Administrative Committee (NAC). The nine members of the Divisional Executive included three RPC members: Dr C.K. Cullen, Chris Hanson, actually a covert CPGB member, and Bert Matlow, an RPC member with Trotskyist sympathies. The Council itself included other RPCers such Jack Huntz from the Party's youth section and Reg Bower, secretary of the ILP's North London Federation. Gaster, although not elected to the council until the end of the year, attended as an alternate.[9]

With Gaster leading the calls, the RPC's stress on the need to develop a revolutionary policy became an important component of pressure for the ILP to disaffiliate from the Labour Party.[10] But the London Division was the only sizeable ILP division to vote for disaffiliation in 1932. Gaster, ill with appendicitis, missed the ILP's 1932 Annual Conference in Blackpool, where Cullen unsuccessfully moved the break with the Labour Party. However, when disaffiliation eventually came at a Special

Conference at Bradford in July 1932, many saw Cullen and Gaster behind the decision. Indeed, the Bradford Conference enthusiastically accepted Gaster's suggestion, described by later commentators as 'insane', that the split with the Labour Party must be definite.[11] Despite the RPC's leftward pressure on the ILP, the CPGB, caught up in the left sectarianism of the Third Period, would have no truck with Gaster and the Committee. They attacked the ILP for their 'deliberate policy' designed to 'confuse the struggle' as 'the greatest crime that has ever been committed against the working class movement'. The RPC were lumped together with the ILP leadership as having 'nothing for anything but the capitalist'. Commenting on the RPC as well as the wider ILP, CPGB leader Harry Pollitt argued 'there can be no talk of unity, no talk of anything in common, there can only be a war to the death'.[12] He was also abusively dismissive of Gaster's ideas, complaining they demonstrated the 'insufferable conceit of the petty bourgeois mind'.[13]

The Communists were scarcely receptive to RPC approaches for unity, and the ILP leadership was concerned about the RPC's activities. However, Gaster's prospects for bringing the ILP and CPGB together were improved by international developments. Following the rise to power of Hitler in January 1933, the CPGB changed its line towards the ILP. No longer was a 'war to the death' required, instead a united front approach was relaunched and eventually both CPGB and ILP leaders accepted a proposal, which had originated from within the RPC, that the two parties should form a United Communist Party.[14] Over the country as a whole, within both parties, there were problems in implementing this new policy of unity. However, in London, under the leadership of Gaster and the RPC, the ILP and the London District of the CPGB made immediate contact and a new and fruitful relationship began.[15] The CPGB's 1933 shift towards the ILP was now matched by a far more positive assessment of Gaster and the RPC. Through the medium of *Labour Monthly*, the CPGB theoretician Rajani Palme Dutt began attempts to influence the Committee. Increasing coverage of the debates within the ILP, he announced a discussion conference on ILP 'Revolutionary Policy' in the March 1933 issue of the journal. Dutt was still careful to distinguish the 'left centrist line' of the RPC from revolutionary Marxism. But for the first time he began to speak of attaining agreement on 'the basic political platform' and to suggest that 'secondary differences should not be allowed to stand in the way of the great objective union of the revolutionary forces in Britain'.[16]

Within the ILP, Gaster's stock continued to rise. He was increasingly acknowledged as the authoritative voice of the RPC and the Committee itself continued to advance. In September, Gaster was elected to both the London Divisional Council and its executive. At the Divisional Conference the following February, dominated by the RPC, he was selected as the London Divisional Representative on the NAC, making him a national figure.[17] He used his new national prominence to push for the development of RPC policy and its acceptance by the ILP. Gaster's Marxism implied 'general acceptance of [Marx's] interpretations of history, analysis of capitalism and its necessary consequences for the workers'. However, the RPC was not immediately attracted to acceptance of the CPGB brand of Marxism. Indeed, in writings, which also related the disdain with which Gaster now treated his religion of birth, he was scathing about the party:

> Blind faith whether in a mystical god-head, or dead economist, or working class leader is an impossible basis for reasoned action. As the religious 'believer' swears that all else are heathen so now it appears as though the rank-and-file of the Communist Party is taught, believes and repeats on all possible occasions that the Communist Party is the Party of the Chosen People and all else are heathen. They go further and suggest that all who are not within the ranks of the Communist Party are consciously and deliberately traitors to the working class movement. Frankly I cannot accept that.[18]

Gaster and the RPC were thus determined to do their own thinking independent of both ILP and CPGB leaderships. Their policy discussions focussed on three issues: workers' councils, joint activity with the CPGB and tactics to encourage the ILP to approach the Third International for sympathetic affiliation.

The CPGB supported the RPC's efforts to promote joint activity and encourage ILP affiliation to the Comintern. The Committee was having considerable success in pushing these policies within the ILP.[19] At the 1933 Annual Conference, the RPC reached the highpoint of its influence within the ILP, and a policy supporting workers' councils was passed on Gaster's recommendation.[20] However, the CPGB was critical of the RPC's stress on workers' councils, dismissing it as a panacea which implied an unacceptably reduced role for the revolutionary party.[21] Thus, despite increasingly frequent meetings between Gaster and CPGB leaders, his relationship with the Communists remained strained.

During 1933 Gaster sat on the ILP's policy sub-committee and argued with considerable skill for RPC policy on the NAC. As the ILP developed its 'new revolutionary policy', Gaster was able to increase the emphasis on workers' councils.[22] However, following this break-through, his influence came under increasing assault, most notably from the Lancashire Division where the ex-MP Elijah Sandham organised a 'Unity Group' to oppose the factionalism of Gaster and the RPC. The following year, under pressure from the Unity Group, RPC progress faltered. Divided over the exact line to take on the formation of a United Communist Party, the RPC failed to issue its 'monthly' bulletin between May and December 1933.[23] Then, under direct orders from Dutt and the CPGB, Chris Hanson, the London ILP Divisional Propaganda Secretary, and his fellow secret CPGB member, Morgan, set up a 'Comintern Affiliation Committee' within the RPC When Gaster discovered Hanson's covert CPGB membership, he and Cullen met with Pollitt to demand the removal of the entrist group from the ILP. When Pollitt refused, the RPC, acting through the London Divisional Council, expelled them from the ILP.[24] However, despite Gaster's attempts to distance the RPC, Hanson and Morgan's activities appeared to give substance to the widely voiced suspicions in the ILP about the relationship between the RPC and the CPGB.

THE ROAD TO THE COMMUNIST PARTY

Gaster's damaged position and changing perceptions of the RPC within the ILP, were reflected at the 1934 Annual Conference in York. Despite Gaster's success in getting the conference to accept proposals moving the party towards forms of democratic centralism and the acceptance of the 'long term' aim of a united party with the CPGB, RPC proposals were generally soundly defeated. Crucially, the conference declined to make further enquiries to the Comintern about sympathetic affiliation and decided that branches had the discretion to refuse co-operation with the CPGB.[25] The RPC leadership accepted that the ILP conference had rejected the 'lead of the left'.[26]

Following these failures, the confidence of Gaster's opponents in London grew and the RPC came under increasing assault in its area of greatest strength. After the 1934 Conference, C.A. Smith, the sometime Divisional Chair, and John Aplin, the Divisional Organiser, who had both declared dissatisfaction with the RPC's factionalism, decided to increase their attacks. The RPC fought back and heavy theoretical controversy came to dominate all events within the London ILP. The Divisional Conference in February 1935 registered the results of these confrontations as the agenda contained a record-breaking 33 items, including a 47 page long policy statement issued by the Divisional Council which included no less than 155 amendments. The Conference was more factionalised than ever before. The RPC used the Divisional Council to present their policy whilst the Trotskyists now commanded a significant presence. The resulting debate was confused, the RPC was far from dominant, and those concerned all agreed that the result was an unsatisfactory compromise between the differing factions within the division.[27]

In this context, Gaster saw the 1935 ILP Annual Conference as an important test of RPC strength and vitality. He had serious disagreements with NAC policy and refused to present it on a number of issues.[28] In particular he was upset with the NAC's line on Soviet foreign policy: the failure of the RPC to prevent a critical attitude towards the USSR being endorsed by the conference caused Gaster considerable anguish. The ILP was becoming committed to positions that Gaster and the RPC strongly disagreed with. The conference also raised serious questions about the position of the RPC, determining that unofficial groups within the party were 'bad in principle'.[29] The Derby Conference had been seen by the RPC as an opportunity to reassert its position and prominence within the ILP. However, the conference decisions had ensured that Gaster and the RPC were increasingly marginalised; there was a growing feeling that the Committee was damaging the party's activity.

In a desperate attempt to alter attitudes, Gaster and the RPC now changed tactics and became much more confrontational. Gaster began with an assault on the ILP leadership's attitudes towards the USSR. Despite earlier ILP decisions not to publish contentious articles, he wrote a long piece for the *New Leader* supporting the USSR's foreign policy. Brockway returned the article and reminded Gaster of the decision to exclude inner-party controversy from the party's national journal. Brockway's decision was endorsed by the Inner Executive.[30] Gaster was determined to make an issue of it. At the NAC, he moved reference back of the Inner Executive minutes, claiming that his article was an uncontroversial elaboration of party policy. He lost, but only by a narrow 8-5 margin.[31]

On the back of this controversy, Gaster gave a speech as the ILP fraternal delegate to the London District of the CPGB which again set out a perspective on USSR foreign policy at odds with the official ILP position. Aplin, the Divisional Organiser, resigned in response and decided to dedicate himself to opposing the RPC in London.[32] Provocatively, the RPC, through the London Divisional Council, started using former ILPer Emile Burns and other CPGB speakers to train ILP lecturers. At the same time, the Divisional Council refused to provide speakers for ILP meetings on the grounds that 'it could not appoint anybody from the London Division who could be expected to speak on behalf of the NAC'. In a similar vein, the Propaganda and Education Section, which had been co-operating with C.A. Smith in the preparation of leaflets, refused to continue its assistance because of 'differences of opinion'. It was clear that a major confrontation could not be long avoided.[33]

Aplin began a vigorous assault on Gaster, who was actively defended by the London Divisional Council. However, the ILP's Inner Executive ruled that the Divisional Council had failed to accept the Conference decisions on Soviet foreign policy.[34] This decision, taken together with the conference attitude towards group activities within the party, meant that the NAC had to act. However, whilst the conference had condemned group activity, it had rejected a disciplinary motion which had been attached to it. The NAC thus decided to issue a statement calling on loyal members to voluntarily cease participation in unofficial groups.[35]

Just when it seemed that Gaster and the RPC had no further role to play within the ILP, the Abyssinian crisis temporarily changed matters. The London Division set up an emergency committee, chaired by Gaster, to deal with the situation. Within the ILP nationally, there was considerable argument over whether the party should seek, through a policy of workers' sanctions, to aid the Abyssinians against Italian imperialism or whether there was nothing to choose between the two 'rival dictators'. The London emergency committee, whose composition transcended factional divisions, came down strongly in support of the workers' sanctions against Mussolini and it was Gaster who was chosen to present the case in the ILP's internal discussion bulletin, *Controversy*. His article had received the unanimous approval of a meeting of the emergency committee at which all members except Cullen were present. However, behind this seemingly innocuous absence lay a crisis in the RPC.[36]

From its foundation to 1935, Gaster and Cullen had stood united as the RPC's twin leaders. However, the Abyssinian conflict divided them and it placed Gaster in opposition to the policy of the CPGB. Cullen supported the Comintern analysis which suggested that the USSR had transformed the imperialist League of Nations when it joined in 1934 and dictated support for the League's economic sanctions against Italy. Cullen also supported the 1935 change towards a broad Popular Front as opposed to a United Front limited to working-class organisations. He argued for an anti-war, anti-fascist alliance, as widely based as possible, rejecting purely working class action. Further, and in line with the Comintern attitude, Cullen suggested the possibility of the capitalist powers using 'military sanctions'.[37] This last point took Cullen beyond what was acceptable to the ILP's Inner Executive, dominated by those who were most opposed to supporting the Negus, Haile Selasse. They decided that Cullen, together with other RPCers who followed his line, should be removed from the National Speakers list.[38] However, Gaster and fellow RPC leader Hilda Vernon were both allowed to remain as National Speakers for the ILP. Both Gaster and Vernon disagreed with the CPGB's position on Abyssinia. They criticised Cullen's 'questionable' statements in an article in the October *RPC Bulletin*. The major difference lay in the fact that Gaster and Vernon sought to keep class struggle at the forefront of policy:

> The problem then presents itself as a conflict between the classes – each attempting to utilise the interests of the other for its own aims … Working class interests are served by the defeat of both imperialisms, and it has therefore to oppose and frustrate Mussolini's aggression and at the same time oppose the Government which represents the equally oppressive interests of British imperialism.[39]

A substantial element of the leadership of the RPC, including Gaster, were now urging a policy closer to Brockway's than to Stalin's. Thus, the October *RPC Bulletin* was forced to begin with a confession:

> Yes, there was a crisis in the RPC … There was a sharp cleavage of opinion on the Abyssinian question and the line we should take on Sanctions and on our attitude to the broad peace movement. There were several conferences of RPC supporters, a few 'personalities' exchanged together with some real straight from the shoulder hitting, a general election of the committee resulting in one or two changes in personnel, a great deal of heart-burning and a devil of a lot of hard thinking, a determination to maintain revolutionary unity, – and the RPC proceeds with its work.[40]

These issues exploded at the summer Divisional Conference of the London and Southern Counties ILP. The regular agenda was suspended so the weekend could be devoted to the Abyssinian crisis. The scene was set for a showdown between the two factions within the RPC, in a situation complicated by the significant Trotskyist presence and the fact that many who attended opposed any form of factional organisation. Gaster moved a motion stressing the necessity of working-class opposition to Italian fascism and imperialist oppression. He found his motion supported by the Trotskyists and Aplin and opposed by Cullen and his comrades in the RPC who moved amendments suggesting the use of the League of Nations machinery. However, it quickly became clear that the combined forces of the RPC dissidents, the Trotskyists and Aplin's supporters who opposed group organisation, comprised a large majority. None of Cullen's amendments were carried and Gaster's statement was endorsed by a five to one majority. The days of automatic RPC success in the London Division were over.[41] When the conference reconvened in October to discuss the adjourned business, there were again sharp divisions. However, by this time, it had become clear to its leadership that the RPC could not expect to have its policy accepted. This was partly because of growing anti-group feeling; a resolution affirming the positive role of groups within the ILP was only carried on the chair's casting vote. However, perhaps the most significant reason the RPC was defeated was because, for the first time, their leaders could not agree amongst themselves as to the correct policy.[42]

The RPC staged a dramatic walkout from the October conference over its failure to accept their platform even though the Committee itself had not been able to agree on what was the correct line. The sensational exit then led to a special RPC conference two days later which voted to join the CPGB. The final issue of *The RPC Bulletin*, issued after the decision, called on 'all revolutionary socialists in the party to follow their example and make application to the Communist Party for membership'.[43] The majority of the RPC resigned *en masse* from the ILP on 31 October 1935 and a torrent of explanatory articles from Gaster and Cullen followed in the Communist press.[44] The reasons given varied, with the 1935 general election policy and ILP failures over Abyssinia at the forefront. The reality of the RPC's failures to make progress and its internal splits over 'revolutionary policy' and Abyssinia were never mentioned. The difficulties of striving to reach an independent position were exchanged for the certainties of CPGB policy and the example of the Soviet Union.

COMMUNIST LIFE

The CPGB accepted most RPC members immediately: Gaster's transition was less straightforward. His anti-party line on the Abyssinian crisis led to concerns over his 'soundness'. Dave Springhall was in temporary charge of issuing party cards and Gaster did not receive one.

The incident suggested to Gaster the sectarianism of the party he was about to join, although Springhall later claimed, unconvincingly, that the card had simply been left in his back pocket. Whatever the case, with Pollitt's return to London, Gaster's party card was quickly 'found'. So began 53 years of CPGB membership. However, the conspiratorial Springhall's suspicions of Gaster did not evaporate and he approached Maire Lynd, the daughter of the well-known Irish Nationalist *litterateurs* Robert and Sylvia Lynd, to keep an eye on the new recruit. Lynd had become a Communist whilst at Oxford and had moved to London to take up a job as literary reader and editor for Heinemann's in 1934. She built up a relationship with Gaster, but not of the kind Springhall had intended: within three years, Jack and Maire were married.[45] Suspicions of Gaster were soon dispelled. He was elected secretary of Marylebone CPGB and in 1937 the branch selected him as their candidate for the council elections. He rapidly made his way onto the London District Committee. He later counted 'Springie' as a close friend and the former sailor danced the hornpipe at Gaster's wedding.

The son of the Haham was untroubled by his rejection of religion. Although his relationship with his parents had never been close, the wedding brought a further deterioration. Gaster's politics had never pleased his family but he had never argued with them over his membership of the ILP or the CPGB. His marriage was a different matter. His father, only a year from death, was especially upset at one of his sons marrying a non-Jew. However, his background did leave one long-term scar. His middle-class upbringing and occupation were never an issue within the London ILP. However, within the more proletarian CPGB, the feeling 'I'm a bourgeois' remained with him, along with a sense that he had to apologise for his existence.

Despite this Gaster was involved in all the major battles against fascism. As an ILP member, he had been at the confrontations with the fascists at the Albert Hall and Olympia. At the 'battle of Cable Street', shortly after he had joined the CPGB, Gaster and his branch were positioned at Gardiner's Corner. Although the fascists never came their way, he always remembered the party instructions: 'don't retreat. If there's a fight, there's a fight'. His sister Lulu, who had followed Jack into the ILP, RPC and CPGB, was also active in fighting fascism and in November 1936 was arrested for throwing a brick through a window of the German Embassy.[46] Yet anti-fascism was neither the reason why he joined nor the main focus for his party work.

It was his role as a lawyer which was increasingly important. He had qualified as a solicitor in 1931. At first he continued to work for the solicitor to the United Synagogue but then established his own practice, first in Basinghall Street in the City, and subsequently, until it was destroyed during the war, in Warwick Court on the corner of High Holborn. His involvement in left legal circles had begun whilst he was still in the ILP and he worked closely with D.N. Pritt at the time of the Reichstag fire trial in 1934-5. After Olympia, he had been responsible for organising the legal response:

> [Afterwards] I rushed home, the arrested people were released and they were directed to Upper Montague Street. By that time I'd collected two or three other lawyers and some of our members were making sandwiches, tea and coffee. As they came in each of us took one or other and we prepared a sheet and gave them advice. Those who were simply charged with obstruction or something like that we told them how to behave and pay the fine and not argue. Those who were charged with obstructing the police or assaulting the police we allocated amongst ourselves to represent them in court. Everyone of them was briefed and represented the next morning in magistrates court, which was quite a feat. A lot of them we got off, a lot we didn't but none of them went to prison.[47]

Within the CPGB, he became more closely integrated into this network. As one of very few left-wing solicitors during the 1930s, along with Harry Thompson, Gaster became a significant background figure in a wide range of party activity. He was particularly involved in the Stepney Tenants' Defence League, working through the best tactics for refusing to pay rent and establishing effective procedures to prove that 'the landlords were blackguards and criminals'. He was also active in international activities and by the late 1930s was, alongside John Strachey, one of the vice-chairmen of the Amsterdam International Against War, at the time when the British section was run by the film actor Basil Rathbone.

On the CPGB London District Committee, Gaster came into close contact with all the leading figures in London Communism: Ted Bramley, who was elected with Gaster to the LCC in 1946; Johnny Mahon, later London Organiser and biographer of Pollitt; and Emile and Elinor Burns, who lived close to Gaster, who had left the ILP many years before him and with whom he appears to have had the most social contact. On the Committee, Gaster's opinions were moulded, and, through contact with Burns in particular, his confidence in his understanding of Marxist theory grew. He came to see his position on the Abyssinian conflict as a pacifist mistake. His earlier apologetic description of himself as having 'not been a profound student of Marx' was replaced with a greater confidence in his ability to dispute Marxist theory with any member of the party.

This was evident as the CPGB struggled to come to terms with the Second World War. Accepting the CPGB view of the Nazi-Soviet pact as a 'master stroke of Soviet Peace Policy' Gaster was utterly convinced that the priority of defending the USSR justified it.[48] He spat venom at the 'weak sisters' who in spring 1940 'disappeared into the Chamberlain camp' after expressing concerns over the pact. However, when the CPGB declared the conflict to be another 'war carried on between two groups of imperialist countries for world domination', Gaster disagreed. He strongly supported the initial line, championed by Pollitt, for a 'war on two fronts', against Chamberlain and against the Nazis and was the only member of the London District Committee to vote against the new line. Gaster, supported by Maire, continued his defence of the 'war on two fronts' position: 'There were terrific arguments … Volume 5 of the selected works of Lenin were closely scrutinised by both sides. We bandied quotation against quotation. It was a very highly theoretical and practical argument about what is an imperialist war and whether there are wars that may be partly an imperialist war but wars which ought to be supported'.[49]

Yet Gaster retained his identity as a 'loyal Communist': these disputes were purely for internal consumption. In public, he maintained appearances and accepted the party line. However, he was much more comfortable when the line changed again to support the war. In 1942, he joined the army but smashed his elbow in a training exercise the day before he was due to be sent to Burma. Declared unfit to bear arms, Gaster spent the war in England. He offered his services as a lawyer but, in what seemed a political move, his appointment was blocked by the War Office. Then his application for the Army Education Corps was turned down and Gaster, again suspecting political motives, turned to his old friend Pritt, who as an MP approached the War Office. Gaster was called for interview, but still did not get a posting. Only when a literacy school was set up in Ipswich by Army Command rather than the War Office was he eventually given an appointment. Even then the War Office attempted to have him moved from a post which gave a Communist a role in army education, but under the protection of his colonel he remained teaching basic literacy skills, and more, until the end of the war.

In 1945 he was amused to be able to force the army to give him leave to act as the election agent for Bill Carritt in the solidly Tory, Abbey Division of Westminster. In 1946 he was elected onto London County Council as a Communist. He chaired the CPGB's Jewish Committee in an attempt to move power away from those with Zionist sympathies. He also worked as the party's full-time Parliamentary Secretary to Phil Piratin and William Gallacher in Westminster for a couple of years in the 1940s until he decided the life of an apparatchik was not for him.[50] In 1956, he was vocal in his opposition to the party line on Hungary, which caused considerable concern within the leadership. However, unlike many Jewish Communists, Gaster stayed a member throughout. During the 1980s, he could be found, far from his ILP roots, arguing his corner alongside the supporters of the *Morning Star*.

Thus, Gaster was far from the stereotypical working-class, East End Jew. Religion, Zionism and family, the mainstays of the narratives of 'Jewish Communism', were not accidental omissions from the chronicle of his political formation.[51] He had no sympathy with Zionism, which he thought 'would ghetto Jews all over the world and give them divided loyalties'. And while his sister Lulu followed him into the CPGB, he did not maintain a close relationship with his parents, although his father was more troubled by his marriage than by his politics. Instead, his life moved between the two worlds, seemingly incompatible if we believe the caricatures, the middle-class 'sandal-wearing vegetarian' London ILP and the proletarian, Jewish Communist Party.

Nor did Gaster evolve as a Stalinist sectarian. Despite the way in which he left the ILP, he retained a close personal relationship with and affection for many of its leading members. After years of friendship, he attended Brockway's memorial tribute in 1988 and, despite his long membership of the CPGB, he retained a peculiar personal affection for James Maxton: 'Jimmy Maxton was the most lovable man. He was a quite lovely man and an idealist socialist of the best kind ... He was a marvellous character. He was a personality. You couldn't help being fond of Jimmy ... His integrity, his absolute honesty. He was incorruptible'.[52] Speaking after more than half a century of party membership, he still suggested his time in the ILP lay behind his frequent dissent from the Communist Party line:

There was an innate loyalty in the Communist Party to the leadership which I'm afraid my training in the ILP had rather dented. I was always more sceptical, because ten years in the ILP right, left and centre, in a rather open way, disqualified one from being an obedient take-it-with-out-question member of the Communist Party and I never was, even unto this day.[53]

Yet a fundamental question remains. Gaster's RPC struggled unavailingly to find an elusive 'third way' between communism and social democracy. Their solution centred upon workers' councils and drew on older, syndicalist, sympathies within the ILP. It also involved intense admiration for international communism. Bringing these ideas together, Gaster argued for a distinctive British socialism within an organised international framework. However, the two pieces of his jigsaw, the ILP and CPGB would not fit together. When the RPC failed to move the ILP, Gaster had to make a choice. The lure of the certainties of the CPGB must have been attractive to the internally divided RPC. However, the real attractions lay not in the realm of policy but in an assessment of the USSR. As Gaster recalled, he 'was very much in favour of the Soviet Union and the CPSU. Everything in those days was very black and white you know'.

We can draw some tentative conclusions from these fragments of Jack Gaster's life. The experiences revealed are inevitably more complicated than the conventional orthodoxies. Contrary to the conclusions of recent work on London Jewish communism, ethnicity provides no explanation of why Jews such as Gaster joined the CPGB. He was not an East End working-class Jew drawn to communism by anti-fascist struggles, despite his prominence as a Communist Councillor for Mile End. Neither, on the other hand, was Gaster a weird ILP crank, adopting socialism as a fad as did the bearded fruit-juice drinkers of George Orwell's London ILP. Instead, the experiences of Gaster and the RPC underline the difficulties of maintaining activity related to but not inside the CPGB in the 1930s. Despite the fiasco of Class Against Class and the difficulties in moving towards Popular Frontism, the attractions of the Communist International and the USSR, for Gaster as for many others, in the end proved too great.

I would like to thank Jack Gaster for talking to me about his life and for his extremely helpful comments on earlier drafts of this piece. Thanks to John McIlroy, Alan Campbell, Andy Flinn, Kevin Morgan,

David Howell, Keith Gildart, Linda Lawton, Jason Hepple and Sarah Cohen for their insights and encouragement.

NOTES

1. F. Brockway, *Inside the Left*, 1942, p240; G. Alderman, *The Jewish Community in British Politics*, Oxford 1983, pp115, 161; S. Bornstein and A. Richardson, *Against the Stream: a history of the Trotskyist movement in Britain, 1924-38*, 1986, p128; P. Piratin, *Our Flag Stays Red*, 1978, p86; N. Branson, *History of the Communist Party of Great Britain 1927-1941*, 1985, p114; F. Beckett, *Enemy Within: the rise and fall of the British Communist Party*, 1995, p43.

2. Branson, *op. cit.*, pp141-2; R. Dowse, *Left in the Centre: The Independent Labour Party 1893-1940*, 1966, p195; S. Bornstein and A. Richardson, *Two Steps Back: Communists and the wider labour movement 1935-45*, 1982, pp16-17.

3. H. Pollitt, 'Communists and the ILP', *Communist Review*, February 1933, p56.

4. Moses Gaster's papers are in University College, London. His political views are discussed in N. Rose, *Chaim Weizmann*, 1986, G. Alderman, *The Jewish Community in British Politics*, Oxford 1983, S. Kadish, *Bolsheviks and British Jews: the Anglo-Jewish community, Britain and the Russian revolution*, 1992.

5. Personal information, here and where not referenced in the remainder of the chapter is drawn from an interview with Jack Gaster, 17 August 2000. Further information can be found in two other interviews: British Library, National Sound Archive C609/06 and Imperial War Museum 1988, Acc. 10253/4. Extracts from the former are presented in D. Weinbren, *Generating Socialism: recollections of life in the Labour Party*, Stroud 1997.

6. Weinbren, *op. cit.*, pp80-4.

7. C.K. Cullen, 'Memorandum on the present political and economic situation and the ILP', p4.

8. National Museum of Labour History, Manchester, CP/IND/MISC/16/1, ILP London Executive Council, 13 December 1931, 10 September 1932; London Divisional Council, 3 April, 8 May 1932; London Division Organisational Committee, 31 August 1932; Summary of discussion at Meeting of Divisional Representatives with NAC, 25 March 1932.

9. CP/IND/MISC/16/1; Interview with Reg and Hettie Bower by Kevin Morgan, October 1999.

10. *New Leader (NL)*, 29 January 1932.

11. *NL*, 8 January, 4 March, 5 August 1932; K. Middlemass, *The Clydesiders: a left wing struggle for parliamentary power*, 1965, p270.

12. H. Pollitt and F. Brockway, *Which Way For the Workers? Report of debate 18 April*, 1932, p9; cf. H. Pollitt, 'The Bradford ILP Conference and after', *Labour Monthly (LM)*, August 1932, p487.

13. H. Pollitt, 'The Communists and the ILP', *Communist Review*, February 1933, p56; cf. CP/IND/MISC/16/4, Letter from C.K. Cullen to Bellamy, 5 August 1932; cf. J. Gaster, 'ILP "Revolutionary Policy" – Discussion', *LM*, January 1933, p32.

14. R.P. Dutt, *For a United Communist Party: an appeal to ILPers and all revolutionary workers*, 1935.
15. ILP Archive Series II, Part 2, card 60, Agreed statement on meeting between representatives of London Divisional Council of the ILP and the London District Committee of the CPGB, 23 March 1933.
16. Editorial statement and Labour Monthly conference announcement', *LM*, March 1933.
17. CP/IND/MISC/16/1, London & South Agenda, 20 September 1932; *NL*, 17 February 1933.
18. Gaster, *op. cit.*, p34.
19. ILP Annual Conference Report, 1933.
20. *RPC Monthly Bulletin*, January-February 1933; ILP Annual Conference Report, 1933.
21. W. Rust, 'Towards a United Revolutionary Party', *LM*, July 1933, p429.
22. See, for example, British Library of Political and Economic Science, Coll. Misc. 702/4 NAC, 24-25 June 1933.
23. *RPC Monthly Bulletin*, March 1934.
24. Gaster interview, 1988, pp8-9; Gaster interview (NSA); 702/6 NAC, 11-12 February 1934; 702/7 NAC, 9-10 June 1934.
25. *NL*, 6 April 1934; ILP Annual Conference Report, 1934; *Labours' Northern Voice*, April 1934.
26. *London RPC Bulletin*, June 1934.
27. *NL*, 2, 9 February 1935.
28. 702/9 NAC, 22 April 1935.
29. *NL*, 3 May 1935.
30. 702/9 Inner Executive (IE), 15 April 1935.
31. 702/9 NAC, 19 April 1935.
32. 702/10 IE, 19 June 1935; NAC, 29 June 1935.
33. 702/10 Executive Committee Report, 29-30 June 1935.
34. 702/10 Executive Committee Report, 2-3 August 1935.
35. 702/10 NAC, 10-12 August 1935; Hull University, Haston papers, DJH 5/8 NAC Circular Letter.
36. J. Gaster and the London Emergency Committee, 'Abyssinia – Where does the ILP stand', *Controversy*, October 1935.
37. C.K.C., 'The war crisis', *RPC Bulletin*, October 1935.
38. 702/10 IE, 24 October 1935.
39. J. Gaster and H. Vernon, 'The war situation – and the League', *RPC Bulletin*, October 1935.
40. 'Foreword – Crisis in the RPC?', *RPC Bulletin*, October 1935.
41. *NL*, 4 October 1935; M. Upham, 'The history of British Trotskyism to 1949', unpublished PhD thesis, University of Hull 1980, pp103-4.
42. *NL*, 1 November 1935.
43. Upham, *op. cit.*, p104; *RPC Bulletin*, November 1935.
44. *Daily Worker (DW)*, 1, 5 November 1935; C.K. Cullen 'Why we broke with the ILP', *LM*, December 1935.
45. 'Obituary: Maire Gaster', *Guardian*, 1 October 1990; Beckett, *op. cit.*, p86.
46. *The Times*, 7 November 1936.
47. Gaster interview, 2000.
48. Gaster interview, 1988.

49. *Ibid.*
50. Gaster interview, 2000.
51. See H. Srebnick, *London Jews and British Communism 1935-1945*, 1995, pp11-19.
52. Gaster interview, 1988.
53. *Ibid.*

Visitors and Victims: British Communists in Russia between the Wars

BARRY McLOUGHLIN

Emigrants from Britain to the USSR in the inter-war years constituted a heterogeneous contingent. Few of them were political immigrants as distinct from repatriates of Baltic or Russian origin expelled from Britain for political reasons during the 1920s. Furthermore, the number of qualified engineers and craftsmen from the United Kingdom who signed contracts with Soviet plants during the first Five Year Plan seems to have been relatively low, totalling hundreds rather than thousands.[1] On the other hand, the Communist Party of Great Britain dispatched cadres to the USSR for schooling or employment. The majority studied or taught at the International Lenin School (ILS). Other trusted party cadres worked in the *apparat* of the Executive Committee of the Communist International, in the headquarters of the Red International of Labour Unions, in the Marx-Engels Institute and for the international service of Radio Moscow (*Inoradio*). The English-language newspaper, *Moscow Daily News* (1930-39), also offered employment, usually on a part-time basis, as did publishing houses and magazines seeking English translators. Many of the British passport-holders residing in Moscow had known one another in London – as colleagues in the offices of the *Daily Herald*, the Labour Research Department (LRD), the Russian Trade Delegation, the Soviet Embassy or Russian-owned companies like *Arcos* and *Russian Oil Products*.

British migration to the USSR was greatly influenced by the CPGB, and those whom it chose for work in Russia were frequently known beforehand to the Russian bureaucracy. Another distinguishing feature of British immigrants, as against those from countries where the Communist Party was illegal, was the relative safety that a British passport conferred. The Russian authorities feared reprisals from London if British subjects were arrested in the USSR, in particular a breach in diplomatic relations, as had been the case between 1927 and 1929, or a trade embargo on Soviet imports to Britain.

The following account cannot claim to be exhaustive and is based mainly on memoirs and files that have been de-classified in Moscow since 1991. A great deal of the British Foreign and Commonwealth Office archival material which might have thrown light on individual biographies is no longer extant: the bulk of the correspondence to and from the British Embassy in Moscow was destroyed in 1941 and later. This irreparable loss is offset to a certain extent by the Moscow files pertaining to the transfer of British Communists to the Soviet party. [2]

This essay adopts a biographical approach, but, for reasons of space, omits to treat the 150-odd British subjects who studied at the ILS between 1926 and 1937. Similarly, the scope of this essay does not allow for an examination of the use of British Communists for clandestine operations of the Russian state. Many of these were graduates of the Lenin School, or of the courses given by OMS, the communications and courier service of the Communist International. Instead, the emphasis is directed towards the question: How did British arrivals in Moscow cope with Russian reality, including its darkest sides? Four female biographies are presented in this light. A final section deals with the repression of Britons in the USSR, and the reaction, if any, of the CPGB leadership to their disappearance. A thorough analysis of this complex issue is hampered by regulations governing accessibility to Russian archival documents of a sensitive personal nature.[3]

EXPELLEES FROM BRITAIN AND SHORT-TERM ECONOMIC IMMIGRANTS

Those arriving from the UK to take up employment in Soviet industry can be divided into two categories, persons expelled as 'undesirable aliens' and craftsmen on one-year contracts. Some hundreds of non-British nationals originally from the Tsarist Empire were expelled from Britain in the summer of 1917 because they refused to serve in the Allied armed forces.[4] Over twenty similar cases, mostly Latvians or Lithuanians, can be documented for the 1920s, presumably those affected by the Alien Restrictions Act (1923).[5] These were foreign-born CPGB members expelled from British territory before or after the 1926 General Strike or in the wake of the break in diplomatic relations with the USSR one year later. Michael Prooth (Prutovskii), for example, a book-keeper by profession and activist in the CPGB Stepney branch, was arrested in May 1926 under the Emergency

Powers Act, sentenced to five months hard labour and subsequently deported.[6] Edward and Amalia Gates (Götz) were expelled as 'undesirable aliens' in 1925 after the police had found Communist literature in their collier home near Glasgow.[7]

By contrast, H.W. and Germaine Emery were political refugees in the accepted sense of the term. Emery was a pre-CPGB bourgeois socialist who left a good job to work in a factory. He joined the party on its foundation. Both had been involved in a raid on a munitions factory mounted for the IRA Supply Department in April 1922. The husband managed to escape from custody and flee to the USSR in July 1922, and his pregnant wife, a Swiss citizen who had trained as a nurse in Birmingham, was deported to her native country in September 1922. Some months later Germaine Emery joined her husband in Moscow, where she worked in several departments of the ECCI before being appointed secretary of the Anglo-Saxon Bureau in the International Commission of the Soviet Central Committee. The fate of the couple remains unclear, but their initial experiences in Russia were overshadowed by the death of their baby and the long delay in having their CPGB membership recognised in order to join the Soviet Party.[8] The CPGB made life in Russia difficult for the Emerys on the grounds that they had never consulted the party about their adventures, and had involved CPGB headquarters in financial outgoings to facilitate their flight, while their return to Britain might expose King Street to unwelcome state scrutiny. The CPGB refused to support the couple's return to Britain, confirming their membership to the Russians only in 1926 – after several years' correspondence.[9]

The sparse data available on CPGB members employed in Soviet industry reveals that at least three had formerly worked with *Arcos* in London: Milly Capps, who took up a secretarial post in the Chelyabinsk tractor works in 1932; Harry Alder, invited to work in a starch factory in Yelets; and Gladys Cattermole, the wife of the Young Communist League executive-member Douglas Wilson, who was hired by the Moscow agency *Elektroimport*.[10] Two further CPGB cadres were involved in 'socialist construction': John Samwell, a carpenter who had worked at the Elstree film-studios was given a one-year contract with the Moscow Building Trust; and Eric Godfrey, who was entrusted with the management of the project department in a factory of the Moscow electro-technical complex *Elektrozavod*.[11] A final category of British-born skilled workers engaged by Soviet factory management comprised young men who either had been rejected out of hand as unsuitable for the ILS, or who had completed the course or were suspended and sent to a factory in the provinces to show their 'proletarian mettle'. Abraham Fagin was commandeered to a job in Gorky, and the ILS graduates of a three-year course, Max Halff (1928-31) and Alan Eaglesham (1930-33), were dispatched to Odessa and the Moscow factory No. 24, respectively.[12]

Halff, from a poverty-stricken Russo-Jewish background in Manchester, had been deported from Britain in 1928 and is said to have become a 'Comintern agent' in later years.[13] By contrast, Eaglesham was born into a privileged family in August 1902 in Half Morton, Dumfriesshire. His father was a clergyman of the United Free Church of Scotland, but his son did not take the cloth and studied at Edinburgh University. Alan worked as an agricultural labourer during college vacations and was active in the Edinburgh branch of the party (1920-24). Further study was terminated through lack of funds and Eaglesham set off to see the world. He tramped around Australia, worked as a labourer and joined the CP. Moving on to New Zealand, he acquired union official status after a series of unskilled jobs, including a stint as a miner. On his return to Britain at the end of the 1920s, he attended a teacher's training course and found work as a sailor before being delegated to the ILS in summer 1930.[14]

The only account found to date of how a young British male came to terms with Soviet factory realities was written by a non-political observer sympathetic to the USSR who wished to see that part of the world before going up to Balliol College. Peter Francis, in spending the months December 1936 to October 1937 in Russia, was probably the last foreigner to be granted a worker's visa to enter the Soviet Union. His first formal applications for employment in the USSR were not answered, but Francis remained undaunted, attended Russian classes at the London School of Slavonic Studies, and, unusually for an ex-public schoolboy, took a job in a small London firm manufacturing plastic moulds. Later, while working in a Birmingham plastics enterprise, Francis was fortunate to meet the Russian delegation leader Frumkin, the director of the All-Union Synthetic Resin Moulding Industry. The Soviet functionary arranged for the apprentice-fitter a contract post in the bakelite manufacturer *Karbolit* near the town of Orekhovo-Zuyevo south of Moscow. Francis got the job on false pretences, for, when talking to Frumkin in German, he translated his trade as 'Ingenieur' (engineer). This impressed Frumkin who no doubt was not aware that in industrial Britain the term also denoted skilled metal-workers.[15]

Francis was fortunate in that *Karbolit* was a clean and well-run factory. He noted the comparatively high number of supervisory employees and the tendency of his colleagues on the bench, also in their early twenties but of robust peasant stock, to say 'Gimme a sledge!' when a moulding press broke down.[16] The response Francis received from a foreman to his question concerning the difference between incompetent operatives and 'deliberate wreckers' also throws light on the prevailing factory-floor culture: 'The FIRST time he wrecks anything, he's just incompetent. The SECOND time he's a wrecker'.[17] Francis, viewed in retrospect, seems very much the innocent abroad, fortunately unaware of the terror unfolding around him. He emphasises that NKVD officers treated him with courtesy when he was seeking accommodation during a summer journey through the Soviet Union or he was applying for his exit visa home.[18]

WORKERS IN INTERNATIONAL ORGANISATIONS AND SOVIET LEARNED INSTITUTIONS

The sojourn in the USSR of CPGB functionaries within the bureaucracy of Soviet state, party, trade union and internationalist bodies rarely lasted longer than one year. Bob Stewart was the permanent British representative to the ECCI in the years 1923-24 and again in the following decade. Other holders of this post included Ernest Brown (1925), J.T. Murphy (1926-28), Robin Page Arnot, Alex Hermon and J.R. Campbell (1928-32), Jimmy Shields (1932-33), Peter Kerrigan (1935-36), Page Arnot, Shields and Ben Francis (1936-37), J.R. Campbell (1938-39) and Douglas ('Dave') Springhall (1939). Besides holding responsible posts in CPGB headquarters at King Street and editing the *Daily Worker* (1933-35), Shields had also served as General Secretary of the Communist Party of South Africa between 1925 and 1927. He was asked by Dmitri Manuilsky to serve in the Cadres Department of ECCI in 1936, and to supervise the Cadres Commission in King Street on his return.[19]

The various sub-sections of the Comintern and RILU *apparat* had a permanent need for *referenty* (consultants) or *praktikanty* (trainee consultants) from Great Britain. Page Arnot was assistant-director of the Eastern Department of ECCI in 1929, while Bob McIlhone and Max Raylock were key advisors in the Anglo-American Secretariat, and in its successor organisation from 1935, the Secretariat, led by the French Communist André Marty. Posted as *referenty* to ECCI in the 1920s were the Welsh miners Dan Richards and Jack Jones, the journalist Hugo Rathbone and a member of the Central Committee of the CPGB, Lily Webb. British Communists were also sought by RILU

(Margaret McCarthy and Bert Williams), the Agrarian Institute (Madge Palmer), International Red Aid (Ernie Cant), the Soviet trade unions (Dora Roberts) and the Marx-Engels Institute (Ralph Fox, Jane Tabrisky, Olive Budden and Nancy Williams).[20] British employees of the English broadcasting unit of Comintern Radio or Moscow Radio included Pat Sloan, Maggie Jordan, John Gibbons, Vera Harvey, Doris Hart and Olive Stoker. Jordan, for example, was a mill girl from Shipley, who had, like Gibbons, attended the Lenin School and later worked in a Bradford spinning mill. She returned to Moscow in 1934 and was chief correspondent in the foreign section of Radio Moscow until her departure for Great Britain in 1939.[21]

Those few British cadres resident in Moscow during the Great Terror of 1937-38 had to cope with the fallout caused by the purges and arrests which decimated the Comintern staff and paralysed decision-making.[22] Permission to enter and leave the country, to receive medical attention or be assigned adequate accommodation, was delayed time and again.[23] For instance, Pollitt complained to Page Arnot in October 1936 that no visa had yet been issued to George Hardy, who was due in Moscow 'to report on the recent mission he had carried out', possibly as a courier for the Comintern's Department of International Communication.[24] In Moscow a similar case unfolded. Page Arnot wrote directly to Comintern chief Dimitrov that 'Comrade Morrison' (George Coyle), a trainee lecturer at the ILS foreseen by King St as the new District Secretary for Tyneside, was still in the Russian capital seven weeks after the receipt of Pollitt's urgent telegram recalling him.[25] Max Raylock's sojourn in the Stalinist bureaucratic limbo was more prolonged. His employment as an expert on Britain and Ireland within ECCI ended in June 1937, and he was given a daily allowance to cover expenses before departure. By the end of the year, however, his repatriation papers, despite Pollitt's direct intervention, had not been completed and the allowance was curtailed.[26]

FOUR WOMEN

Four remarkable women have left accounts of their Russian experiences – Margaret McCarthy, Jane Tabrisky (Jane Degras), Freda Utley and Violet Lansbury, the daughter of the Labour Party leader George Lansbury. With the exception of Lansbury, all broke with Soviet-style Communism, not least because of what they had seen or been subjected to in the USSR. Their memoirs contain common features, particularly the problems of keeping oneself properly housed and fed in Moscow during the first Five Year Plan. Romantic liaisons with

Russians or Communist émigrés, they emphasise, could not become legally binding without risk as British women who married foreigners at that time lost their UK citizenship.

Margaret McCarthy, from Oswaldtwistle in Lancashire, grew up with politics. Her maternal grandfather was a socialist miner, the father of her father an ardent Sinn Feiner. Margaret joined the YCL in 1926 and participated in a British youth delegation to the Soviet Union in 1927. Working in a weaving mill in Accrington, she was involved, together with CPGB activists Lily Webb and Rose Smith, in the struggle against the 'more looms' system and wage reductions in the textile industry.[27] McCarthy was invited, as one of eight young industrial workers from abroad, to work in the Moscow headquarters of RILU for one year from June 1931. Known as 'Clyde' in the Anglo-American Section, she compiled, among other reports, a long analysis of the British National Unemployed Workers' Movement for the RILU Executive. Due to institutional wrangling between RILU and ECCI bureaucrats, McCarthy and her colleagues soon lost permission to lunch in the Comintern's *Hotel Lux*. Faced with few alternatives in food-starved Moscow, she finally obtained a pass for the Lenin School and could dine in the canteen although, as a mere evening-student, she was not entitled to this privilege. Her final break with the CPGB was largely influenced by her treatment on returning to Britain. When she asked the party leader Harry Pollitt what tasks the Party had in mind for her, he gave her £2 for the train-fare home to her mother and answered, 'Oh, I don't know. I suppose you could get married'.[28] Severely shocked by the Comintern's 'line' on the defeat of German communism at the hands of Hitler ('tactical retreat'), she left the CPGB in 1934 following a series of acrimonious exchanges with party functionaries in Glasgow.

Margaret McCarthy's disillusionment with Communism was a cumulative process influenced by her cultural adaptability. Her father was an Irish patriot and she spent her formative teenage years in America. Due to two sojourns in Germany as a guest of the youth movement of the German party in the late 1920s, she felt drawn to the compact social world of German communism. While attending the Fifth World Congress of the Communist Youth International in Moscow in August 1928, McCarthy was warned by a member of the Executive Committee of the British Young Communist League to confine her friendships to her own delegation as 'the Germans only wished to obtain ... information as to the influence and numerical strength – or rather weakness – of our own league'.[29] Her estrangement from British 'leading comrades' was due in no small part to unacceptable social behaviour, a 1920s variation of the 'laddism' still with us:

> The British delegation suffered, in its out-of-Congress moments, from that peculiar manner which characterises so many Britons abroad: not being able to let their hair down gracefully ... One of the favoured forms of amusement was to seize a small and hysterical young Londoner, who clung around the YCL leadership, strip him naked and pour cold water over him. The story of this and similar exploits was whispered around the Youth delegations, but were stopped by the intervention of a young Scottish miner, one of the more balanced and manly among our crowd.[30]

Trying to adapt to unemployment and the harshness of Depression Britain after her return, McCarthy's sense of hopelessness was exacerbated by what she perceived to be a vast change in the kind of person who had joined the CPGB in Accrington since 1931. The worker-students from the National Council of Labour Colleges, active trade unionists and ex-ILP members driven left by the events of May 1926, had drifted from the fold. Their replacements were desperate and totally destitute individuals 'yearning for violent action'. Later, she alleges, most of these CP neophytes joined the British Union of Fascists branch opened personally by Oswald Mosley in the town.[31]

Jane Tabrisky was born in London on 3 February 1905, the daughter of a cabinet-maker and a female metal worker. Although hampered by poor eyesight, she won scholarships to secondary school and the London School of Economics, where she was secretary of the ILP branch. In 1925 she graduated with First Class honours and joined the CPGB, later becoming local organiser in St Pancras. Invited to work at the Marx-Engels Institute in Moscow because of her linguistic skills and economics degree, Jane Tabrisky spent 1930 to 1935 in the Soviet capital.[32] She became a close friend of the textile expert Freda Utley, who later wrote of her: 'Jane felt she could no longer stand living in Moscow. She was not tied unhappily to Russia by a husband she loved and she pined for the freedom of England'.[33]

Violet Lansbury, another confidante of Freda Utley in the Soviet metropolis, kept the 'true faith', even if she did return to Britain after a thirteen-year absence in 1938. Violet was born on 4 December 1900 and joined the *Daily Herald* as a typist in 1919. Her autobiography is intriguing for what it does not reveal or attempts to play down. She maintains, for instance, that she had little to do with 'the chiefs' in the trade delegation of the Soviet Embassy in London, her employer between 1920 and 1925.[34] Violet, in fact, was entrusted with far more than the shorthand and typing tasks she describes in her book, acting as personal secretary to Maxim Litvinov, the leader of the Soviet delegation to the Hague Conference in June-July 1922. A member of the YCL since 1923, Violet was instructed by the CPGB to cut her links to the Party and join the Russian Party cell in the Embassy. She carried out, with Albert Inkpin, the Secretary of the CPGB, 'secret business' and functioned as the 'permanent mediator', via the Embassy, between the CPGB and the Communist International. In this latter function she co-operated with David Petrovsky, the Comintern representative for Great Britain and Ireland who used the pseudonyms 'Max Breguer', 'A.J. Bennett' and 'Humboldt'.[35]

In Russia Violet Lansbury studied at the Communist University in Sverdlovsk, and after a series of jobs, worked in the Foreign Workers' Co-operative Publishing House (1931-38). She supported, in her autobiography at any rate, the trumped-up charges against 'bourgeois specialists' in 1930 ('Industrial Party'), and those concocted against Kamenev, Zinoviev and Bukharin in the show-trials of 1936 and 1938. Of more interest for our topic, she not only believed the espionage indictment against the British engineers of Metro Vickers Electrical Co at the public show trial in April 1933, but was employed in round-the-clock shifts to translate the statements of the Russian defendants and witnesses.[36]

Violet's friend, Freda Utley, also came from a left-wing family: her father was Secretary to the Fabian Society and a friend of Engels. Born on 23 January 1898, Utley's first job was as a private teacher at seventeen. During the Great War she worked as a clerk in the War Office and won a scholarship to London University in 1920. She graduated from King's College with a First Class honours degree in history, received an MA scholarship and was given a fellowship by the London School of Economics. Utley lectured for the Workers' Education Association and taught English to the Russian staff at Arcos. Following the expulsion of her Russian husband Arcadi Berdichevsky (Soviet Trade Delegation) from Britain in September 1927, Freda was invited by Moscow to study the Soviet cotton industry. In the ensuing years she lived for periods in Japan and China with her diplomat husband and wrote popular works on the Sino-Japanese conflict.[37]

Life in Moscow was difficult for the couple because Freda could not accept a permanent job on account of her wish to accompany her husband on his foreign postings, which meant that she herself had no right to a ration-card or an apartment. The short-term assignments she did accept in the early 1930s brought home to her the realities of Soviet life: for example, the starvation rations available in the canteens of textile mills as compared with the privileged and unreal world of Comintern headquarters. A short period working as a referent in the Anglo-American Department of the ECCI was seen by Utley as futile – the directives and memoranda drawn up by her and others for the CPGB were mainly exercises in self-insurance and platitudinous abstraction. Later, as an expert for textile exports within the People's Commissariat for Light Industry, Utley observed that the selling price was very much a secondary consideration, covering approximately 20-25 per cent of production costs, while fulfilment of the plan remained paramount. The economic situation had improved by 1936, and Freda and her husband could finally live together with their son for the first time. She also profited from the friendlier attitude shown to British, American and French Communists during the Popular Front era.

However, the political atmosphere within the USSR soon deteriorated, and her husband Arcadi was arrested in April 1936. She entrusted the care of her son Jon to her mother in England and returned to Moscow to fight for her husband's release. An official in the State Prosecutor's Office led Freda to believe that Arcadi had been arrested because of a remark he had made years before when on trade business in Japan. She was allowed to bring him food parcels and linen regularly after queuing with hundreds of distraught women outside the Butyrka prison. If the prisoner signed a receipt for the package, the family knew that he or she was still alive in a Moscow prison and had not yet been sent to the Gulag. Called back to Britain by her publisher to correct the proofs of *Japan's Feet of Clay*, Freda Utley was refused a re-entry visa to the USSR. She lost her Moscow flat, including its contents, and the money she had put in the care of friends was stolen by the NKVD. The sporadic postcards of Arcadi Berdichevsky from the Siberian mines stopped in 1937.

With the help of Bertrand Russell, appeals for Berdichevsky's release were organised by Freda, and letters were signed by the Webbs, George Bernard Shaw, Kingsley Martin and Harold Laski. Laski approached the CPGB leadership, but even private representations from that quarter were categorically ruled out. Rajani Palme Dutt justified this in a letter to Laski: 'Least of all have we in other countries who have made a complete mess of our own Labour movement ... any right to pose as superior critics and censors of those who have shown in practice that they are able to judge correctly the necessary measures to defeat the capitalist enemy'.[38]

The Utley affair was also mentioned in Harry Pollitt's correspondence with Page Arnot, the permanent British representative at the ECCI. In his letter of 27 October 1937, Pollitt admitted that the main obstacle 'in getting Labour people interested in Spain is the argument ... of the trials and executions in the Soviet Union'. Conceding that conventional Soviet-style arguments were failing to convince influential Labour circles, Pollitt continued:

> Take such a person as Lasky [*sic*]. He had promised to write an article in commemoration of the 20th Anniversary of the Revolution for the *Labour Monthly*. He has since written to Dutt that he will not write any article commemorating the Russian Revolution so long as Freda Utley's husband is in prison and letters he had written to Litvinov and Stalin had been unanswered. Take another example. He made it a condition of his appearing at the Left Book Club rally in connection with China that Freda Utley should be one of the speakers. I was placed in a difficult position because if I had refused to have gone it would have meant losing a big opportunity of getting our propaganda over, and I finally decided that in spite of Utley's presence I should take part in the meeting. She is absolutely foul in the way she is getting propaganda against the Soviet Union across ... In my speeches I am dealing everywhere with this question and it has been discussed in all inner party meetings. We have done everything we can to get the [Daily] Herald to take a definite line but it is of no avail.[39]

VICTIMS

The most spectacular case involving the detention and trial of British subjects in the USSR between the wars was that of the engineers of Metro Vickers Electrical Co Ltd, arraigned at a show-trial in April 1933. The timing of this judicial farce was no coincidence as it was staged shortly after Stalin's speech (7 January 1933) to the Central Committee on 'wrecking' in industry. Metro Vickers Electrical employed Russian specialists for the construction and maintenance of electrical power stations – engineers of bourgeois origin who came from the 'dying classes' excoriated in Stalin's brutal tirade. Furthermore, a temporary Anglo-Soviet trade agreement had been suspended shortly beforehand, following the new Dominion trade agreement signed in Ottawa.[40]

Forty-two employees of the British firm were arrested in March 1933; seventeen were brought to trial. In mid-March the British subjects under indictment were released from investigative custody after two days of intensive interrogation, a most unusual concession in Soviet legal practice. Sir Esmond Ovey, the British Ambassador to Moscow, was recalled for consultations to London. He threatened Soviet Foreign Minister Litvinov with legislation in the House of Commons 'to impose an embargo on Russian imports to Great Britain ... in order to secure fair treatment' for the British engineers.[41] The prosecution case in the show trial (12-19 April 1933) rested on trumped-up charges of espionage, wrecking and bribery. Ten native Russians were sentenced to terms in prison ranging from 18 months to 10 years. Three of the British subjects in the dock were condemned to expulsion from the USSR within three days; the other two received prison sentences of two and three years. The latter were released in July 1933 following the imposition of a British trade ban on Soviet imports.[42]

Other British victims of Stalin's terror had little in common, save for the decisive fact that they had never been UK subjects or had renounced British citizenship for a Soviet passport. An early case concerns Abraham Landau, a twenty-two year old London Jew, sent by the CPGB to work in the headquarters of the Communist Youth International. He was arrested in his room in *Hotel Lux* on 27 January 1923 and executed two weeks later on an espionage charge.[43] No less than the brother-in-law of CPGB leader Arthur MacManus, William Wheeldon, a Communist from Derby who emigrated to Samara in 1926 to work as a teacher, is said to have been executed at some unknown date and place.[44]

Fragmentary evidence exists on a number of individuals. Len Wincott, one of the leaders of the 1931 Invergordon mutiny in the Royal Navy, was arrested in 1944 and freed twelve years later, in the face of demands for his release from sections of the British left but not the CPGB; Kathleen Barnes, a resident of Moscow since 1938 and a teacher at a military academy, spent the years 1950 to 1955 in confinement; Bernard Isaacs, arrested in 1938, survived his camp term, but his brother Moshe, convicted in 1947, died in the Gulag.[45] Finally, Gabriel Raffe, adopted by a Russian family after his British mother had died, was swooped upon by the secret police when leaving the British Embassy in February 1951. Originally charged with 'treason', Raffe was subsequently convicted of 'anti-Soviet agitation and propaganda'. The gates of the Gulag opened for him and countless other prisoners in 1954, during the first stirrings of a Soviet 'thaw'.[46]

In contrast to the experience of members of illegal Communist parties temporarily domiciled in Moscow, there is only one documented case known to date of a person close to the British party leadership who was arrested in the USSR and for whom King Street made energetic interventions – Rose Cohen. These supplications were made confidentially in Moscow and, as in the case of Fred Utley's spouse, the public attitude of the CPGB to Cohen's arrest after it was publicised in the British press in April 1938 was craven. King Street refused point blank to help, and Cohen's old friends at the LRD could find only nine signatories from the liberal and left-wing intelligentsia to sign a 'studiously moderate' letter of protest which was printed in the *New Statesman* in November 1938.[47]

Rose Cohen was born of Jewish parents in London on 20 May 1894. Her tailor father enabled her to complete secondary school education. Her first job after leaving school was in the Education Department of London County Council. She joined the National Guilds League in 1916, the ILP in 1917 and the CPGB in August 1920. Later employed in the Labour Research Department, where Harry Pollitt fell in love with her, Rose Cohen spent a period in 1923-24 working for the Comintern, presumably abroad and in a secret capacity. On her return to London she was employed by the Soviet Embassy and by the *Arcos Steamship Co*. Given a 'confidential' post in King Street from March 1926, Rose married the Comintern representative David Petrovsky and left with him for Moscow in April 1927 'to work in the Communist International'.[48]

Details of this assignment are unknown, but Cohen did attend the 1930 ILS class for English-speakers before joining the staff of the *Moscow Daily News*, the newspaper which was launched under the editorship of the American socialist Anna Louise Strong in October 1930.[49] Cohen was entrusted with directing the paper's foreign department. This post, along with her husband's career, may have played a part in her arrest and subsequent judicial murder. Petrovsky, known to his English friends as 'Max', was born in Kiev as David Lipez in 1886 and joined the Jewish Socialist Bund at sixteen.[50] He studied at Brussels University and, following years of exile in Sweden and the USA, returned to post-revolutionary Russia. In 1919, he joined the Bolsheviks and enlisted in the Red Army. Following the Civil War, Petrovsky helped to re-organise the new State's third-level education system, wrote and was engaged in publishing. When he joined the ECCI *apparat* in 1924, Petrovsky changed his name to Max Breguer. He met Cohen on Comintern business in Paris, and the entire CPGB leadership when he was appointed ECCI representative to Britain and Ireland in 1924.

In the course of the implementation of the ultra-left policies laid down by Moscow in 1928-29, Petrovsky's supervisory role in British Communist affairs ceased and he was shunted off in September 1928 to head the Agitation and Propaganda department of the International.[51] Accounts of his sharp fall from grace two years later are inaccurate or exaggerated as he became a member of the presidium of the Supreme Economic Council and was put in charge of all institutes of learning within the People's Commissariat of Heavy Industry.[52] By virtue of his influence, Petrovsky may have been instrumental in saving Ivy Litvinov, the English wife of Maxim Litvinov, from arrest when her husband was in disgrace: he arranged for her to teach English at a teacher training college in Sverdlovsk, where she stayed until the worst was over.[53]

Petrovsky was arrested on 11 March 1937 and executed the following September. He is said to have been buried, with other ex-functionaries of the Comintern, in a mass grave beneath the turreted walls of Moscow's Novospassky Monastery.[54] Terrified and alone with her son Alyosha, Rose had few visitors after Petrovsky's arrest. Ivy Litvinov was an exception, despite the plea of her prominent and jeopardised husband that visiting relatives of 'an enemy of the people' could have untold repercussions.[55] Rose Cohen tried in vain to revoke the application for Soviet citizenship she had made in early 1937 when under pressure to hand up her British passport. The NKVD arrested her on 13 August 1937. Her case – 'spying for British Intelligence' – came before the Military Collegium of the Supreme Court on 28 November 1937. The verdict of death by shooting was carried out the same day.[56]

A colleague of Cohen's at the *Moscow Daily News* found himself in a similar predicament. The translator and journalist Patrick (Padraig) Breslin, born in London in 1907 of Irish parents who returned to Ireland in 1920, made the disastrous decision in 1936 to renounce his Irish passport and apply for Soviet citizenship. He had been persuaded by his first wife Katja, who in turn had been confronted with this question again and again by her senior officers in the Japanese section of the espionage department of the NKVD. Breslin, now trapped in the USSR as Cohen was, had grounds for wanting to return home. In 1936 he had fallen in love with and married Daisy McMacken, a Belfast Republican with strong Communist sympathies who worked as a linguist in the Foreign Workers' Publications Cooperative. But she returned to Ireland in 1937 to give birth to daughter Mairead, whom Breslin was fated never to see. Shortly afterwards, in April 1938, Katja fell victim to an internal NKVD purge and was arrested. Patrick and the grandparents looked after the children of Breslin's first marriage, Genrikh and Irina. The children were later dumped in one of the notorious orphanages of the NKVD, the fate of many offspring of 'enemies of the people'.

Pat Breslin was arrested shortly before Christmas 1940. He underwent over fifty nocturnal interrogation sessions before being sentenced in September 1941 to an eight-year term in the Gulag. Sick and feeble, he died on arrival at the slave labour camp in Kazan one year later. The NKVD dropped the espionage charges during the long custodial investigation, knowing that enough 'evidence' existed to brand the Irishman 'a socially dangerous element'. While such an indictment could be and often was based on such harmless incidents as telling jokes against Stalin, Breslin's *vita*, as his interrogators learned, showed a strong iconoclastic streak. He had broken with the religious world of his parents and joined the Communist Party of Ireland (CPI) at fifteen, becoming a regular contributor to the Party weekly *Workers' Republic*. The 'first' CPI was wound up by the Comintern in 1923 on the recommendation of Arthur MacManus and because Moscow felt that Jim Larkin, recently released from an American prison, had retained his popularity from the 1913 Dublin Lock-Out and should establish a new Comintern section in Ireland. But as Communist activities subsequently receded because of Larkin's preference for trade union work, Breslin turned to other philosophical interests and joined the Irish Theosophical Society. Three years later he was expelled from the ILS for his espousal of far eastern philosophy and rejecting the tenets of dialectical materialism.

Breslin's dismissal from the Lenin School in January 1930 brought no immediate disadvantages. He was asked to stay as a translator in the school administration and later taught English at other Moscow universities of the Comintern. By now fluent in Russian, Breslin travelled the country and received many translation commissions, notably some poems of Mayakovsky, the short story 'The Road' by Isaac Babel and excerpts from the thirteenth century Georgian epic by Shota Rustaveli, *Knight in the Tiger Skin*. His colourful past as an ILS dissident did not cloud his friendship with the Scottish CPGB functionaries Jimmy Shields and Tom Bell, nor with the American journalists he knew from Moscow's tight-knit Anglophone colony. Informers' reports on Breslin's outspoken views played a significant part in the indictment, credible expressions of dissatisfaction with the collectivisation of agriculture, Soviet elections, the draconian labour legislation of 1940 and the Hitler-Stalin pact.[57]

As with Rose Cohen, George Hannah was another victim for whom the British party is said to have made supplications. The details of his imprisonment and indictment are vague: work as a translator at Moscow's Foreign Language Publishing House and at Radio Moscow, arrest in the late 1940s and return from the Gulag to Moscow about 1957.[58] Hannah was born in Leyton in 1902 and joined the CPGB at twenty years of age. He enlisted in the Royal Signal Corps of the British Army in 1924 and perfected the trade he had learned – radio-mechanic. After service in India Hannah left the Army in 1933 and was sent to Moscow by the CPGB in February 1934 to work as a radio-operator for the Comintern.[59] His wife was expected to join him at the OMS school near Moscow but because of 'domestic difficulties' she refused to leave Britain. Hannah's reaction to this blow can be judged by the fact that his superiors thought his subsequent behaviour 'very strange'.[60] There are two versions of why Hannah left OMS in December 1937: the head of the Cadres Department of the Comintern, Belov, held that 'Murray' (Hannah's Russian pseudonym) was dismissed 'because we could no longer trust him'. Hannah believed his removal was part of a reduction in departmental staff.[61]

He moved on, firstly to the State Pedagogical Institute for Foreign Languages. His arrest after the war – in 1948-49 thousands who had survived the Gulag were re-arrested – was on suspicion of espionage, the run-of-the-mill charge against foreigners and their Russian contacts, acquaintances or friends. During interrogation he learned that Pollitt, his friend, was 'a British government agent'. 'Evidence' for this ridiculous accusation had been collected ten years previously, during the interrogation and torture of the leading Comintern figures Knorin, Pyatnitsky and Bela Kun, and was to serve as 'proof' for a projected fourth great show trial, this time against the members of the Executive Committee of the International.[62] Hannah initially believed that his arrest was due to an error, but he realised during the long journey east to the camp that his fate was shared by thousands of others.

CONCLUDING REMARKS

The full story cannot yet be told. But it is clear that despite the burning faith with which most of them arrived in the USSR, not a few Communists from the British Isles experienced disillusion, suffering, and in a few cases death, as Soviet communism degenerated into Stalinism during the inter-war years. Yet, set against the experiences of most Communist exiles domiciled in the USSR between the wars, those of the British expatriates represented a special case. Their sojourn was generally a limited one, unlike the open-ended immigration of Communist refugees fleeing from fascist or dictatorial regimes. Whether sent to Moscow on a party remit or hired by a Soviet industrial enterprise, the holder of a British passport was psychologically not attuned to permanent residence in Stalin's Russia. Britons had, in other words, a country to return to, unlike the Germans, Italians or Bulgarians.

'British insularity', as a national predisposition not absent from the imaginative world of CPGB members, can be seen as a blessing in disguise in the Moscow environment, a self-defence mechanism used to measure the relativity of 'Soviet life'. The long democratic tradition of Britain, the wide base of popular as distinct from Marxist-orientated culture and the comparably wide scope of action open to British Communists in cross-party, left-wing movements were factors which, it may be argued, conditioned many CPGB cadres to trust their own sense of tradition and place and to be sceptical, if not caustic, about Stalinist criteria of what a good cadre should be. Rejecting or questioning the worst excesses of Comintern doctrine, however, did not seriously undermine the loyalty many British emissaries or trainees sent to Moscow continued to pay to the Soviet experiment. The 'British aversion to continental theorising', feelings expressed in internal correspondence by Pollitt, were commonplace sentiments adhered to by most British socialists outside the narrow constituency of inter-war British communism.[63]

Considering Stalin's view that the Communist International was 'working for the enemy', the possibility of effective intervention to help arrested foreign Communists was extremely narrow. Comintern Secretary Dimitrov intimated as much to Gallacher and Pollitt in connection with the disappearance of Rose Cohen.[64] When Ernst Fischer, the permanent representative of the Austrian Communist Party, sought assistance from Dimitrov in 1938 in respect of the numerous arrests affecting political refugees from Austria, he was told to 'trust Soviet organs' and not to push the matter.[65] Even in the Kruschchev era, Communist Parties were merely told that the cadre in question had been rehabilitated. Fictitious death certificates were issued to the aggrieved families on request, crude forgeries stating that the prisoner had died during the Second World War from natural causes.[66] Any open debate within the British party on Stalinist mass-repression, whether in 1937-38 or in the post-war years, would have split the CPGB and led to the expulsion of its initiators, not least at the behest of the Moscow 'friends'. Furthermore, apart from their internalised complete identification with the Soviet Union, close family ties with that country predisposed CPGB leaders not to pursue the matter in Moscow, nor indeed to speak openly about it in Britain. After all, the stepson of the veteran Communist leader John Ross Campbell was a veritable hostage in the USSR after he had accepted Soviet citizenship in 1939, while Rosa Rust, the daughter of the ultra-orthodox CPGB boss Bill Rust, was left parentless in Ivanovo International Children's Home after her mother had precipitately returned to London in 1937.[67]

For suggestions, references, copies of rare books and archival documents, I am indebted to the following: Monty Johnstone, Andy Flinn, Emmet O'Connor, Mairead Breslin Kelly, Lara Kelly, Tony Coughlan, Kevin Morgan, John Halstead, John McIlroy and Alan Campbell.

NOTES

1. No definite statistics for British *spezialisty* have been found. According to calculations made in early 1935, an unknown number of Britons featured in a total of 1,370 'other nationalities' directly employed by the People's Commissariat for Heavy Industry; see State Archive of the Russian Federation, Moscow (GARF) 5451/19/595.
2. John Fisher (PRO) to author, 8 July 1997; Rachel O'Flynn (FCO) to author, 24 June 1997. For a confirmation of this deplorable policy, see A. McLeod, *The Death of Uncle Joe*, 1992, pp3-4.
3. The most important documentation in this regard (cadre dossiers of the CPGB and NKVD prosecution files) may be viewed only by the victim, family members or persons of their trust who produce a letter-of-attorney. Access to prosecution files of the Soviet secret police is governed by the Rehabilitation Law of 18 October 1991, that pertaining to other personal files by the Archival Law of April 1994.
4. A. Monkhouse, *Moscow 1911-1933. Being the Memoirs of Allan Monkhouse*, 1933, pp236-8.
5. Leslie Kajaminoff Saunders, born in Poland at the turn of the century, specifically mentioned this Bill in the autobiography he submitted to the Comintern. Saunders was forced to leave the United Kingdom after the General Strike. See Russian State Archive of Socio-Political History RGASPI 17/98/787: 3.
6. RGASPI 17/98/774: 4-7.
7. RGASPI 17/98/701: 13, 14, 18.
8. RGASPI 17/98/824: 4, 9-12, 14, 15.
9. Visiting Moscow in 1925, William Gallacher stated openly he would 'see to it' that Emery would 'have no opportunity to work in the British Party'. The reason for Gallacher's hostility was the allegation that Emery had worked for the IRA in 1921-22 without the permission of the CPGB leadership RGASPI, 495/100/225: 1-2.
10. RGASPI 17/98/754: 1, 7, 10; 17/98/766: 2, 11, 13; 17/98/732: 8.

11. RGASPI 17/98/784: 1; 17/98/706: 2, 3.
12. RGASPI 531/1/39: 14, 40.
13. M. McCarthy, *Generation in Revolt*, 1953, p115.
14. RGASPI 17/98/750: 1-3.
15. P.G. Francis, *I Worked in a Soviet Factory*, 1939, pp24-5.
16. *Ibid.*, pp52-3.
17. *Ibid.*, p54.
18. *Ibid.*, pp215-18.
19. For an account of his first tour of duty, see Bob Stewart, *Breaking the Fetters*, 1967, pp137-46; RGASPI 495/18/1085: 114.
20. This information is taken from RGASPI 17/98 files.
21. RGASPI 495/14/220: 16; 17/98/796: 3-7; 17/98/811: 1-2; Employment in broadcasting may have been part of the training envisaged for British couriers and radio-operators of the OMS service.
22. Exact figures on the number of Comintern officials who fell victim to purges in the late 1930s are difficult to compute, as many were arrested long after dismissal and others seized by the NKVD while still in office. One indicator is the fact that membership in the Russian Party cell in Comintern headquarters fell by 57 per cent between January 1936 and April 1938. See F. Firsov, '"Säuberungen" im Apparat der Komintern', in H. Weber and D. Staritz (eds), *Kommunisten verfolgen Kommunisten. Stalinistischer Terror und 'Säuberungen' in den kommunistischen Parteien Europas seit den dreißiger Jahren*, Berlin 1993, pp49-50.
23. Page Arnot reminded ILS rector Kirsanova that the promised medical attention for the ILS students 'Citrine' (Bill McGregor) and 'Evans' (Margaret Dickens), soon to depart for Ireland and Britain, respectively, had not been provided to date. See RGASPI 495/14/243: 60, Page Arnot to Kirsanova, 20 March 1937. Constance Haverson ('Irene Anderson'), the granddaughter of George Lansbury and a courier for OMS, was expected to share one room in Hotel Lux with her aunt Violet Lansbury and Violet's ex-husband because OMS 'repudiated liability' for her. She refused this ménage-a-trois 'on moral and political grounds'. See RGASPI 495/14/243: 31, Ben Francis to Dear Comrade [Dimitrov?], 29 October 1937.
24. RGASPI 495/14/220: 106, Pollitt to Page Arnot, 29 October 1936.
25. RGASPI 495/14/243: 56, Page Arnot to Dimitrov, 11 March 1937.
26. RGASPI 495/14/243: 179, Raylock to Page Arnot, 27 December 1937.
27. See the recollections in McCarthy, *op. cit.*; S. Bruley, 'Women and Communism: a case study of the Lancashire weavers in the depression', in G. Andrews, N. Fishman and K. Morgan (eds), *Opening the Books. Essays on the Cultural History of the British Communist Party*, 1995, pp73-5.
28. McCarthy, *op. cit.*, p218.
29. *Ibid.*, p125.
30. *Ibid.*, pp133-4.
31. *Ibid.*, pp238-9.
32. Unless stated otherwise, information is from her party transfer file (RGASPI 17/98/800). Under her married name Jane Degras, she compiled three volumes of documents on the history of the Communist International, published by the Royal Institute of International Affairs

between 1956 and 1965.

33. F. Utley, *Lost Illusion*, 1949, p131.

34. V. Lansbury, *An Englishwoman in the USSR*, 1940, p5.

35. RGASPI 17/98/734: 6.

36. Lansbury, *op. cit.*, pp172-4, 318-19, 309.

37. Her impressive list of publications for the inter-war period included: *An Illustrated History of the Russian Revolution*, translation, 1928; *Japans's Feet of Clay*, 1936; *Japan's Gamble in China*, 1938; *China at War*, 1939.

38. K. Morgan, *Harry Pollitt*, Manchester 1993, p175.

39. RGASPI 495/14/243: 162-3.

40. Monkhouse, *op. cit.*, p285.

41. *Ibid.*, p303.

42. *Moscow Daily News*, 18, 19 April 1933; O. Gordievsky and C. Andrew, *KGB. Die Geschichte seiner Auslandsoperationen von Lenin bis Gorbatschow*, Munchen 1992, p163.

43. *Rossiiane* 4-6, Moscow 1995, p148.

44. RGASPI 17/98/693: 1-2; M. Durham, 'Russians wrong about Briton who "died in Stalin camp"', *Independent on Sunday*, 6 September 1993; S. Rowbotham, *The Friends of Alice Wheeldon*, 1986.

45. Wincott's memoirs, published in the Brezhnev years when the author was still living in Leningrad, do not mention his detention. L. Wincott, *Invergordon Mutineer*, 1974; W. Kendall, 'The Communist Party of Great Britain', *Survey* , 20, 1. 1974, pp125-6; Memorial Archive, Moscow (MAM) 1/1/397; 1/2/91; 1/2/3059.

46. MAM 1/2/4787.

47. The details of the CPGB's attempts to save Rose Cohen or to find out about her fate are well-known and will not be repeated here. See Morgan, *op. cit.*, pp.33, 126-7, 174-5; F. Beckett, *Enemy Within. The Rise and Fall of the British Communist Party*, 1995, pp69-77; M.B. Reckitt, *As it Happened. An Autobiography*, 1941, pp148-51.

48. RGASPI 17/98/724: 4.

49. RGASPI 531/1/32: 6. Her attendance was 'on a voluntary basis'.

50. Unless otherwise stated, information on Petrovsky is taken from B. Lazitch and M.M. Drachkovich, *Biographical Dictionary of the Comintern, New, Revised, and Expanded Edition*, Stanford 1986, p361; V. Piatnitskii, *Zagovor protiv Stalina*, Moscow 1998, p458; RGASPI 495/65a/13497.

51. G. Adibekov et al, *Organizatsionnaia struktura Kominterna 1919-1943*, Moscow 1997, p159.

52. For example, that he was expelled from the Russian Party in the early 1930s because of Trotskyist sympathies (Vilém Kahan, 'The Communist International: the personnel of its highest bodies', *International Review of Social History*, 21, 2 1976, p171); or removed from Comintern employment in 1928 and shot shortly afterwards because of incidents in the Ukraine during the Civil War (A. Kuusinen, *Der Gott stürzt seine Engel*, Wien-München-Zürich 1972, pp72-3).

53. J. Carswell, *The Exile. A Life of Ivy Litvinov*, 1983, pp140-5, 207.

54. C. O'Clery, *Melting Snow. An Irishman in Moscow*, Belfast 1991, pp121-2.

55. Carswell, *op. cit.*, pp207-8.
56. Beckett, *op. cit.*, p71; GARF, NKVD investigation file no. 29883 Patrick Breslin, information of 9 April, 27 May 1941.
57. This account is based on Breslin's Party file in RGASPI, his NKVD dossier and his prison file.
58. *Independent on Sunday*, 6 September 1993.
59. RGASPI 17/98/762: 2.
60. PRO HW 17/17 (intercepted radio traffic), Telegram from Pollitt to Arnot and Henri, 31 October 1934; telegram from Moscow to West, 13 December 1934.
61. RGASPI 17/98/762; 495/14/243: 35-7.
62. Piatnitskii, *op. cit.*, pp133-4. For the background to the 'Anti-Comintern Block' indictment, which petered out into a series of single secret court sessions in 1938-39, see R. Müller, 'Der Fall des "Antikominten-Blocks' – Ein vierter Moskauer Schauprozeß?' in H. Weber et al (eds), *Jahrbuch für Historische Kommunisforschung 1996*, Berlin 1996, pp187-214.
63. K. Morgan, 'Harry Pollitt. The British Communist Party and International Communism' in T. Saarela and K. Rentola (eds), *Communism National and International*, Helsinki 1998, pp199, 203.
64. F. Firsov, 'Aus den Tagebüchern Dimitroffs. Komintern und Stalinistischer Terror', *Mittelweg 36*, Hamburg, April-May 1998, p82; Beckett, *op. cit.*, pp71-2.
65. E. Fischer, *Erinnerungen und Reflexionen*, Reinbek bei Hamburg 1969, pp359,365.
66. *Istochnik*, 1, 1993, pp83-4, KGB-Chairman Semichastnii to Central Committee CPSU, 26 December 1962.
67. McLeod, *op. cit.*, pp267-8. For Rosa Rust, see the chapter by Andrew Flinn in this volume.

Afterword: Living History

DAVID HOWELL

'A hell of a thing to be History! – not a student, a historian, a tinkling reformer, but LIVING HISTORY ONESELF, being it, making it, eyes for the eyeless, hands for the maimed ...'[1]

So reflects Ewan Tavendale, the young Communist in *Grey Granite*, the final book in Lewis Grassic Gibbon's *A Scots Quair*. The time is recognisably the early 1930s, the location is the fictional city of Duncairn. The multi-voice and fractured narrative presents in its very form the problem of constructing an urban solidarity to replace the lost world of the Scottish peasantry. Young Ewan seeks his purpose through political agitation, culminating in the organising of an unemployed march to London. From this fiction, it is a short shift to David Proudfoot (see chapter 7) in the all too real Fife coalfield of the 1920s, seeking to construct a new radical solidarity among his fellow miners. Proudfoot met apathy spiced with transient enthusiasms. He faced hostility not just from the coalowners but from the hierarchy of the Fife Mineworkers' Association. The obstacles could depress an already pessimistic temperament. Did Proudfoot, hardened with his zealous commitment to the party, ever reflect that it was 'A hell of a thing to be History'? For him, his commitment led to victimisation, long term unemployment and resignation from the Communist Party.

The identification with 'History' expressed by Ewan Tavendale, which perhaps acted as compensation for the isolation or defeats of the present, can be presented as a characteristic feature of the Marxism that came to dominate the international left after the Bolshevik revolution and the subsequent isolated survival of the Soviet Union: 'Trotsky identifies History with himself, Lenin identifies himself with History', in Edmund Wilson's couplet.[2] Such identification can be highlighted as a means whereby morality is banished from politics; a teleology replaces the need for complex and decisive choices. Yet the sense that 'History' was progressive was deeply embedded within pre-1917 socialisms, whether the Marxism of the Second International or the self-consciously ethical socialism of the Independent Labour Party (ILP). Indeed, it was a significant thread within the broad Radical culture of those who made, in their various ways, the complex transition from British Liberalism to some form of Labour or socialist commitment. The optimism was evident in the sentiments that accompanied the Labour Party's political advance in the 1920s. The electoral complexities and parliamentary compromises that produced and sustained the first Labour government mattered little to Labour Party loyalists. Instead, the fact of office was best seen as a signpost to future triumphs: hence the adulation accorded to the living symbol of the advance, Ramsay MacDonald, in his 1924 election campaign. Given such expectations, the record of the 1929 government and the consequential setbacks in by-elections and municipal contests were chastening experiences. The collapse of the government in August 1931 provided an appropriate solution. Those once revered as leaders were now reviled as renegades. Their pictures vanished from party committee rooms; their earlier contributions were expunged from official party memories. But 'History' could be rehabilitated.

The parallels are suggestive. They support the judgement found in the individual studies in this book that Communists were not a species apart, defined through a supposedly unproblematic characterisation as Stalinist or totalitarian. Rather, in several respects, they shared assumptions, sentiments, practices, prejudices, with those in the wider labour movement who were sometimes comrades and sometimes opponents. Sometimes this could indicate a politicisation that pre-dated the Bolshevik revolution. Of those whose stories are told in this book this was most clearly the case for Dora Montefiore. Her socialist identity, for many years articulated through the Social Democratic Federation and its successors, was informed significantly by two problematic relationships – that of Second International socialist orthodoxy with the inequalities of gender, and the contradictions manifest in labour and socialist attitudes to empire. Others were also influenced by their earlier involvements. Rose Smith, much younger than Montefiore, had also been active in the immediately pre-war and wartime socialist movements. She chose to work with those whose commitment was to socialist organisations outside the Labour Party, though the trajectory of the British Socialist Party offered sharp lessons in the crippling lack of space typically available for such mobilisations. Arthur Horner's pre-party experience was very different again. A participant in the richly radical but minority mobilisations within the South Wales Miners' Federation (SWMF), he imbibed from them political and industrial sentiments that often fed into the early Communist Party of Great Britain . Yet an emphasis on a combative, rank and file centred trade unionism could be at odds with the hardening emphasis on the central role of the party.

Not only did Montefiore and Horner have political identities that were initially formed prior to the foundation of the party: they also rested, in part, on institutions other than the party. For Montefiore, her commitment to feminism was central. The activities and institutions through which this had been expressed had always gone beyond an uncomplicated party identity. The problems that would have faced Dora Montefiore had she remained a Communist activist were not the exclusive experience of those restricted to the familiar agenda of Comintern instructions and British responses. Both Communist and Labour Parties in the 1920s witnessed substantial erosions of the spaces available for women's mobilisations on specifically feminist issues. The parties' spheres for women's activities increasingly came to be constructed around a conception of economic and social priorities that was based on a claim of a shared class identity and a denial of the relevance of gender-based distinctions. The consequential problems were encountered within the CPGB by activists such as Rose Smith. She had many Labour counterparts.[3]

Horner's work as a trade unionist in the SWMF was so central that it precipitated for him a major crisis as a Communist. This was a spectacular manifestation of what was a potential tension for any Communist trade unionist. The politics of Horner and of the Scots, Proudfoot, Allan and Moffat, were coloured by their local experiences: the problems of the coal industry during the inter-war years as manifested in their Districts; and their assessments of how best to improve miners' conditions; and the prospects for the party in specific coalfields. Horner's South Wales was never so radical as some of the Fed's pronouncements might suggest. The political character of most SWMF MPs and the political style of an Agent such as Arthur Jenkins made this clear.[4] And after the defeats of 1921 and 1926, non-unionism was a serious problem; after 1926, breakaway unionism established some bases. In spite of these problems the SWMF retained its central place in coalfield communities, and, as such, it informed Horner's politics. In contrast, longstanding criticisms of the Old Guard leadership in Lanark and Fife produced a configuration of splits, right-wing contempt for union procedures and a haemorrhage of membership. If the leaders of these coalfields' lefts were, in James MacDougall's view, 'made in Moscow', many components of their politics were supplied from Blantyre, Buckhaven and Lumphinnans. In such lives there was demonstrated a complex interplay between community experiences, the dynamics of union politics and party political rivalries. The Scottish Communist miners were politicised as members of the party but they were never simply party men.

Similarly, Arthur Reade and Randall Swingler can be located within that complex process through which a significant minority of upper middle class progressives moved to socialism during and after the First World War. But the chapters on these men also demonstrate complexities. Firstly there was the difference of chronology – the party joined by Reade was not the party joined by Swingler. Accordingly, the terms through which this transition is addressed have to be handled with sensitivity as regards context. Secondly, the profile of Swingler demolishes simplistic images of well-heeled intellectuals' attraction to Stalinism. The analysis of these two figures thus contributes to a broader debate. The complexities of progressive recruitment – whether to the Labour Party, Communist Party, or to the cause of socialism more broadly – cannot be captured in a few simplistic images and ahistorical concepts. For example, several high profile and upper class recruits to Labour left their former Liberalism appalled at the method and content of Grey's pre-war diplomacy; but this was only one route amongst several. The pacifistic Arthur Ponsonby was joined later on the Labour benches by Christopher Addison, a supporter of the war and Minister in the Lloyd George Coalition.[5] Similarly, if understandings of progressive politics could lead some to Labour or to Communism, in other circumstances the politics of progress could be expressed through support for the National Government, or for appeasement. Once again, the complexities of Communist lives fit into a broader pattern.

This wide range of experience is evident in a distinctive fashion in the experience of Jack Gaster, the last of those recorded here to become a Communist recruit. Politicised through the ILP in its radicalising, post-General Strike and pre-disaffiliation years, his initial commitment was to a party that claimed to offer an ethical and revolutionary alternative to the CPGB. The setbacks experienced by the Revolutionary Policy Committee within the post-disaffiliation ILP led to Gaster's shift to the CPGB. The provenance of his new allegiance indicates the problems in the 1930s of maintaining a credible left politics outside the CPGB. It also demonstrates that choices between parties were not sharply posed alternatives – whatever the rhetoric employed by partisans. Once again continuities were significant.

There is one Communist life story told here which seems exempt from such emphases on complexity and continuity. William Rust's rise within the party was rapid. He mastered the organisation, grasped the complexities of the British party's relationship with Moscow and skilfully employed Comintern approval as a resource. Careerist, zealot or a blend of both, his career seemed to personify the party's failure. Indeed, his premature death at the party headquarters in 1949 came at a time when the Cold War appeared to guarantee his party's decline. Yet to describe Bill Rust as the personification of the authoritarianism, manipulations and deceits of Stalinism is too neat. If the content of his bureaucratic politics owed much to the distinctiveness of British Communism, one could also consider Rust as an organisational autocrat. The sociologist Robert Michels, applying Weberian views on bureaucracy to socialist parties before 1914, argued that working-class emancipation necessitated organisation but that organisation inevitably generated oligarchs.[6] They certainly had come to dominate the SPD and all other pre-war socialist parties. Although there are problems in Michels' insistence on an iron law, and in his underlying positivism, the type he noted was a commonplace. Approved socialist discourse served as cement in the construction of bureaucratic controls. Rust can be placed within a framework that denies his status as Stalinist monster. His personality is one issue; understanding him as a political type quite another.

This characterisation of Rust suggests that these Communist lives should be located in a context that is both comparative and cognisant of the specific historical circumstances. The latter were often bleak. Mining trade unionists, for instance, lived with the legacies of industrial defeats. The CPGB remained small, overshadowed by the Labour Party, and by the late 1920s had been cast out by the larger organisation. In this frustrating and often discouraging world, the fact of the Soviet Union could be a consolation. Not surprisingly, most Communists aspired to be the model revolutionaries envisaged by the Comintern, whatever the unexpected and sometimes problematic dimensions of the latest model. Yet within Britain, the broader labour movement had to remain a key point of reference. Whatever the rhetoric of Class Against Class, and the visceral attractions of the denunciation of reformist politicians and trade union bureaucrats, isolation was neither feasible nor desirable. Continuities and similarities have been suggested between Communist lives and those of their Labour counterparts. And this comparison can be profitably taken further.

Much of the characterisation of orthodox Communist autobiographies and biographies applies to their Labour equivalents. As Labour's parliamentary status grew, so the party's publicists began – in the style of nineteenth century nation states – to construct a usable tradition. S.V. Bracher's *The Herald Book of Labour Members* offered epic and sentimental portraits. *The Book of the Labour Party* constructed the approved party identity on a broader canvas.[7] A pile of autobiographies chronicled the passing from poverty (crow scaring or a workingman's cottage) to acceptance (Westminster/Windsor Castle).[8] These mythic odysseys had similarities not only with earlier Lib-Lab autobiographies, but also in several respects with their Communist equivalents. Colourful portraits of early life in working-class communities were all too often succeeded by stilted accounts of arrival, not in Moscow, but in Westminster, and sometimes in Whitehall. If Communist rebels discovered the discipline of orthodoxy, their Labour contemporaries learned of the essential decency of political opponents. Similarly, Labour biographies could be carefully crafted in the service of the party. For example, Arthur Henderson's post-1931 emergence as a party icon, the antithesis of the reviled MacDonald, was reflected in and facilitated by Mary Hamilton's 1938 biography. In the book, Henderson's protracted, and for several years ambiguous, journey from Liberalism to Independent Labour became a simple story of a decent, honest artisan who from the beginning realised his primary loyalty, as he would subsequently in 1931.[9]

Beyond the myth making, we can see these Labour lives not just as party lives, but as complex, elusive, ambiguous – just like their Communist counterparts. For example there is the story of J.R. Clynes. He is typically remembered as a mild mannered autodidact, the one-time piecer in a cotton mill who went on to become an official of the Gasworkers, a member of the ILP, a wartime Minister, and leader of the Parliamentary Labour Party in 1921-22. As a Cabinet Minister in the first two Labour governments, he was an accommodating go-between, attempting to maintain a harmonious relationship between Labour's leadership and the Trades Union Congress – a moderate, decent Labour figure, discreet, flexible and wise. Yet this unobtrusive man had strong and sometimes contradictory views. Vehemently opposed to direct action in national politics, he placed total faith in the ballot box and the achievement of a parliamentary majority. But in 1926, as President of the recently amalgamated National Union of General and Municipal Workers (NUGMW), he played a major part in limiting the scope for elections within the union. Thereafter, principal officers would not be subject to re-election; this was a response to the fact that in 1926 they had been challenged – though not seriously threatened – by candidates backed by the Minority Movement. This restriction of participatory opportunities was one element in a much broader campaign to marginalise Communist influence within the union, some of the rhetoric and tactics of which foreshadowed the style of McCarthyism. The campaign enjoyed widespread support within the union, not least from Will Thorne, its General Secretary, and one-time advocate of New Unionism. Yet Thorne had been a comrade of Eleanor Marx, and on his election to the Commons in 1906 had cited Eleanor's father as a formative influence. However he had gone on to become a wartime patriot and a member of the trade union establishment, and by the late 1920s his politics were far removed from those of the East End agitator he once had been.

Thorne, Clynes and many others provided abundant evidence that shifts away from an earlier idealistic radicalism, towards bureaucratic manipulation and partisan abuse, were not an exclusively Communist phenomenon. Younger NUGMW officials showed a similar pattern. For example, Charles Dukes was gaoled for his opposition to military conscription during World War I: by the late 1920s, as the NUGMW Lancashire District Secretary, he was attacking Communist union members, unhindered by any liberal reservations. Dukes subsequently became the union's General Secretary, and he ended his career as Lord Dukeston, a director of the Bank of England. His union was influential in Labour politics, but its internal democracy was limited. Family dynasties became a significant force within the union; the oligarchy was acquiesced in by most of its members.[10]

The NUGMW represented an extreme case of the rise of the anti-Communist Right within Labour politics, but from the mid-1920s the phenomenon was commonplace. Particularly after 1926, most trade union leaders responded to criticism with a tougher line against the Left, and typically achieved at least some of their objectives without the disintegration that characterised Scottish mining trade unionism. Often attacks were directed at Communists, but the target could be any person or group seen as potentially dangerous to the emerging compact between the Labour Party leadership and the dominant element within the TUC. Hostility was directed also at the Miners' leader, A.J. Cook, and at the ILP as it fell increasingly under the control of the Left. One manifestation of this development was the style and decision making of Labour Party Conferences. By 1928, MacDonald's authority seemed effectively uncontested as the major unions underwrote the party leadership. From the chair, George

Lansbury's socialist rhetoric sanctified the proceedings. Criticism was difficult and fruitless. Communist politics in the 1920s increasingly involved the removal of dissent; parallel developments within the Labour Party and the trade union movement should not be neglected.

Such developments included styles of argument that are usually characterised as Stalinist. One Stalinist tactic was to condemn any rank-and-file opposition to the leadership on the grounds that it undermined the whole organisation and thus played into the hands of its enemies. Thus, in the years of the Popular Front, Trotskyists were frequently equated with fascists: objective consequences were what mattered and criticism threatened the solidarity of the anti-fascist forces. Exactly the same kind of argument was made in the chaos that threatened the coalfields after 1926. Miners' leaders attacked the Minority Movement as splitters who could be equated with Spencerite breakaway unionists. To criticise was to play the coalowners' game.

Communist lives were not a special kind of life, captured in the easy categorisation of Stalinist or totalitarian – nor were Communist a peculiarly principled brand of socialist, devoted, self-sacrificing yet blind to Stalinist crimes. Above all, they were not just labour and socialist people with some kind of Stalinist additive. These categorisations are insensitive to change over time, and they neglect shared patterns of behaviour. Demonstrations of principle, altruism and devotion to a cause, but also manipulation and fraud, were to be found across the labour movement. Indeed, the Labour Party and many trade union networks offered scope for individual advancement in a way closed to Communists. On the other hand, the case of the Electrical Trades Union would later demonstrate that in a union where Communist Party membership had become a passport to a union career, many Communists could become embroiled in the oligarchic tendencies and corruption of which they were usually so critical. Frank Haxell, after all, was another Communist life.[11]

Alongside all these complex similarities stood the fact of the Soviet Union. But its prominence in individual Communist lives varied between individuals, and its significance fluctuated over time. Furthermore, the authority of the Comintern rarely necessitated commands imposed on the recalcitrant. Rather, a Communist identity typically included a wish to meet Comintern standards of revolutionary wisdom; but this desire was tempered by the complexities of individual identities. Superficially, this dimension imposed on CP members a distinction that cut across all similarities with the rest of the Left: Communists, in accepting Comintern authority, became blind to

British exceptionalism; confined, on this account, within the limits of the one revolutionary road, they neglected the potential within the British context. But these were the lives of Communists with diverse national identities. The content of such identities and their relationships to Communism merit further exploration. The relationships between individuals' activities within national and local institutions, and their sincerely avowed Communism, were usually complex. Once again any notion of a simple distinction collapses.

There is another reason for scepticism about such a notion: there have been moments when socialists far removed from the CPGB have experienced the appeal of authoritarian political systems, which have seemed to offer solutions to some of the problems of an irrational and malfunctioning capitalism. Communist *and* Labour lives need to be viewed in their complexities. The certainties of familiar identities and distinctions should be queried.

In December 1932 an Old Etonian Labour politician who emphasised 'Practical Socialism' visited a famous dictator. The politician praised the energy of the regime. Its public works policies contrasted with depressed and economically orthodox Britain. He confided in his diary: 'There is no living man it would have thrilled me more to meet'.[12] But Hugh Dalton never met Benito Mussolini again.

NOTES

1. L. Grassic Gibbon, *A Scots Quair*, 1973, p459.
2. E. Wilson, *To the Finland Station*, New York 1953, part 3, chs 4 and 5.
3. See P. Graves, *Labour Women*, Cambridge 1994.
4. R. Jenkins, *A Life at the Centre*, 1991, pp10-11.
5. R. Jones, *Arthur Ponsonby*, Bromley 1989; K. and J. Morgan, *Portrait of a Progressive*, Oxford 1980.
6. R. Michels, *Political Parties*, 1915.
7. S.V. Bracher, *The Herald Book of Labour Members*, 1923; and second edition 1924; H. Tracey, *The Book of the Labour Party*, 1925.
8. See G. Edwards, *From Crow Scaring to Westminster*, 1922; J. Hodge, *From Workingman's Cottage to Windsor Castle*, 1931.
9. M. A. Hamilton, *Arthur Henderson*, 1938: for example, at p30 on his shift from Liberalism.
10. Clynes, Thorne and Dukes are all profiled in Bracher's *Herald Book*. For the union's anti-Communism, see its *Reports*, 1926-28.
11. J. Lloyd, *Light and Liberty*, 1990, chs 16-21.
12. Dalton's own published account is in his *The Fateful Years*, 1957, pp33-5. See also B. Pimlott, *Hugh Dalton*, 1985, pp214-15, with diary comment cited at p215.

Who's Who

COMPILED BY JOHN McILROY

Noah Ablett (1883-1935): South Wales miners' leader, industrial unionist and one of the authors of *The Miners' Next Step*, the famous 1912 programme for union reform.

William Adamson (1863-1936): Secretary of the Fife miners' union from 1908 and Labour MP for West Fife from 1910, he was an influential, anti-communist right-winger within the federal Scottish miners' union. In the face of Communist victories in the Fife union, he led a breakaway organisation and was beaten by Willie Gallacher for the West Fife seat in 1935.

Robin Page Arnot (1890-1986): Foundation member of the CPGB, Secretary of the Labour Research Department and British representative to the Comintern, he was later a historian of the British miners.

Joan Beauchamp (1890-1964): Involved with the suffrage movement and the No-Conscription Fellowship, 1914-18, and editor of its journal, the *Tribunal*, she joined the CPGB at its foundation from the National Guilds League. She worked for the Labour Research Department and *Labour Monthly* in the 1920s.

Tom Bell (1882-1944): A founder member of the Socialist Labour Party in his native Glasgow and a founder member of the CPGB in 1920, Bell held a succession of leading positions in the party through the 1920s. Author of the first history of the CPGB.

Ted Bramley (1905-89): Played a prominent role in the CPGB as a party worker in London where he was a councillor; he was on the national executive from 1932 to 1948.

Archibald Fenner Brockway (1888-1988): An opponent of the First World War, he was a prominent leader of the ILP from 1922 to 1946 when he joined the Labour Party. He was MP for Eton and Slough between 1950 and 1964, when he joined the House of Lords.

Nikolai Bukharin (1888-1938): Old Bolshevik, supporter of Stalin and leader of the Comintern, 1926-28. He was expelled from the CPSU Politbureau in 1929 on the basis of his 'right wing' tendencies, and executed by Stalin in 1938.

Emile Burns (1889-1972): Ex-ILPer associated with the Labour Research Department and a Communist from his early twenties, he was a member of the CPGB Executive for over two decades from 1935 and occupied many positions within the party apparatus, particularly relating to cultural and educational activities.

Elinor Burns: Joined the CPGB in 1923 and played a prominent role in the London cooperative movement. A member of the CPGB Executive from 1943 to 1956, she was married to Emile Burns.

John Ross Campbell (1894-1969): A former Paisley shop assistant and member of the British Socialist Party, he was a fixture on the CPGB Executive, 1923-65. Briefly Party Secretary in 1929, he later edited the *Daily Worker*.

Edward Carpenter (1844-1929): Sheffield poet, writer on sexuality, women and the family, and supporter of the Social Democratic Federation.

Walter Citrine (1887-1983): A Liverpool electrician who was General Secretary of the Trades Union Congress between 1923 and 1946, he was an apostle of moderation and an opponent of Communism.

J. R. Clynes (1869-1949): Leader of the National Union of General and Municipal Workers and minister in Ramsay MacDonald's Labour governments of 1924 and 1929.

Claude Cockburn (1904-81): CPGB fellow traveller, member and *Daily Worker* journalist who wrote under the pseudonym of 'Frank Pitcairn'.

Jack Cohen (1905-82): Member of the YCL Executive in the 1920s and the CPGB's first National Student Organiser in the 1930s, he was later the CPGB's Coventry organiser and worked in the party education department.

G. D. H. Cole (1889-1959): Labour Party intellectual and prolific writer, he was associated with the National Guilds League, the Labour Research Department, the Fabian Society and workers' education in the 1920s; and with the Socialist League in the 1930s.

Tom and Amy Colyer: After their deportation for the USA in 1922, both were active in the Left Wing Movement which attempted to build a united front between the CPGB and the Labour Party left. They resigned from the CPGB in opposition to party domination of the movement and were later active in the ILP.

A. J. Cook (1883-1931): South Wales Miners' leader and briefly a member of the CPGB in 1921, he remained a close collaborator of the party until 1928. He was General Secretary of the Miners' Federation of Great Britain from 1924 until his early death.

Robert Conquest (b.1917): sympathetic to the CPGB in the 1930s, he became a popular and painstaking critic of Russian communism.

Idris Cox (1899-1989): South Wales miner, politicised by attending Central Labour College. Joined CPGB in 1924. Full-time party worker from 1927 until 1969. Strong supporter of Comintern line during Third Period.

Helen Crawfurd (1877-1954): Leading opponent of the First World War, prominent ILPer and militant suffragist. Joined CPGB in 1921 and remained a member until her death.

Dr C. K. Cullen (d.1966): Medical Officer of Health in Poplar who left the ILP with Jack Gaster, subsequently playing little prominent role in the CPGB though remaining an active local member.

Eugene Debs (1855-1926): Influential American socialist from Terre Haute, Indiana. Prominent in the Industrial Workers of the World, he was the Socialist Party's Presidential candidate from 1900 to 1920.

Maurice Dobb (1900-76): An economist and economic historian who joined the party in 1922 and was on the executive of the Labour Research Department and the Plebs League in the 1920s. Later a Fellow of Trinity College, Cambridge, he was a lifelong CPGB member.

Rajani Palme Dutt (1896-1974): Of Indian and Swedish parentage, he was the CPGB's leading political intellectual for four decades. Editor of the *Workers' Weekly* and the *Labour Monthly*, he was Party Secretary of the CPGB, 1939-41.

Max Eastman (1883-1969): American sympathiser of Trotsky. He translated Trotsky's work into English and in *Since Lenin Died* provided the first account of the struggle inside the Russian party in the mid-1920s; later edited the *Reader's Digest*.

Elizabeth Wolstenholme Elmy (1833-1918): Manchester headmistress, radical suffragist and pioneer of women's rights, who survived to work with the insurgent women's movement of the early twentieth century and see women win the right to vote in 1918.

W.N. Ewer (1885-1977): Close associate of Palme Dutt and Page Arnot, and Foreign Editor of the *Daily Herald*; left the CPGB in the late 1920s and became a virulent anti-communist.

Arthur Ewert (1890-1959): Joined the German Communist Party in 1919 and later worked for the Comintern in the USA, China and Brazil.

Ruth Fischer (1895-1961): A leading member of the left wing of the German CP from 1919, she became its leader in 1924. Never a favourite of the Russians, she was expelled from the party for leftism in 1926. Later in the Trotskyist movement.

Ralph Fox (1900-1937): Novelist, playwright, literary critic and CPGB propagandist, he was killed fighting in Spain in 1937.

Eddie Frow (1906-1997): Communist and engineering union activist, notably in Manchester, who joined the CPGB in 1924. Founder, with his wife Ruth, of the Working Class Movement Library, Salford.

William Gallacher (1881-1965): A member of the ILP and then the Social Democratic Federation/British Socialist Party, he was a leader of the Clyde Workers' Committee during the First World War. The Paisley-born Gallacher was a fixture on the Executive of the CPGB, and MP for West Fife, 1935-50.

Reg Groves (1908-88): Supporter of the leftist line in the unions encouraged by Palme Dutt in 1928-29. He then moved towards Trotskyism and was expelled from the CPGB in 1932.

Charlotte Haldane (1894-1969): Labour Party entrist who joined the CPGB after her son was killed in Spain; married to J. B. S. Haldane.

J.B.S. Haldane (1892-1964): Celebrated scientist and CPGB fellow traveller who became a party member in 1942. He left the CPGB in opposition to the party's support for the views of the Soviet scientist, Lysenko.

Wal Hannington (1896-1966): A popular Londoner best known for his leadership of the National Unemployed Workers' Movement in the interwar years. He was always involved in the Amalgamated Engineering Union, of which he was a full-time official for many years from 1942.

Keir Hardie (1856-1915): A pioneering Scottish socialist, feminist and anti-imperial-ist, he played a central part in the fight for independent working-class representation and the separation of labour from liberalism.

Arthur Henderson (1863-1935): Leading Labour Party politician; Home Secretary in the 1924 government and Foreign Secretary in 1929.

Walter Holmes (1892-1973): A well-known CPGB journalist, he moved from the Fabian Research Department to the *Daily Herald*. In the late 1920s he edited the *Sunday Worker* and thereafter spent many years at the *Daily Worker* where he was associated with the 'Workers' Notebook' column.

Thomas Hodgkin (1910-82): Came from an academic, Quaker family and joined the CPGB in 1937 after working as a civil servant in Palestine. He was later prominent in university adult education and became an authority on African politics.

J.F. Horrabin (1884-1962): A journalist, cartoonist and cartographer, he was identi-fied with the movement for independent working-class education and edited *The Plebs* magazine. A founder member of the CPGB, he left the party in 1924 and was subsequently Labour MP for Peterborough, 1929-31.

Winifred Horrabin (1887-1971): Secretary of the Plebs League, she left the CPGB shortly after her husband in opposition to the party's attempts to control independent working-class education.

Allen Hutt (1901-73): Lifelong CPGB member, typographer, journalist and wit; later President of the National Union of Journalists and editor of *The Journalist*.

Douglas Hyde (1911-96): Joined the CPGB in 1928 and became an organiser for the Spanish Medical Aid Committee. A Labour Party entrist in the 1930s and *Daily Worker* journalist in the 1940s, he left the party in 1948 after becoming a Roman Catholic.

Albert Inkpin (1884-1944): General Secretary of the British Socialist Party, 1913-20 and of the CPGB, 1920-29, he was essentially an administrator and manager. Removed in the leadership purge in 1929-30, he later worked for the Friends of the Soviet Union.

Derek Kahn (d.1944): Oxford University Communist and editor of the literary journal, *Left Review*, he was killed in Burma in 1944.

Lev Kamenev (1883-1936): Old Bolshevik and leader of the party with Stalin and Zinoviev; later in the United Opposition with Trotsky and Zinoviev. Executed after first Stalinist show trial in 1936.

Alexander Kerensky (1881-1970): Member of the Social Revolutionary Party and leader of the provisional government overthrown by the Bolsheviks in 1917.

Peter Kerrigan (1899-1977): Scottish engineer and fixture on the CPGB Executive after 1927, he was prominent in the leadership in the 1930s, represented the party in Moscow and was a commissar in Spain.

Alexandra Kollontai (1872-1952): A Menshevik who became a Bolshevik and a pioneering writer on the family and sexual relations. A leader of the Workers' Opposition in the CPSU, she later became a supporter of Stalin.

Elsa Lanchester (1902-86): Socialist dancer and actress who frequented Communist circles in the 1920s and later married the actor and filmstar Charles Laughton.

George Lansbury (1859-1940): Joined Social Democratic Federation in 1889 after rejecting Liberalism. A Labour Party member, he was sympathetic to the Russian revolution in 1917 and sympathetic to the CPGB – several of his children were active in the party. He was editor of the *Daily Herald*, 1919-22, and leader of the Labour Party, 1931-35.

Jim Larkin (1876-1947): Irish socialist and trade union leader, who in the 1920s was involved in attempts to establish a Communist Party in Ireland and attended congresses of the Comintern and the RILU.

V.I. Lenin (1870-1924): Leader of the Bolsheviks, strategist of the 1917 revolution and after 1924 the icon of world communism.

Cecil Day Lewis (1904-1972): Schoolteacher, poet and, under the pseudonym Nicholas Blake, writer of detective stories, he was briefly in the CPGB in the 1930s.

Alexander Lozovsky (1878-1952): Secretary of Red International of Labour Unions, 1921-37; later a victim of Stalin's anti-semitism, he was shot in 1952.

Rosa Luxemburg (1871-1919): Key figure in European socialism, particularly in Poland and Germany. A Communist critical of the Russian revolution, she was assassinated by paramilitaries in Berlin in 1919.

J. Ramsay MacDonald (1866-1937): Leader of the Labour Party and Labour Prime Minister, 1924 and 1929-31; Prime Minister in the National Government, 1931-35.

Margaret MacDonald (1870-1911): Social worker, ILP activist and wife of Ramsay MacDonald.

John Maclean (1879-1923): A graduate of Glasgow University, he was a schoolteacher who joined the Social Democratic Federation in 1902. He led the opposition to the First World War in its successor, the British Socialist Party, and was its greatest propagandist. Imprisoned three times during the war, he was admired by Lenin but refused to join the CPGB, advocating a separate Scottish Communist Party.

Arthur MacManus (1889-1927): A leading member of the Socialist Labour Party, he was prominent in the wartime shop stewards' movement. As the first 'President' of the CPGB, he played a significant role in the party in its earliest years.

Harry McShane (1891-1988): Glaswegian engineer and shop steward who was a member of the BSP until 1920. Closely associated with John Maclean's agitation among the unemployed in the early 1920s, he joined the CPGB in 1922 and was a prominent member of the National Unemployed Workers' Movement. He resigned in 1953 but continued to adhere to revolutionary socialism.

John Mahon (b.1901): Son of the veteran socialist, John L. Mahon and a lifelong member of the CPGB, he played an ultra-leftist role during the Third Period but was perhaps best known as its London organiser in the 1940s and 1950s.

Dmitri Manuilsky (1883-1959): An uncritical supporter of Stalin, he was a member of the ECCI between 1924 and 1943, and played a leading role in the Third Period between 1929 and 1934.

Tom Mann (1856-1941): Prominent member of Social Democratic Federation and leading trade unionist in the pre-war militancy in Britain, he was General Secretary of the Engineering Union between 1919 and 1921 and a prominent CPGB figure until his death.

André Marty (1886-1956): A leading member of the French Communist Party which he represented in Moscow from 1932. A member of the Comintern Secretariat from 1935, he was commander-in-chief of the International Brigades in the Spanish Civil War.

Jimmy Maxton (1885-1946): A graduate of Glasgow University, he joined the ILP around 1904. A strong opponent of the First World War, he was MP for Bridgeton, Glasgow, and a leading ILPer until his death in 1946.

William Mellor (1888-1942): Oxford graduate and Guild Socialist, he was a foundation member of the CPGB and a journalist on the *Daily Herald*; left the CPGB in 1924.

Alex Moffat (1904-1967): Younger brother of Abe Moffat. A leading young Communist in Fife in the 1920s, a County Councillor, and organiser of the United Mineworkers of Scotland in the 1930s; he temporarily left the CPGB in 1956. President of the Scottish Area NUM, 1961-67.

Mary Moorhouse: Guild Communist, foundation member of the CPGB and a member of the group around Palme Dutt, she was involved in party press work, organising students and women, as well as in courier activities for the Comintern. She later married Eino Pekkala, the first husband of Dutt's wife, Salme.

Sir Oswald Mosley (1896-1980): Conservative then Labour MP. Prominent on the left, 1924-31, he founded the New Party in 1931 and the British Union of Fascists in 1932.

J.T. Murphy (1888-1965): Leader and theorist of the wartime shop stewards' movement. A leading Communist throughout the 1920s, he was expelled from the party in 1932 in a rather obscure argument over trade between Britain and the USSR.

J.T. Walton Newbold (1888-1943): Economist, pedagogue and propagandist, he was elected Communist MP for Motherwell in 1922 but lost his seat at the next election and left the CPGB in 1924.

Conrad Noel (1869-1942): Christian Socialist and Vicar of Thaxted, active in the British Socialist Party and the National Guilds League; a sympathiser of the early CPGB.

Sylvia Pankhurst (1882-1960): Prominent suffragist who established the Workers' Socialist Federation in 1918. Expelled from the CPGB in 1921 over party control of the WSF paper, the *Workers' Dreadnought*. Supported the Workers' Opposition in Russia and left communism elsewhere in Europe.

Cedar Paul: A famous translator of Marxist works, folk singer and, with her husband Eden Paul, a mainstay of independent working-class education. A former member of the ILP and the Workers' Socialist Federation, she was a foundation member of the CPGB and a prominent activist in the 1920s, particularly interested in working women, birth control and proletarian culture.

Will Paynter (1903-1984): Welsh Communist miners' leader who eventually succeeded Arthur Horner as President of the South Wales Miners' Union in 1951 and the National Union of Mineworkers in 1959.

Iosif Piatnitsky (1882-1938): Joined Bolshevik Party in 1903 and became treasurer of the Comintern in 1921. He was on the ECCI, 1923-1935, arrested in 1937 and executed in 1938.

Harry Pollitt (1890-1960): A Manchester-born foundation member of the party and its General Secretary, 1929-39 and 1941-56.

Morgan Phillips Price (1885-1973): Publicist of the Bolshevik revolution in Britain and an intimate collaborator of the CPGB between 1920 and 1924, when he was the Labour parliamentary candidate for Gloucester. Later a Labour MP, 1929-31 and 1935-59.

D.N. Pritt (1887-1972): Well-known barrister, CPGB fellow traveller and vocal supporter of the Moscow trials; from 1935 Labour MP for Hammersmith.

Raymond Postgate (1896-1971): Socialist journalist, historian and *bon viveur* who resigned from the CPGB in 1924 in reaction against the Bolshevisation of the party.

Stewart Purkis (1885-1969): CPGB activist in the Railway Clerks' Association and enthusiast for the Comintern's leftist line in the unions after 1928, he became a leader of the Balham Group, expelled from the CPGB for Trotskyism in 1932.

Karl Radek (1885-1939): Joined the Bolsheviks in 1917 and was briefly secretary of the Comintern and always influential in international affairs. Although he recanted his support for Trotsky in the 1920s, he later perished in the Gulag.

Edgell Rickword (1898-1982): Poet, critic and an editor of the cultural journals *Left Review* and *Our Time*. Joined CPGB in 1934 and left in 1956.

Andrew Rothstein (1898-1994): Son of Theodore Rothstein, émigré and later Soviet minister, who played an important role in the foundation of the CPGB; he was in the leadership of the British party throughout the 1920s before falling victim to the purge of the leadership during the Third Period.

Dora Russell (1894-1986): Fellow of Girton College Cambridge, and enthusiast for the Russian Revolution, social reform and birth control. Married to the philosopher Bertrand Russell, she divorced him in 1932.

Herbrand Sackville, Earl De La Warr (1900-1976): After joining the Labour Party, he was Under-Secretary of State for War in MacDonald's 1929 government. Followed his leader into the National Labour group before joining the Conservatives in 1945.

Richard Schüller (1901-57): An Austrian Communist, leader of the Communist Youth International and on the ECCI from 1923.

Jimmy Shields (1900-49): Greenock-born Scottish Communist who joined the CPGB in 1921. He emigrated to South Africa on health grounds and was appointed chair of the Communist Party there between 1925 and 1927. He was elected to the CPGB Executive in 1929, played a role in the United Mineworkers of Scotland and was twice editor of the *Daily Worker*.

Alexander Shliapnikov (1884-1937): Commissar for Labour in the first Soviet Government and subsequently leader of the Workers' Opposition in the Russian party in 1921, he was expelled from the CPSU in 1933 and perished in the Stalinist purges.

Charles Montagu Slater (1902-56): Journalist, novelist and playwright, he joined the CPGB in 1927 and remained active until his death.

Norah Smythe: A member of the Women's Social and Political Union who worked with Sylvia Pankhurst in the Workers' Socialist Federation. Resigned from the CPGB in 1921 in protest against Sylvia's expulsion and continued to collaborate with her into the 1930s.

John Sommerfield (b.1908): Joined CPGB in 1930 and fought in Spain. Left the party in 1956; continued to publish novels and short stories into the 1970s.

Boris Souvarine (1895-1984): Founder member of the French Communist Party and member of the ECCI; supported Trotsky in the 1920s.

George Spencer (1872-1957): President of the Nottinghamshire Miners' Association (NMA), and Labour MP for Broxtowe between 1918 and 1929, he adopted a defeatist attitude during the 1926 mining lockout and negotiated a return to work. After establishing a breakaway union, he was expelled from the NMA and MFGB in October 1926.

Douglas 'Dave' Springhall (1901-53): A former sailor, associated with the Workers' Socialist Federation, he was a YCL leader in the 1920s and a Political Commissar in the International Brigade in Spain. He was subsequently imprisoned for spying for the Soviet Union in 1943 and expelled from the CPGB.

Josef Stalin (1879-1953): General Secretary of the Russian Communist Party from 1922. The elaborator of 'socialism in one country', by 1930 he dominated the Russian party and the Comintern, systematically eliminating his opponents, amongst others, most publicly in the show trials of 1936-8.

Bob Stewart (1877-1973): A Scot from Dundee who was a temperance advocate, he played an important role in the CPGB in the 1920s, holding a range of leading positions and representing the party in Moscow before taking a back seat in the 1930s.

John Strachey (1901-63): An intimate collaborator of the CPGB in the 1930s after he left Oswald Mosley's New Party, he was later a Labour Minister.

Jack Tanner (1890-1965): Leading London engineering activist and prominent in the shop stewards' movement, he was a delegate to the Second Comintern Congress. Apart from the Third Period, he worked closely with the CPGB until the late 1940s. President of the AEU, 1939-54, he became an energetic anti-Communist.

Wally Tapsell (d.1938): National Organiser of the YCL, CPGB Executive member and manager of the *Daily Worker*, he was killed serving in the International Brigade in Spain.

R.H. Tawney (1880-1962): Influential Labour Party intellectual, social thinker and advocate of workers' education.

William Temple (1881-1944): Liberal churchman who became Archbishop of York and Canterbury; associated with the Workers' Education Association.

J.H. Thomas (1874-1949): Leader of the National Union of Railwaymen, and minister in the 1924 and 1929 Labour governments.

Mel Thomas (b.1904): Welsh miner and CPGB activist in Maesteg through the inter-war period, and later member of the South Wales NUM Executive.

W.H. Thompson (1885-1947): Husband of Joan Beauchamp and uncle of the historian A.J. P. Taylor, he acted as a solicitor for the CPGB during this period, most notably in the trial of the twelve party leaders in 1925. His firm became well known as legal advisors to the British trade unions.

Lev Davidovitch Trotsky (1879-1940): With Lenin, the leader of the revolution and creator of the Soviet State. An opponent of the *troika* of Kamenev, Zinoviev and Stalin from 1923, he headed the United Opposition with Kamenev and Zinoviev, 1926-27. He was expelled from the Soviet Union in 1929 and murdered by Stalin's agents in Mexico in 1940.

Eugen Varga (1879-1964): A Hungarian Communist who joined the Russian Party in 1918 and became an influential adviser to Stalin.

Hilda Vernon (1902-82): Left the ILP with the Revolutionary Policy Committee to join the CPGB. During the 1930s she was involved with work among the unemployed and women.

Melvina Walker: Former ladies' maid and docker's wife, she was a member of the Women's Social and Political Union and Workers' Socialist Federation. Active in anti-war agitation and campaigns for equal pay in the East End of London, she joined the CPGB with Sylvia Pankhurst.

William Weinstone (1897-1985): Lithuanian-born founder member and leading cadre of the Communist Party of the United States which he represented in Moscow between 1929 and 1931, displaying consistent support for Stalin.

Harry Wicks (1905-89): A leader of the YCL, student at the Comintern's International Lenin School and one of the pioneers of British Trotskyism.

Ellen Wilkinson (1891-1947): Born in Manchester, attended the university and was involved in suffragist movement and the ILP. An organiser with the Shopworkers' Union, she joined the CPGB in 1920, left in 1924, and was elected Labour MP for Middlesborough East a few months later. Minister of Education in the 1945 Labour government.

Jock Wilson (1884-1976): Scottish born, Liverpool-based seamen's organiser and member of the ILP, he was a leading figure in the CPGB throughout the 1920s until the leadership purge in 1929-30 when he emigrated to Australia.

Tom Wintringham (1898-1949): Joined the CPGB in 1920, working on its press and becoming an expert on military affairs. He fought in Spain and was expelled from the party in 1938 because his American wife, Kitty, was regarded as an *agent provocateur*.

Clara Zetkin (1857-1933): Pioneer German socialist, prominent in the Second International and from 1919 in the German Communist Party and the Comintern.

Grigori Zinoviev (1883-1936): An old Bolshevik and President of the Comintern, 1919-26, he was a member of the ruling triumvirate in the Russian party but broke with Stalin in 1926. Subsequently led the United Opposition with Trotsky. Executed by Stalin in 1936.

Contributors

Alan Campbell teaches in the School of History, University of Liverpool. He is the author of the two-volume *The Scottish Miners, 1874-1939* (2000).

Gidon Cohen is a researcher on the Communist Party of Great Britain Biographical Project at the University of Manchester. He has recently completed a PhD on the ILP in the 1930s.

Andy Croft is a poet, historian of labour movement culture and part-time teacher. He lives in Middlesbrough and is working on a biography of Randall Swingler.

Nina Fishman teaches at the University of Westminster. She is the author of *The British Communist Party and the Trade Unions, 1933-45* (1995) and is currently working on the life of Arthur Horner.

Gisela Chan Mang Fong is an adjunct Assistant Professor of history at Concordia University, Montreal, Canada. She is currently researching the history and development of the Asian diaspora in Southern Rhodesia/Zimbabwe before and after 1980.

Andy Flinn is a researcher on the Communist Party of Great Britain Biographical Project at the University of Manchester. He recently completed a PhD on political militancy in Lancashire in the inter-war years.

David Howell is Professor of Politics at the University of York. His latest book is *Respectable Radicals: studies in the politics of railway trade unionism* (1999). He is working on a study of Ramsay MacDonald's Labour Party.

Karen Hunt teaches history at Manchester Metropolitan University. She is the author of *Equivocal Feminists: the Social Democratic Federation and the woman question* (1996) and is writing (with June Hannam) a book on socialist women.

John McIlroy is a Reader in Sociology at the University of Manchester. He is the editor, with Alan Campbell and Nina Fishman, of the two-volume *British Trade Unions and Industrial Politics, 1945-79* (1999).

Barry McLoughlin is a freelance researcher into international communism. He lives in Vienna and has written on Irish, Austrian and British communism.

Kevin Morgan teaches politics at the University of Manchester. The author of a biography of Harry Pollitt and an editor of *Socialist History*, he is currently working on a study of Bolshevism and the British left.

Index

INDEX

254